# A PARTHENON ON OUR ROOF

ADVENTURES OF AN ANGLO-GREEK MARRIAGE

THE PARTHENON SERIES
BOOK 1

PETER BARBER

Illustrated by
CHARLY ALEX FULLER

Second Edition, 2023
Illustrations by Charly Alex Fuller
Printed in Kopa
ISBN  978-1-916574-11-3

KAKTOS PUBLICATIONS
Laskaridou 35
17676 Kallithea
Tel. +30.210.38.40.524 - +30.210.38.44.458
www.kaktos.gr • info@kaktos.gr

t

# CONTENTS

# MAP OF GREECE

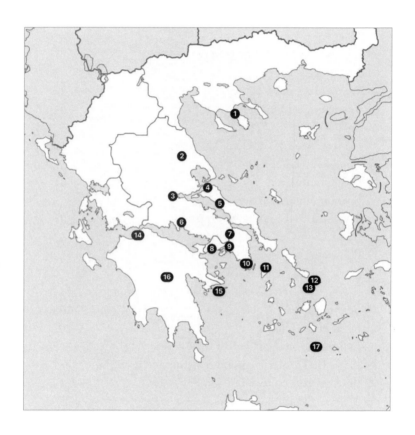

## KEY

# 1

## MEET ALEX

It was a hot July day and Alexandra and I were driving through the Peloponnesus. We had the windows open and were enjoying the breeze as the car hugged the side of the mountain on the narrow, winding road. To our left, broken crash barriers reminded us of the very real dangers. Miniature glass churches filled with plastic flowers and oil burners dotted the roadside, shrines to the many less careful motorists who'd veered off the tarmac and plummeted to their end thousands of metres down, into the abyss.

The smell of fresh mountain herbs wafted through the open windows; oregano and sage baked in the hot sunshine, releasing their fragrant oils in a bouquet of warm, sweet Greek air. The constant chatter of crickets drowned out the thrum of the engine as we began our descent towards the sea. The route became less serpentine and although we were still high in the mountains, we could now make out olive groves far below us. We were on the way down at last. As I navigated a long bend, the road ahead straightened out and allowed me to pick up speed.

Suddenly and without warning, the car launched into a spin. I stamped on the brake, but to no avail. We were out of control. I had already been nursing my complaining twenty-year-old Citroen. It did not like the heat and struggled to climb even the smallest of hills in the city without belching black smoke and making worrying grinding noises. Chugging up this thousand-metre mountain had almost been the end of it, so when we'd finally crested the summit, I was relieved. If it did give up now, I thought, we might at least be able to coast down to the next village. No such luck.

With my foot jammed down on the brake pedal, we'd come out of the spin but were now skidding sideways towards a large oak tree. Until this point, I'd been happy. I was in a beautiful country with a wonderful person beside me. I'd started a new life and having recently turned forty, I had everything to live for. But now all my hopes and dreams were about to be snuffed out. We were going to crash.

The spinning and braking had no effect; we were hurtling

towards the tree at a horrifying speed. Then everything went into slow motion. I spotted a small dirt track beside the fast-approaching oak. Would this be our route to a miraculous escape or a one-way ticket off the deadly cliff edge and into the ravine? I had an instant to decide which would be less lethal. If we hit the tree, we were unlikely to survive, so the dirt track seemed the only option. I held my breath, took my foot off the brake and regained the steering. In a microsecond I steered towards the track, aimed for the tiny gap and stared straight ahead. It took us into an olive grove on a steep slope. We were still travelling fast, but I somehow steered around the trees without too much pressure on the brake in case we skidded again. At last we came to a stop, just metres from the cliff edge.

Everything was quiet. Even the crickets had ceased their chatter in the expectation of watching another tourist fall off the mountain, no doubt looking forward to having one more shrine on which to perch and soak up the sunshine.

I glanced to my right to see my fiancée with a frozen expression on her face. 'Are you okay?' I asked softly.

She nodded, then fixed her eyes on mine. 'I'm so sorry,' she whispered.

'Don't be silly. It's not your fault.'

She stared down at the floor. 'But it is. I pulled the hand-brake.' Lifting her head, she added hesitantly, 'It was only a joke.'

While I was trying to absorb this information, I heard applause coming from the top of the olive grove. Half a dozen motorists had left their cars and were standing on the ridge, clapping and cheering with shouts of 'Well done!' and 'You're a jackal!'. They'd been following close behind us when the car had gone into its spin. They'd had ringside views and had enjoyed the performance.

Although Alex and I had yet to be married at this point, we

had our lives together all planned out. Or so I thought. I'd been spending more and more time with her in her native Greece so that we could get to know each other. Our cultural differences were bridged with humour, and we passed most of our time laughing as our two worlds slowly merged. Looking back on her handbrake stunt, I think she may have been testing me; she wanted to ensure I was a survivor before making the ultimate commitment. Just as in ancient Greece, where young men would be sent into the mountains to hunt and kill a bear armed only with a sharp stick before they could be accepted as true warriors, so I was tested on a mountain road in the Peloponnesus. Before I was permitted to join the Greek culture, I had to show my worth.

If only Alex had consulted me first, I'm sure we could have found another way, preferably at sea level. But Alex is not one of those fireworks that just sizzle. She's the sort that goes bang and shakes windows and makes the earth tremble. She is loving to her family and friends. But you need to get your facts right, otherwise you'll be found wanting once the forensic examination begins. If you are her friend, it's for life. Upset her, and you pay with blood.

She spits on me when I look well – the 'ftou, ftou, ftou' spitting sound being a way of warding off the evil eye. She has the face of an angel and a smile that will draw you in, but her mind is like a scalpel; she will dissect any idiotic statement, put it under the microscope and ensure the full examination of every syllable uttered before allowing further discussion.

I do not suffer fools, but in my private life, I don't get to meet many. This is because they don't get past Alex. Before they get to me, they have been fact-checked and sent back to school for a year before being permitted to try again.

When Greek philosophers would rather drink hemlock than bend to public opinion, you know you are dealing with a stubborn race: they asked Socrates what his punishment should be for corrupting the minds of the youth of Athens and not believing in the gods of the state. He suggested a good meal. His accusers turned down this request and gave him the choice of exile or hemlock. He chose the latter.

# 2

## LUNCHES UNDER THE BOUGAINVILLEA

Alex grew up in Glyfada, a seaside resort on the southwestern perimeter of Athens, and once I'd passed the fiancé test, I went to live there too. Her family had built their house there in the 1950s, when Glyfada was still a fishing village with dirt roads. By the year 2000, when I arrived on the scene, the place had grown into a bustling suburb of Athens, the playground of the capital, with land prices to match the better parts of London. The house, however, had remained unchanged. It had seen better days.

In Greece, family is more important than anything else, so it is unusual for a daughter to leave the family home. It is more normal for the family to divide the property or even build another storey on top. Some large families build four or five extra floors over the years to accommodate them all. Alex's family home had just two levels. Her parents, Debbie and Zissis, occupied the semi-basement, and Alex lived upstairs. This arrangement worked to a point. They all theoretically had their own space and privacy, but everyone ignored that and continued to live as one big, contented family.

When Alex and I first got together, she was living alone in Glyfada. Her father, a cruise director, was at sea, and her mother was temporarily living in England, taking care of relatives. Alex worked as a beauty therapist and had her studio in a room on the upper floor of the house. As her parents were away, the lower level stood empty, awaiting their return.

Alex made it her mission to introduce me to the real Greece right from the very start of our relationship. I had been to the country before, but on a holiday, so my experience was of sandy beaches, welcoming hotels and travel reps taking us off to quaint tavernas where plate smashing was the highlight of the evening. Alex was determined to correct that image, and quickly.

On my first afternoon, she showed me around the Glyfada house, took me to my room and left me to unpack. Showered and changed, I emerged feeling refreshed. Alex was waiting, fully dressed for the evening. She looked magnificent in a low-cut blouse, short leather skirt and knee-high boots, and she smelled of perfume. We were going to a music bar.

We stepped out of the taxi near the docks in Piraeus, Athens' port area. Lights from the moored ships danced across the calm water. There was a slight tang in the air of diesel fumes, and the rhythmic beat of music emanated from a dark alley nearby. Alex led me towards the sound.

'Will there be plate smashing?' I asked.

'Doubtful,' she replied. 'We don't do that in Greece.'

We entered the club. It was even darker than the alley outside. I took a breath and my lungs filled with the fug of cigarette smoke. We made our way through the crowded room. There were no chairs or tables; people just stood in groups, drinking spirits at the wooden bar that extended along one wall. The band occupied the opposite wall. This comprised a bearded man sitting on a stool and enthusiastically beating a series of tom-toms, a bouzouki player strumming his sparkling white instrument, a small man playing a guitar, and an older chap blowing into a clarinet. Everything was amplified via huge speakers in each corner, making conversation impossible, so we simply merged into the crowd and communicated with expressions and hand signals.

On the small dance floor, women were gyrating in time to the music, but this was no disco-style dancing; it was much more eastern, organised and rehearsed, more like belly-dancing, and even more erotic. We grabbed a drink, and Alex stepped onto the floor to join them. It was the sexiest thing I'd ever seen. She echoed the rhythmic beating of the drums with well-practised movements. This was real Greek dancing, and it was incredible to behold. It was nothing like the *Zorba* style I'd seen before, where people stood in a line with arms outstretched to each other's shoulders; this was the way the locals did it. Slowly, men who'd been standing around the perimeter advanced and joined in. Some showed their appreciation by kneeling beside a dancing woman and clapping in time with the music to encourage her. Others remained on their feet, took the hand of one of the dancers and lifted it to allow her to swivel under his arm before continuing her own moves.

Although this club was in the seedier part of Piraeus and looked to be dark and threatening, it was not. There were no bouncers on the door; they weren't needed. Women felt safe there, and the men weren't in competition with each other and didn't need to prove themselves. They didn't hassle the women. Everyone was there to have fun.

By the end of the evening, my ears were numb. We were both hungry, so Alex suggested a seafood restaurant on the harbourfront nearby. The sweet smell of barbecued fish and hot charcoal assailed my senses before we turned the corner and saw the brightly lit restaurant. A single table ran the entire length of the room. The benches to either side of it were full of diners busily peeling shrimps and breaking crab shells with small hammers. There were no cloths; the tables were spread with newspaper, on which were heaped untidy piles of freshly cooked shellfish. This was the ultimate finger food, and polite table manners were not required. You just squeezed into a space on a bench, grabbed a shrimp, threw the shell on the floor and ate. When a pile was exhausted, the server simply rolled up the newspaper, replaced it, and dumped a fresh heap of assorted fish on top.

During those first few months of our relationship, I was grateful to have the time with Alex in Glyfada without the family at home. I had only met her mother on a couple of occasions and had not yet met her father. It gave us a chance to get to know each other without distractions. But Alex missed her family. She was used to the constant noise, the ins and outs of the extended family and the non-stop visits of the neighbours. Without all that, she felt lonely. I spent most weekends with her, but I still needed to fly back to the UK every Monday morning to run my business, and she had her own work to attend to.

After a while, though, the family came back. They arrived like a hurricane. Suddenly the house sprang to life.

Alex's mother's actual name was Despina, but she was known to everyone as Debbie. She was a large, loud lady with no volume control. Debbie's father had been a ship's captain, and I'm sure he taught her to use her voice as a foghorn before she could walk; after that, she never learned how to tone it down. Having been so blessed, there was no need to get near a person in order to have a chat with them, and certainly no need to leave the house – she just had to speak up a bit. To communicate with her neighbours and hold conversations with friends across the road, or even further down the street, she simply yelled through the window of her tiny subterranean kitchen while standing at the cooker. Her friends might be preparing their family meals too, or sitting in their gardens scrubbing vegetables, or sweeping their paths. There were no secrets on that street; everyone knew everything about everybody.

Some days I would sit and listen happily to these long-distance conversations, comparing Alex's 'village', as the locals still called Glyfada, even after its gentrification, to the north London neighbourhood where I grew up. We rarely saw our neighbours, never mind heard them. If we wanted to visit, we would make an appointment. Glyfada was different. I knew from my daily walks that here it was normal to be surrounded by a cacophony of screaming voices struggling to be heard above the traffic noise or the roar of aircraft on their descent into nearby Ellinikon Airport.

If something particularly sensitive was to be discussed, then coffee was required. These were the only times that Debbie's volume button was turned down. A conversation held over coffee was not the sort you could shout across the neighbourhood. They usually concerned a local affair and a discussion about who was currently sleeping with whom. When a neighbour made it clear they wanted a private chat, everyone knew that the gossip would be juicy and they all wanted a piece. Such conversations happened after lunch. The women would shower, change into their best outfits, and come for coffee. The loud yelling of the morning was now replaced with a huddle on the patio, a lot of quiet whispering, and the occasional sharp intake of breath and series of incriminating nods in the direction of the victim's house.

Whenever I asked Alex about these uncharacteristically subdued meetings, she'd reply, 'Oh they're just digging holes. In Greece, the expression is "bring the shovel, we're burying someone".'

The patio was where nearly all the socialising took place. It was the heart of the home, a thin strip of land between our house and the neighbour's, with a floor made up of uneven, random stone blocks. A vibrant bougainvillea covered the wall to one side, spreading uncontrollably and sometimes dropping its confetti of deep red flowers onto the table. The table was actually three wobbly tables pushed together, with a selection of even wobblier chairs arranged around it and a plastic table-cloth stretched over the top. A few stray ashtrays were scattered across it, along with the inevitable coffee cups, perpetually refilled. It was here that we discussed all family business, local gossip and plans for the future. And it was here that we gathered for Sunday lunches.

Sunday is a day of conviviality in Greece, where lunches extend long into the afternoon and you never know who will drop by. Debbie's basement kitchen was just below the patio, and she would always cook enormous quantities on Sundays, singing at the top of her voice as she passed a never-ending series of vast plates out through the little kitchen window to the table. Stuffed tomatoes, meat casseroles, fried calamari, fried eggplants, courgettes dipped in a light, tasty batter, the ubiquitous dishes of rice and fried potatoes... It was open house, after all. And she was right: people always turned up to eat her food, so nothing went to waste.

On my first ever family Sunday at the house, I was surprised to discover that Debbie did all her cooking wearing nothing but her bra and knickers. I was sitting on the patio and glanced down into her dark kitchen to see her standing by the fryers, which were perched on top of a pair of flaming gas rings, clad only in her underwear and cheerfully belting out a tune. For me, this was so refreshing. She was showing me in her way that I was part of the family and she felt comfortable to be herself. After the cooking was done, she would emerge onto the patio freshly showered, dressed in her usual leggings and flowered top, ready to join the fun.

Most lunchtimes we would carry out extra chairs to squeeze around the already packed table as other friends and cousins arrived. Everyone knew that they were always welcome in this house. We usually continued sitting and chatting and eating in the narrow passageway under the bougainvillea until the sun disappeared; then the bottles of ouzo (Greek brandy) and soft drinks were brought out with buckets of ice to see us nicely into the night. This was how Alex's family lived every day, and it was perfect.

Debbie was the kindest woman I'd ever met. She had a smile that matched the long days of Greek sunshine, and it never left her face. She would laugh easily at any situation, but she was also tough and logical and patient. I never saw her angry. She would defuse the most troublesome situations with a smile and a wave of her hand while pointing out the flaw in any argument, restoring familial harmony within moments. She showed me a better way to live, and her daughter, who I am now proud to call my wife, has continued the tradition.

In fact, if it hadn't been for Debbie, I might never even have got together with Alex. Debbie was there at our first meeting and there again at our second encounter, some twenty years later.

Alex and I first met in north London when I was just sixteen and she an innocent fifteen. Debbie and Zissis owned a house in Northwood Hills and were close neighbours of Elton John, who at that time was still known as Reg and used to play his music in the local pub. Zissis had moved the entire family there when his cruise company had asked him to run the London sales office. Alex went to school at the Potter Street Comprehensive and I worked in a nearby butcher's shop. She and her friends would pass by in the mornings and give me a wave. She was the most beautiful creature I had ever seen and I would always make sure that I was near the window, cleaning or arranging trays, at the time I expected her to walk by.

One afternoon, a girl in school uniform came into the shop and handed me an invitation to Alex's birthday party the following Saturday. Unable to think of anything else for the rest of the week, I looked forward to the weekend with a combination of excitement and terror. I had never spoken to this girl of my dreams. What birthday present should I buy? What would I say? How should I act? Was she expecting me to be cool and laid-back, or should I just be my normal fumbling self?

Saturday finally arrived. I followed the directions on the invitation and found the house. I didn't want to be the first to turn up, so I hid around the corner until I saw others knocking, then rushed over to join them. Alex opened the door. She was a vision of loveliness in a short glittery skirt, a belt of wooden beads, a tight gold Lycra top and a gold scarf to finish it off. She kissed her guests on the cheek as they entered the hallway. I felt myself blushing as I waited for my turn. She put her hands on my shoulders, said, 'Geia sas, to ónomá mou eínai Alexándra,' then kissed my bright red cheek.

Her mother arrived behind her, shook my hand and welcomed me. She put her arm around her daughter and said, 'Welcome! We are Greek. Alexandra does not understand much English yet, but she is learning.' Then she translated. 'She said her name is Alexandra, what's yours?'

I shook Alex's hand and introduced myself. With that, she smiled and turned away to join her other guests.

I didn't speak to Alex again that evening and I left the party alone. It hadn't gone the way I'd hoped, but at least we'd spoken and she might remember me the next time she walked past the butcher's.

The following Monday, I waited by the shop window for her to pass. She didn't come. Nor did she appear the next day, or the one after that. After a torturous week, I found out that she and her family had left England and gone home to Greece. I had no address for her and no way of getting in touch. I was devastated.

A few months later, I gave up my job in Northwood to continue my education. Alex did the same. Unbeknownst to me, she went on to get married at nineteen and was then divorced by twenty-one. I also married young and lost my wife to illness. Some days I would think of Alex and wonder how she was. We had never really spoken and didn't know each other, but I was certain that one day we would meet again.

## 3

# THE FORGIVEN

I f Debbie was the heart and soul of the house, Alex's father, Zissis, was the control. But he was often away from home. As a cruise director, he spent much of his time at sea, sailing around the Greek islands and the Mediterranean in summer, cruising the Caribbean in winter.

Zissis was born into the Greek community in Istanbul, Turkey, the only son of a doctor. He'd had a strict upbringing, which he tried and usually failed to replicate in his Glyfada family home. I came to know when his return to Glyfada was imminent: the plastic tablecloths were upgraded to cloths of fine linen, we had our coffee in bone-china cups with saucers, and the non-matching cutlery was thrown into a drawer and replaced with the silver set that was saved for his visits. Plastic tumblers and assorted glassware were hidden in the cupboard and cut-crystal glasses were laid out instead. There was no more cooking in bra and knickers; Debbie stopped singing and dressed formally in her best clothes and impeccable make-up.

Having seen the family prepare for his homecoming, I had a picture in my mind of a stern man. Although there was still laughter and fun in the house, the atmosphere was slightly muted in anticipation, and everything seemed to become more formal. His reputation as a man of integrity and unbending principles preceded him. He had lofty standards and high expectations of his family and I'd already heard stories from Alex about potential boyfriends having been chased away in the past because they didn't meet his criteria. Somewhat nervously, therefore, I agreed to drive Alex to Piraeus to meet him.

There was an impressive ship tied up at the dock. Its pure white hull gleamed in the afternoon sunshine. A slim, balding man walked down the gangplank towards us. Alex ran up to meet him and kissed his cheek, took him by the hand and led him towards me. He held out his hand as she introduced us. Zissis was fluent in several languages and, luckily for me, English was one of them. We chatted amiably during the short drive home. He didn't seem too bad, certainly not the ogre that

I'd expected, having witnessed the furious tidying-up ready for his arrival. Perhaps I was missing something?

That evening I dressed for dinner, just in case.

The lower section of the house, where Debbie and Zissis lived, was dank and pretty dilapidated. It was a semi-basement, reached via an entrance to the side of the building, down three marble steps. A cast-iron lattice door panelled with multi-coloured stained glass opened onto a bare stone floor randomly scattered with rugs. It was always dark and shaded down there, mostly as a defence against the hot Greek summers, allowing the home to stay cool. Although there were windows in every room, these always had the shutters closed to stop the sun penetrating.

In addition to Debbie's tiny kitchen with its ground-level window that opened onto the side patio, there were two bedrooms and a living room. The living room contained a few wooden chairs, a large oak dining table that was always covered in papers, and an old upright piano with assorted bric-a-brac on the lid. The principal seating area comprised two threadbare armchairs and a small sofa arranged in front of the oil-burning boiler whose black pipe disappeared into the chimney breast.

The house always smelled musty. Dampness continually crept through the walls, causing enormous chunks of plaster to fall off the rendered stone. Polythene had been stuck on with masking tape to cover the bald patches, and over these were hung a patchwork of framed old photographs, a few oil paintings, and a poster of the harbour in Castella where Debbie had grown up.

One corner of the living room was dedicated to prayer.

Here, propped on a table and leaning against the crumbling wall, stood a large hand-painted wooden icon showing the infant Jesus in the arms of Mary, both graced with gold halos. Little oil burners flickered continually, the everlasting flame announcing that religion was alive in this house, and rosary beads lay neatly alongside another icon and a clutch of post-cards depicting lesser saints. Almost every house in Greece had a corner like this, with an oil burner always lit and an icon or two of a favourite saint. In our case, because of the family's seafaring history, it was St Nicholas, patron saint of sailors.

I had assumed that the younger generations wouldn't place so much store in faith and saints, but I was disabused of that one night, when, coming home late by bus from the airport to Glyfada, I had a pack of rowdy youths as fellow passengers. For most of the journey they were climbing over seats and loudly singing the praises of their local football team. But when we passed a brightly lit church, every single one of those young men turned towards the church, bowed their heads and crossed themselves, and did not resume their antics until we were clear of it again.

Visitors to the house would pay their respects to the icon too. Every Sunday, Debbie's aunties from Piraeus would arrive for coffee. In Greece, visiting for a coffee usually means staying for the whole afternoon and evening and being treated to a full meal, large quantities of drinks and lots of entertain-ment. The aunties would all turn up together, and they all looked the same: small, elderly women with sparkling eyes and peaceful smiles, always dressed entirely in black and all of them wearing hairnets over their blue-rinsed hairdos. They would enter the house in a line, and with a rhythmic tapping of their walking sticks on the stone floor they'd visit the icon in the corner, taking it in turns to light a candle and cross themselves. Then the tapping resumed as they marched in line to the patio to start the afternoon with a traditional Greek coffee.

Now the gossip flowed. As none of them had televisions or radios, the news shared was of the family. They discussed new recipes, recent additions to their sons' and daughters' houses, who in the village was sleeping with whom, and who had died recently. They spoke no English, and my Greek was still limited to niceties such as offering coffee, but none of this seemed to matter as they included me in their conversation and I just nodded and smiled, happy to be part of the family.

Alex helped me out by translating difficult words or filling in the details when I lost the thread. The phrase 'o sinhores' (the forgiven one) kept cropping up whenever they discussed their late husbands. This interested me as I wondered what crimes the men had committed that required forgiveness. Alex translated my question, which resulted in howls of laughter around the table. When you pass away, the aunties explained, the Orthodox Church forgives all your sins so you can go straight to heaven. 'So we don't need to mention their names again; we simply refer to them as "forgiven".' I wasn't the only one to have been confused by this. The aunties were already widows when Alex was a child, and as she sat listening to their chatter she used to wonder whether all of them had been married to the same man, Mr O Sinhores. Or was it just that all the husbands happened to have had the same name?

One afternoon, once I'd served everyone coffee, the aunties' talk turned to a neighbour of theirs in Castella whose o sinhores had brought shame on the family by not melting. He'd been recently dug up from his resting place and found to still have some flesh on his bones.

I was horrified. 'Why on earth would they dig him up?' I asked.

Alex translated as I listened intently to the explanation.

Apparently, there's a shortage of graves in Greece, and if there is no family grave nearby then relatives of the deceased will rent one at the local cemetery, usually for three to five years. After this time, the grave is opened and the bones are removed by family members and washed in wine. If the family has enough money to continue the rental, the bones are then reburied; if not, they're put into a box and stored in a part of the church known as the ossuary, a building resembling an archive with filing cabinets full of bones. Relatives come and visit the bones, occasionally removing them from the box to pay their respects or to ask a priest to bless them. But use of the ossuary still incurs rent, and for some even this smaller fee can be unaffordable. If the relatives don't show up for an exhumation or have stopped paying rent at the ossuary, the bones are thrown into the 'digestive pit', a subterranean mass grave.

Under Greek law, it's illegal to keep bones anywhere other than a registered cemetery. In the UK, we are permitted to keep the ashes of our cremated relatives, but no Greek houses can have the bones on their mantelpiece. So the bereaved have to keep paying the rent for the grave or for a space in the ossuary.

Having presumably only recently recovered from the funeral of their loved one, relatives not only need to go through another set of rituals but must also hold the bones to bathe them in wine and avoid the indignity of the digestive pit. When the grave is opened, it's a good sign if the body has decayed, leaving clean bones. It means that the earth has accepted them and they were good people. If there is still decaying flesh on the bones, this is taken to signify that they were not so good and that the earth has refused their body. When this happens, the relatives will generally blame the medication, radiotherapy or chemotherapy given to the poor patient before they died, claiming it to have been a preservative. In such cases, they pay additional rent on the grave and the body is reburied for another period before undergoing the same process.

This unfortunate chap had not had the good manners to decompose properly and so had become the subject of local gossip, bringing shame to his grieving widow.

'Don't you have the same custom in England?' one of the aunts asked.

'No,' I said. 'We tend not to dig up our dead relatives. And anyway, our deceased are usually cremated.'

Silence descended on the table as the aunties absorbed this shocking revelation. It was their turn to be horrified. Cremation might have been common practice in ancient Greece, but in modern Greece the Greek Orthodox Church forbids it, considering it to be blasphemous to the human body, which is 'the temple of the Holy Spirit'.

'But some of your saints are still on show in churches, laid out in glass boxes,' I reminded them. 'They didn't melt; in fact they smell of perfume.'

The chatter ceased and they all turned to look at me.

'That's because they are saints,' one of the aunties explained patiently, a sympathetic expression on her face. She clearly felt sorry for the stupid foreigner who didn't understand.

'But how did they know they were saints when they buried them?' I persisted.

Now they looked at me accusingly. Alex kicked my leg under the table and fixed me with a piercing stare. I was obviously treading on dangerous ground. This theological discussion seemed likely to get me into trouble, so I changed the subject.

I decided that in future I would refer to my Grandad Wilfrid as 'o sinhores'. He was the black sheep of our family. Unfortunately, we'd made the mistake of cremating him, so even a name change wouldn't be sufficient to ease his passage to heaven.

Sometimes the gang of sombrely clad aunties were joined by another elderly lady. This was Auntie Olga. Although she was around the same age and size, she was never dressed in black but always wore a flowery dress. Her spectacles had enormous diamond-studded wings which looked like sparkling extensions to her eyebrows, and her hair was always freshly coiffed. She didn't have an o sinhores as she'd never married. Olga was considered to be 'a little loose' and was a hot topic among the other aunties because of her long-term and ongoing affair with a local married doctor.

Through the course of these afternoons with the aunties, an assortment of cousins, neighbours and friends would also drop by the house, adding to the party. At some point, the aunties would disappear back inside and then the sound of Debbie playing the piano would radiate through the window, accompanied by the reedy voices of the aunties as they all joined in for a song or two.

Alex's extended family made me feel welcome from the moment they met me, and the same was true of her neighbours, especially when I was accompanied by Lady. Lady was the family pet, a sweet-faced, medium-sized, middle-aged dog of unknown heritage with a brindled coat and long ears that hung down towards her shoulders. Lady didn't belong to us, and nobody could remember her arriving; she just turned up one day and stayed.

She had never worn a lead but would follow us whenever we left the house, sit outside shops to wait for us and stay at the kerb of busy roads ready for instructions to cross. When we sat down at a pavement cafe, she would snooze under the table.

She didn't understand English, so I needed to learn a few words before allowing her to follow me when I went out alone. The local people loved Lady. They all knew of me, being a foreigner, and, realising that I didn't speak or understand Greek, would announce themselves in the street by saying good morning to Lady and offering a smile to me as they stroked her head. After a few weeks of daily walks, I would also get a 'Good morning, Petros' from the locals. It delighted me. I was slowly fitting into village life.

Sometimes, I'd spend too much time wandering around the village. Lady would get bored and make her own way home. She would be happily sleeping in the garden under a tree when I returned.

As in all Greek homes, cats wandered freely around the gardens. Our garden was no exception. Lady ignored the cats, and they ignored her. Neither would acknowledge the other's existence, and that kept the peace. This did not alter, even at mealtimes. Lady knew that we would feed the cats with a few bits and pieces but that she would receive a bowl of dog food. The cats would hiss and fight over the scraps while Lady watched on. But when Lady received her bowl, they stayed well away, leaving her to eat in peace. She always left a little food in her bowl. It was her way of showing that she was the preferred animal. This morsel would stay uneaten for many hours as she lay next to the bowl while the cats watched and waited for an opportunity to snaffle it. Before finally abandoning the bowl, she would finish the last bite and slowly walk away, leaving the cats again disappointed. The biggest cat-lover on our street was Stella, an elderly lady who lived on the third floor of her recently constructed apartment block. She owned several cats and they seemed to do little but spread themselves over her balcony wall and doze in the sunshine. One year, during an earthquake that struck Glyfada, the buildings shook so much that four of her cats fell off. But Stella soon replaced them with a new crew of feral felines from the neighbourhood.

Stella was a talker, and she liked to corner me and hit me with a barrage of Greek, spoken so rapidly I never saw her take a breath. It didn't seem to matter to her that I didn't understand a word, especially in my early months in Glyfada, and I spent many an encounter with her, walking backwards trying to make my escape while hopefully nodding and smiling in the right places. Most of her conversations with other neighbours were undertaken from her balcony, with her screaming out her observations at the top of her voice. The locals all knew that she just liked to talk and never expected an answer, so they were content to let her pour out her opinions and simply nodded when required as they hurried past.

The upper level of the Glyfada house was brighter and airier than Debbie's home, and this was where Alex and I lived. This part of the house had been designed by Debbie's father, Jannis, to look like a ship's bridge (he was a sea captain). It comprised two curved bay windows on each side of a broad-based marble staircase that narrowed slightly as it reached the veranda, and a recessed front door with porthole windows to either side. The veranda was our equivalent of Debbie's side patio, and Alex and I would sit up there, at the glass table, observing the goings-on down on the street below. On warm summer evenings, after the fierce heat of the day had subsided, our jasmine hedge would emit a heady perfume as we chatted long into the night.

Our living room was at the front of the house, with well-positioned windows that allowed the sunshine to flood in along with a slight breeze, keeping the edge off the overpowering heat. Alex's studio was here too. Her clients came to our house for their therapeutic massages, skin treatments and make-up appointments. The kitchen always had a tub of wax bubbling away on the stove, ready for the next client's hair treatment. The therapy room had a small balcony, which was at almost eye level for anyone walking past. I always ducked and averted my eyes, in case Alex had a client, but often I'd hear a 'Yasou, Peter!' through the open window. Many a time, I'd turn my head to reply, and there would be one of Alex's clients, stark naked on the massage table, waving at me.

Ellinikon Airport, at that time Athens' main international airport, was so close to Glyfada that we would automatically pause our conversation every time an aircraft flew over us on its final approach. When the wind direction changed, the planes would take off in our direction, rattling the windows and setting off all the car alarms in the village. But we were used to this.

When Alex was younger, she knew the timetable of most of the departing airlines and would use the noise to cover her secret night-time flits to the local discos. Coming home at the end of a night out, she'd wait patiently outside the house for a noisy one that would allow her to slip back unnoticed through her bedroom window. The Russian planes were the best because they were really loud.

The teenaged Alex had a passion for discos, and luckily for her, Glyfada was fast becoming fashionable for its bars and nightclub. She began to hone escape skills that even a wartime POW would have been proud of. She knew every creak of the window and the best way to open the door without inconvenient clicks. She learned how to make her empty bed appear as if she were still in it, and she familiarised herself with the breathing patterns of her mother and grandmother, listening for gentle snores to ensure that they were fully asleep and not just pretending so as to catch her out. In Greece, the girl child was always watched more closely than the boy, but ironically it was Christos, Alex's brother, who got discovered more often than not when he tried the same escape tactics. He has never been as sneaky as his sister.

# 4

## WAR HEROES AND CALAMARI

For all its decades of joyous gatherings and cherished traditions, the Glyfada house was old and crumbling. It felt out of place in what was nowadays not a fishing village but a glamourous suburb of Athens. After sitting tight watching five-storey apartment blocks rise around us, Alex and I had decided that it was time to join the fashion. We could no longer see the sun; being the last small house left in the street, we were permanently in shadow. It made sense to add to the recent explosion of developments by knocking down our beloved house and replacing it with a multi-storey version.

If our plans came together, things would change forever. We would leave this house of laughter. I already had so many happy memories there, and I was but a recent addition to the family. I could only imagine the sadness of Alex and Debbie, as they had lived most of their lives in this home, where even the stones were warm and welcoming.

By now, having been married to Alex for five years, I'd forged a close relationship with Debbie and Zissis. Debbie was generous beyond belief, a wonderfully loving person who set an example that was easy to follow. Nothing was too much trouble. She was open with her feelings, always had a smile in her eyes and was forever looking for a reason to laugh. More straight-laced and reserved, Zissis was the realist who ensured her generosity had a limit. It was an excellent combination. But how would the two of them react to our radical rebuilding proposal?

Alex and I had begun our negotiations with potential developers in secret. We wanted to minimise the stress and heartache for Zissis and in particular Debbie by doing the legwork first, sourcing the best possible contractors. After a few weeks and several interviews, we had finally settled on an architect. He had built other apartment blocks in our street, so he had the local knowledge. Now we just had to convince Debbie. We flew in from London with our nerves on edge.

I knew we had entered Greek airspace because the light changed. The Aegean sparkled in the sunshine as we passed over Thessaloniki, the city no more than a sprinkle of sand on a green mountain. I could see the three green fingers of land reaching into the sea, an unmistakable sign that we were nearly home. Alex poked me gently in the ribs and interrupted my daydream. She was trying to explain yet again what to say, but more particularly what not to say to the architect during tomorrow's meeting.

The plane circled the outskirts of Athens, turned sharp left over the island of Aegina, its heaps of pistachio nuts drying in the sun just about visible if you squinted. Another left turn over Vari, a favourite destination for spit-roasted-lamb lunches, before we flew low over Glyfada and touched down just up the road at Ellinikon, Athens' international airport. Minutes later, we were at the house, picking up Debbie and Zissis ready for lunch in Castella, where we would break the news.

Castella is a suburb of Piraeus, a picturesque fishing harbour encircled by tavernas nestled together in a curve overlooking the sea. Debbie was born and raised there, together with her younger brother Vasilis, so whenever we had the chance, we would take her to Castella for lunch and enjoy listening to tales of her youth. Today we had a different agenda.

Every taverna had a server outside, waving menus at passing cars and pedestrians, trying to tempt us in to try their speciality, all of which were fish-related. We quickly scanned the restaurants through the flexi-glass walls around the outdoor tables, rejecting the ones with real cotton tablecloths as they were likely to be expensive, and finally opting for a charming-looking establishment right on the harbour; we could have walked through and boarded a boat without touching the shore. The chairs had been painted Aegean blue and each table had just an ashtray and a bottle of olive oil perched on top. We were led to the one nearest the sea.

Zissis took charge, ordering the food and chatting to the server, discussing the options. In Greece, only tourists generally get a menu. With Greek diners, the waiter will stand or, more usually, as on this occasion, sit at the table and explain the best dishes of the day.

I was gazing over the water, appreciating the beautiful scenery and watching the grey mullet dart between boats in search of the bread and pieces of shrimp shell being fed to them by the children on the next table. Alex squeezed my hand and whispered, 'We need to talk about the house.'

I turned back. The waiter had left to take our order to the kitchen. It was time to broach the subject with Debbie and Zissis. Although we had been casually discussing the possibility of development with them for a while, they were unaware that we'd been meeting with architects and were well into the details. We needed to ask for their blessing.

In Greece, property passes to the daughter, and this family was no exception. Debbie, being the legal owner, controlled all matters in relation to the Glyfada house, and her permission would be necessary if we were to rebuild. At this point, Alex and I were spending more time together in England, and her parents were living permanently in Glyfada. Zissis was still travelling with his job on the cruise ships but was working less now as he prepared for his imminent retirement.

As the wine arrived, I poured out four glasses, handed them around the table and delivered my prepared spiel. Debbie and Zissis both listened intently as I explained that we could have three nice new flats in the fresh development and a shop which could be rented as an income for the future. Debbie sipped her wine and looked at Alex. A rare frown crept across her face and her eyes dropped as she considered our proposal. I could see that she was battling with our wish to progress and improve our situation, but this was her home, lovingly built for her by her father many years ago.

Debbie's father was Jannis. He was a sea captain and part owner of a large cargo ship based in Piraeus. The family lived in Castella, in a house overlooking the harbour, just up the hillside from where we now sat. The house had been demolished to make way for a petrol station in 1965, but the small natural harbour had remained unchanged. The same traditional fishing boats of the village sat peacefully tied to the harbour walls, waiting for the next generation of fishers.

In Greece, it is customary to give your daughter a home as her wedding present. So when the time came for his only daughter to wed, Jannis set about buying a piece of land. Debbie chose Glyfada, a location she loved, just a short twenty-minute drive around the coast from Castella. Her father had allowed her the decision as he wanted her to start her marriage in the best way possible.

Debbie's father was a playful man. When not at sea, he would spend his time at home and around the village. He was a strict captain and ruled his ship with an iron fist, but at home he was a kind, humorous husband and dad. Debbie would have us in fits of giggles as she recounted his practical jokes – how he once waited until the local priest and a party of nuns came to the house for coffee and then ran in wearing his wife's dress and shoes and danced around the room. Like Debbie, he loved his food. If a dinner party was planned, her mother, Bia, would cook each dish and immediately take it to the neighbour's house for safekeeping while he was out, otherwise he would certainly have consumed the lot immediately upon his return.

Alex also has fond memories of her grandfather and remembers him taking her down to the kafenio near the harbour in Castella to meet his friends. Cafes play an important role in Greek social life and are far more than simply a place to drink coffee – you expect to be there for at least two hours – so Alex used to get bored. As a seafaring man, Grandfather Jannis knew knots and would use this expertise to tie a rope around her waist, giving her the freedom to wander around and play. He would sit chatting to his friends while holding her on a line like a fish. When she neared the water, he would just reel her back in.

During the Second World War, while the Germans occupied Greece, Jannis worked with the resistance and for the British. He used his knowledge of local maritime conditions to rescue Allied soldiers and ferry them away from the occupied territory under cover of darkness, aiding their escape. One night, as he was transporting three Allied soldiers to a rendezvous with a British submarine that was about to surface a few kilometres offshore, a German patrol boat, acting on a tipoff, boarded his boat just outside the harbour. The Germans captured everyone on board.

The Allied soldiers were sent to a prisoner-of-war camp and Jannis was taken to the local Gestapo headquarters for questioning. The Greek resistance movement was known to be one of the most ferocious in Europe and when it began having an impact on the occupation, the Germans passed over control of the population to the ruthless Gestapo. They requisitioned a building at 6 Merlin Street in Athens for their headquarters, and this served as the main interrogation centre and contained torture chambers and prison cells. Anyone suspected of belonging to the resistance or committing other acts of defiance was taken to this terrible place. Some never came out. Hundreds of individuals who passed through the doors of 6 Merlin Street were either tortured to death or sent to the nearby concentration camp at Chaidari. The Nazis left corpses hanging from trees for days as a warning to other citizens.

When the Germans withdrew from Athens in October 1944, the building returned to civilian use. In the 1980s, it was converted into a shopping centre, so the site of the former Gestapo building now houses a beauty retail outlet, and the area where the torture chambers were is now full of cosmetic displays. Outside the building stands a memorial to those who were detained, tortured or killed at 6 Merlin Street. It includes a carving of a bound prisoner, one of the original torture chamber doors, and several plaques, one of which reads: 'Free people were led through this door.'

Like his fellow resistance fighters, Jannis was also tortured at 6 Merlin Street. The Gestapo were trying to make him give away his friends and allies. Jannis didn't break after the first day and was left to reconsider through the night. He then withstood a second day of brutality. Realising that he would never assist them, the Germans put Jannis in front of a military tribunal, who sentenced him to death. He was transported to the Chaidari concentration camp, located in the grounds of a Greek army barracks in a suburb of Athens. Chaidari was the largest and most notorious of the camps in Greece, nicknamed the 'Bastille of Greece'. During its one year of operation, it's estimated that 21,000 people passed through the camp, including Jews, Italian POWs and Greek political prisoners. The Jews were transported north, destined either for Auschwitz or for Germany to work as forced labour; the other prisoners were detained at Chaidari for questioning by the Gestapo. Approximately two thousand inmates were executed at the camp.

Jannis, however, was among the few who managed to get out of there alive. One of his closest friends happened to be a German sea captain who'd been a fierce, clandestine, critic of Hitler before the war. His ship had been requisitioned by the German state to carry supplies and was docked at Piraeus.

When the captain found out that the Gestapo had captured Jannis, he dreamed up an elaborate escape plan together with Jannis's comrades in the resistance. Part of his ship's cargo was a consignment of German officers' uniforms, some of which were destined for the SS headquarters. So he and a few of his like-minded crew dressed up in SS uniforms and went to the prison camp. As they appeared to be high-ranking officers and German, it was fairly straightforward to convince Jannis's low-ranking guards to hand him over into their custody, and so Jannis got away.

Once free, he went into hiding to recover from the wounds he'd sustained during his torture at the hands of the Gestapo. His resistance group contacted the British army, who arranged the next phase of his escape. They took him to a rocky cove near his home village, Castella, where a British boat was waiting to ferry him to an Allied submarine out at sea. We know nothing about the fate of his German friend, or the details of his torture, as Jannis would never discuss it. But when he finally returned to his family, years later, he wore a patch over a glass eye.

Because the Gestapo had sentenced Jannis to death, he was now a wanted man. He had no option but to flee Greece, leaving his family to fend for themselves. Debbie was only twelve years old. She first recounted her father's story to me as she sat with me in one of the Castella tavernas, gazing wistfully at the small boats in the harbour. The family endured great hardship after her father fled. The Greeks were starving. A famine had begun, and people were running out of food. Her father's resistance comrades did what they could to help his family, but food was scarce, so they went hungry. Since I'd become part of this family, I'd been impressed by the tremendous amounts of food Debbie prepared on a daily basis. She spared no expense and always cooked much more than we could eat. She always gave the reason that someone might visit and would probably be hungry. Indeed, this was usually the case, and many people came. Her experience of being hungry as a girl had taught her to appreciate a good meal.

Jannis eventually arrived in British Columbia, Canada on a cargo ship from Turkey, and at once set to work on a plan to help his wife, Bia, and their young children, Debbie and Vasilis. One morning Bia received a visit from a priest who told her she should go to an address in Athens where there were some sweets waiting for her. She duly set off, taking Debbie and Vasilis with her.

On arrival, they were met by one of Jannis's old friends and given a small leather bag. This contained fifty gold sovereigns, worth around £15,000 in today's money. With this wealth, not only was Bia able to buy food on the black market, but she could also assist other starving people in Castella.

Jannis had secured a position with a Canadian shipping line and joined the war effort against the German navy as captain of a cargo ship. He was involved in the Battle of the Atlantic, the struggle to supply Britain with essentials in the face of the Germans' attempts to stem the flow of merchant shipping. His salary, converted into sovereigns, kept coming for the duration of the war. Bia continued to feed as many as she could.

Years later, Grandmother Bia was the love of Alex's life. She was mostly responsible for Alex's early upbringing as Debbie worked full-time in the University of Athens teaching music. I met Grandmother Bia when she was much older. She spoke no English, only Greek and French, neither of which I understood at the time, so we communicated with nods and smiles. She would sit in Debbie's tiny, dark kitchen and keep her company while she cooked the family meal. Her face was that of an angel. When she smiled, her eyes sparkled and lit up the room; they were full of wisdom, hiding the years of suffering. She taught Debbie to value and respect the family and a happy home, and Debbie passed this down to Alex, and so to me.

The building of Debbie's marital home started just as Greece was returning to normal following the German occupation and after Jannis's return from exile. Jannis had given his son, Vasilis, a job on his ship and would mentor him over the next few years to follow in his footsteps. Vasilis would eventually captain his own vessel. But before setting out to sea, Jannis arranged for the building of the house in Glyfada to start. They had designed the front of the house to resemble the bridge of a ship, with two curved bays and a marble staircase leading to the upper level. The material would not be brick but large yellow sandstone rocks hewn from a nearby quarry.

Jannis and Vasilis would be away at sea for many months at a time, so Jannis arranged for his cousin to oversee the work. She was experienced with building, was already constructing a row of shops nearby, in Athens, and had a builder who could split his time between the two projects. This all seemed like a good plan until the bills rolled in. Every port Jannis visited, there was a message left through his shipping company demanding money for the building work. He arranged for the invoices to be paid via his employers to keep the construction going. Costs had escalated to more than double what they'd budgeted for, and the family were becoming suspicious. They soon learned that not only had they been paying the builder for his labour and materials in Glyfada, they had also paid for the row of new shops in

Athens too. We could only hope that our own construction project wouldn't go the same way.

The house was eventually completed in 1958 and Debbie finally had a new home in which to embark on married life. At that time, it was the largest and most imposing house on the street. Being stone-built and two floors high, with a sweeping marble staircase, it was quite different to all the other single-storey dwellings on the street. Those had been built from whitewashed concrete blocks, with extensions added over the years as the families grew. Sometimes these were masonry, but more often they comprised rough wooden walls and corrugated tin roofs. All the houses had gardens in which grew pomegranate and fig trees, and perhaps orange and lemon trees too, which flourished in the warm climate.

Soon, Alex and her brother Christos came along. Alex would play in the street with friends from the neighbourhood on the unmade earth road. When she got hungry, she would pick a pomegranate or peel an orange to sate her hunger before being called in for lunch. Whenever she reminisced about her Glyfada childhood, I would reflect on my own in north London. I used to be repeatedly chased away from my neighbours' gardens after scrumping a sour cooking apple or a rock-hard pear. Compared to my young life, Glyfada seemed like the Garden of Eden.

But now nearly all the gardens were gone.

The street was only around 150 metres long, set back from the main village square. These days, there were shops at either end and a couple of restaurants in the middle, and the remaining space was taken up with newly developed apartment blocks fronted by a few eucalyptus trees. Our house was the only original one left. To the rear was a high wall hiding an open-air cinema. The latest films played there nightly, mostly in English. We quickly got to know most of the words of the latest blockbuster, having no choice but to listen to the dialogue three times a night.

By the time I'd finished outlining our plans for the new apartment block that would replace our old Glyfada home, Debbie, Zissis, Alex and I were surrounded by half-empty platters of fish and seafood. For a while, no one spoke. We continued to polish off the last few calamari and gulps of wine.

Debbie was still taking in the news. I could see that she was weighing up the prospect of a better retirement for herself and a future for her daughter. But this would mean losing the home where she had spent her happiest years. Gone would be the bougainvillea and its daily scattering of red confetti on the narrow patio where so many happy memories had been forged. Gone would be the perfume from the jasmine bush that invaded our senses on long hot summer evenings as we chatted and laughed while looking down on the street and shouting our greetings to passing neighbours. A concrete box would now replace this heavenly home. I could understand her hesitancy.

I reached across the taverna table and took her hand. She looked up and met my eyes. There were tears running down her cheeks but a smile played on her lips. She had decided. 'Are you sure this is what you want?' she asked.

I glanced at Alex, who nodded. Seeing Debbie's eyes well up, I was having second thoughts. 'We can delay this for a few more years,' I said.

'You are my son and the husband of my daughter. If you think it's the right thing to do, you have my blessing,' Debbie said. 'Let's do it now.'

## 5

## SWIMMING WITH SHARKS

Normally, the selection of a developer in Greece is by word of mouth and personal recommendation. As most people in Glyfada had already been through a similar rebuilding process, we'd asked around. This proved to be its own challenge, however. Like with most builders the world over, relationships tended to be good at the start of the project, before then rapidly going downhill, until, by the end of the works, all parties invariably hated each other. So, after listening to horror stories from several of our friends and neighbours, we went with the least-hated architect. He had an office in the area, so at least we could monitor him, and, being local, he'd be less inclined to upset us. Or so we thought.

The next day the architect arrived. Stavros was a short, stout fellow with cropped hair and tanned skin. He was wearing a pair of blue jogging pants and an unbuttoned white polo shirt. In one hand he held a string of large blue worry beads, which he nervously fumbled with; they clicked continually while he laid out his proposal. He avoided looking me in the eye, which concerned me, but I put this down to him being nervous so did not follow my instincts, which were trying to warn me.

Alex also picked up on this. She smiled and went deeper into the questioning. After all, we were considering joining with this chap in the most important decision of our lives. Stavros did not know who he was dealing with and was quite unprepared for the grilling to come. When having a serious discussion with Alex, you know you're in trouble when she smiles at you. This ploy has the effect of putting you at your ease and encouraging you to continue digging yourself into a hole. Beware! She's not agreeing with you but gathering information for the imminent attack.

She will sit like a spider in its web, beckoning you in with sweet words while nodding in what appears to be agreement until you lower your guard. Now you are ready to be consumed. Then the famous Greek logic is brought to bear. She will, in just a few words, destroy your argument and make you feel like a clumsy schoolboy reaching for safety after falling into a fast-running river. Stavros was in for the interrogation of his life.

With domestic developments in high-value areas of Greece, it is common to enter a formal agreement with the architect in what is known as adiparohy symphonia. In such arrangements, the architect takes full responsibility for obtaining planning permission, commissioning all technical drawings and covering all demolition and construction costs. In return, he receives an agreed proportion of the finished building. In our case, Stavros was proposing to construct five apartments and two shops. He would keep two of the flats and one shop, and we would have the rest. This seemed a good deal, but we needed to be sure. Theoretically it shouldn't cost us anything as he would receive a good profit for his investment.

Friends who had been through a similar experience advised us to be very careful. We were about to enter the shark pond and we would be on the menu.

As we started our negotiations, we made our demands. He countered with his. After two hours of arguments and counter-arguments and Alex's forensic examination, Stavros was flushed. Trickles of sweat ran down the sides of his face.

We were almost ready to sign. We had discussed everything from the allocation of parking spaces and the exact meterage of the apartments to the colour of the floor tiles. We'd even agreed on a completion date. He promised to deal with all the bureaucratic paperwork and required permissions, meaning that there was nothing further for us to do and nothing to pay. We could simply walk into the building on completion.

The last sticking point was the allocation of floors. Stavros suggested that our apartments would be on the lower level and that he would keep the top two floors. This was not acceptable to us. The top floor was always the most valuable, and we wanted to use the roof terrace for ourselves. This part of the discussion wasn't going his way, but he persisted.

'I will not agree to this,' he said, and slammed his file on the table.

Alex immediately got up from her chair, picked up the scattered paperwork, handed everything back to him, walked over to the door, opened it and informed him that the deal was off. She finished by politely telling him to have a nice day.

He didn't move but looked at Debbie for reassurance. She smiled sweetly at him but said nothing. He pleaded with me and insisted that it was a good deal. I said nothing. He was outnumbered. Realising he would not win, he eventually acquiesced. So we signed the contract. We would get the penthouse, and Debbie and Zissis would have two small flats on the first floor, one of which they could rent out, giving them a small income. The shop would provide rental income for Alex.

This all seemed good, but having engaged in nothing like this before, it was worrying. I had assumed responsibility for the deal and felt a lot of weight on my shoulders. I had to get it right. I continually tried to anticipate all the potential problems that might arise. The project occupied my every waking moment and haunted my dreams.

I was born into a working-class family and grew up in a rented house, so I'd never thought about building. When I left home to make my way in the world, I worked hard and saved enough to put down a deposit for my very own house. I thought this was the ultimate achievement, but I now realised that buying a house in England was nothing compared with building a new apartment block in Athens. In the UK, the system allows you to feel safe as most of the work is done through solicitors and estate agents. Here, we were alone and vulnerable.

More worrying still, the contract was written in ancient

Greek, a language that very few Greeks who are not lawyers understand. Written Greek comes in two versions, modern and ancient, and all legal contracts are written in the latter. The cliche 'all Greek to me' therefore also applied to my Greek family in this instance. Wading through the contract ourselves was pointless. The family had just signed this crucial document on the trust of the architect, which concerned me, and rightly so.

I expressed my fears to the family, who were wonderfully supportive. They told me they had faith, and not to worry, but I couldn't help feeling I might let them down. After all, the original pitch had come from me, so I'd made myself responsible for the success of the project.

The time arrived to say goodbye to our cherished home. We had devoted the last few days to packing up everything destined to be put into storage. Zissis had gone back to sea, leaving us to deal with the move. We were ruthlessly throwing away things that we would no longer require and the pile of discarded items had grown into a small mountain in the front garden.

Debbie was quietly staring at the ever-growing heap of once-prized possessions. Her valued piano was on top. She'd been a music teacher, and not only was this piano the tool of her trade, it had also been the focus of a thousand sunny Sunday afternoons. Friends and relatives used to gather round it and sing as Debbie played medleys of traditional Greek music along with other well-known songs from films and Broadway. Music had always been a source of life in the house. Sundays would be the piano recitals, but on most other days there'd be Debbie singing at the top of her voice while cooking or peeling vegetables.

The collection of treasures accumulated over half a century now sat unceremoniously in a pile, waiting to be thrown away. It was a sad sight. I put my arm around her ample waist and gave her a tissue to wipe away her tears.

Alex was sitting quietly on a stool under the olive tree, dabbing at her own tears with the end of her sleeve. We had all been so busy packing and sorting out which items to save and which to discard, we hadn't been thinking too hard about the enormity of what we were doing. Now we were finished and ready to leave. The sadness had at last hit us all.

I could only imagine how they were feeling about these last hours at their wonderful home. I'd been around for a mere three years and already had so many happy memories there. I decided they needed a distraction. 'Barbecued lamb?' I whispered.

Debbie's eyes sparkled as she shifted her gaze from the depressing accumulation of redundant belongings. She smiled.

We left the packed cardboard boxes, stumbled over the scattered remnants and got into the car. We were going to Vari for lunch.

Vari is a meat-eater's paradise about ten minutes' drive from Glyfada. As we approached the village along the busy airport road, we could see, to our right, the lengthy line of lamb tavernas set back along the slip road. All of them had a representative outside, dressed in traditional Greek costume and dancing in front of the car, trying to wave us into their establishment. We ignored the first few, as Debbie preferred the third one along. The elderly costumed guy outside this restaurant seemed less enthusiastic and was just sitting on the wall with his stick leaning against his knees while he rolled a cigarette. This being Vari's best taverna, he didn't have to work too hard at encouraging us in.

A whole lamb was turning on a spit over a bed of glowing charcoal inside the glass-fronted cooking area. The decor was basic, with old wooden tables and creaky chairs lined up in neat rows on the rough, tiled floor and a few posters on the wall, including one of a sheepdog feeding a bottle of milk to a lamb. The noise of passing traffic mingled with tinny village music coming out of an old black speaker. Its wires dangled down, feeding off the nearby radio.

The smell was mouth-watering. This was fast food, Greek style. We selected a table and dragged another table over to join it. Being hungry, we'd be ordering too much food to fit onto just one. The waiter standing in the corner realised this, turned and grabbed another plastic tablecloth and approached to stretch them over both surfaces.

'Ti tha thelate na phate?' (What would you like to eat?) he asked.

Alex and Debbie temporarily forgot the sadness of the day as they focused their minds on the meal to come. 'What do you have today?' Alex asked.

The server repeated the memorised menu while Debbie and Alex listened. There was spit-roasted lamb, suckling pig, barbecued lamb chops, liver, kidneys, and Debbie's all-time favourite, kokoretsi. This is a selection of unpleasant bits from the inside of a lamb, including the liver, heart, spleen and lungs, which all gets wrapped up with the intestines and barbecued slowly over charcoal with a sprinkling of salt and oregano.

Alex paid careful attention and then said, 'Yes, let's have that.'

The waiter looked at her. 'Which one?'

'Everything,' she replied.

A grin spread over his face. He understood that we were big eaters, and we had become his best friends.

I ordered a kilo of local white wine for Debbie and me, and a coke for Alex. In Greece, wine is sold by weight, so a kilo is equivalent to a litre or around two pints. It arrived swiftly, in a large glass carafe with drops of condensation already forming. They made the wine on the premises from grapes grown nearby and stored it in giant barrels at the back of the taverna. It was rough and bitter, but it complemented the food. And at less than one euro for a litre, we were more than happy.

When dining in Greece with others, it is traditional to order dishes to share, served in the middle of the table. Meat is ordered by the kilo. Salads are large and always shared. This dispenses with formality and is more friendly. On the islands, restaurants also cater for tourists who prefer individual dishes, but Greeks are used to digging into everything on the table.

The food began to arrive. First came an enormous basket of toasted bread sprinkled with olive oil and mountain herbs; a large Greek salad with feta cheese and olive oil followed. There were also courgettes deep-fried in a light batter, a dish of boiled greens picked that morning from the nearby mountain, and a side order of fried potatoes. The gold and glistening barbecued lamb came together with the roast pork, well-done lamb cutlets and Debbie's eagerly awaited kokoretsi.

In England, sadness and loss are usually dealt with by a cup of tea and a chat. In our family we do this over vast quantities of food. Greeks will use a family meal to discuss all sorts of issues, to cope with the loss of a loved one or just to raise their spirits. As we ate and sipped the rough wine, we all felt better. Debbie reminisced about the fun times in our home, and Alex joined in with her memories of night-time escapes through her bedroom window. By the time the meal was finished, our tears of sadness had become tears of laughter as the funny stories flowed.

Once we'd rounded off our lunch with a mountain of yogurt topped with honey running down the sides and pooling around the base, we waddled out and eased ourselves into the car for the short drive home.

We arrived back at the house to find that all the rubbish had gone and that the removal company had taken all the taped-up boxes. Our home was an empty shell.

Our neighbour, Kostas, was peering over the wall at the lifeless building. He had daughters about Alex's age, and they were firm friends. Kostas was the local tobacco baron and owned a wholesale warehouse supplying cigarettes to most of the thousands of kiosks found on street corners throughout Athens. This had made him rich and he owned his entire apartment block outright. But it seemed that this had come at a price. When he talked, he made bubbling sounds at the back of his throat and constantly coughed out unidentified lumps into a tissue after each sentence. Alex was certain that smoking too much of his own product had caused this affliction. He'd also been shot during a robbery at his warehouse. He was proud of this and would often show off his bullet wound and boast about his bravery in protecting his business and not giving in to the thieves. He had been a handsome man, and he knew it. Always immaculately dressed, he drove the finest cars and had made his house into a fortress with high walls and electronic gates.

I glanced across the road and saw our nosy neighbour Pandelis huffing and puffing, trying to ram Debbie's old piano into the back of his van. He had liberated it from the rubbish pile and was likely to be on his way to the flea market to see if he could turn a quick profit. We didn't mind; it was now a relic from our old life and wasn't needed anymore.

The local gossips suspected Pandelis of having a penchant for the darker side of Athens and of being a frequent visitor to the old brothels located south of the city's Omonia Square. He was said to be most disappointed when the alleged brothel in our street finally closed down. I had heard about this place from Debbie only recently, after we'd decided to build our new apartment block. She stormed into the house one day after having had coffee with a neighbour, Mimi.

'She forgets I know where she comes from,' Debbie raged.

It was very rare to see Debbie angry, so I presumed there had to be a good reason. Alex and I sat her down and asked her to relax and tell us what the problem was. Debbie replied that she had been discussing the future development of our house into the apartment block and that Mimi had criticised her for giving away half of our new building. When Mimi had built her apartments, she didn't need to make an agreement with a developer, she proudly informed Debbie, because she was rich enough to employ a builder herself, thereby keeping all the flats and both shops.

Debbie was still angry as she let us in on the gossip. In the late 1950s, when our house was first built, Mimi owned a house on the corner. Debbie noticed that there were a lot of men arriving and departing from the house through the night. She didn't know Mimi as she never came out in the daytime, but the local gossip informed her that this was either a house of ill repute or an illegal gambling den. Nothing had been proved, so it was generally ignored until one day the police raided. They took Mimi away in handcuffs and the house was cleared and boarded up. A week later she was back. Although the house looked to be closed up, with boards over the windows and the garden overgrown, men would continue to visit at all hours of the night. Finally, one day, the bulldozers arrived and knocked down the house and a new construction was started on.

Mimi had become respectable and began to socialise with the neighbours. Debbie got friendly with her and would invite her to the house for coffee. One evening, she turned up crying;

it transpired that Mimi's husband had left her. Debbie consoled her with a glass of cherry brandy and an understanding ear. At which point it all came out. Mimi was indeed the local madam. She had inherited the house, along with a few working girls, as a going concern from her mother, who had originally set up the brothel for German officers during the Second World War. After the war ended, Mimi continued to offer the services of her house to the well-heeled men of Glyfada. Over the years she made a fortune and became a rich woman. Now she was denouncing Debbie for not being rich enough to afford to keep our new building in its entirety.

Kostas came out of his gate to join us while Debbie walked around our home one last time. He proudly pointed at his apartment block next door and puffed out his chest. 'I'm sure your new apartment will be nice, but probably not as nice as mine.' With that, he bade us farewell and went back though his gate.

There was no longer anything to remind us that anyone had lived there. We felt detached now. We walked away without glancing back. That was our old life. From here on, we would focus on the future.

# 6

# SNOWBALLS AND A WOLF CUB

D ebbie immediately returned to the UK to meet up with
Zissis; she would remain there for the duration of the
construction process. Alex and I would oversee the project,
flying back and forth between London and Glyfada over the

coming months, to keep an eye on the building work and in particular on Stavros. In the three years since we had been together, Alex had begun to show me the real Greece, and I had met many warm and generous people. But I had never been involved in business there. Friends had warned me to be careful, and I still had a nagging feeling that we'd embarked on a relationship with a shark who was determined to line his pockets with our heritage. But we had signed the contract, so all we could do was hope for the best while keeping our eyes open.

It was Thursday afternoon by the time we'd packed up the house and waved Debbie off at the airport; on Monday we would complete the paperwork, so we now had a free weekend to fill. As part of our agreement, Stavros had arranged a furnished apartment for us to stay in until our new home was complete, so that's where Alex and I now headed.

It was horrible! Stavros had only completed the rental agreement with the owner that day, having left this until the last minute, so we had no chance to reject it and find an alternative. It was above a shop just off the main road into central Athens. We parked outside, watched closely by an old man sitting on a wooden chair leaning back against a dirty white wall. His eyes narrowed as we approached him. 'We're moving into the flat,' Alex told him. He reached into his pocket, took out a keyring and beckoned us to follow him down a dark hallway to the side of the shop. As our eyes adjusted to the gloom, we noted the flaking paint on the long grey wall.

Stavros had assured us that our temporary apartment was 'very nice'. In reality it was depressingly dark and musty. With the old man already returned to his chair out on the street, we set to work trying to make it a home. I opened all the shutters while Alex mopped over the stone floor. Then she made the beds while I walked to the supermarket for some essentials to render the place a little more habitable. By the time I returned, the flat had been transformed. It was still basic, but it was at least somewhere we could sleep in comfort whenever we came over for a site inspection.

Next morning, we were woken at 5 a.m. by the loud rumble of traffic. We needed a distraction from the grotty flat and any regrets about our now derelict home, something to take our minds off things for the weekend. It was late November but still warm, so I suggested we go to Piraeus and catch the first ferry to wherever it happened to be sailing. Alex had a better idea. 'Let's go skiing,' she declared.

I looked at her the way a parent might look at a stupid child. 'But this is Greece – do you mean waterskiing?' I asked.

'No. Real skiing, with snow and everything,' she replied. 'I know a place.'

I had never heard of a Greek ski resort. But after a two-hour drive, we arrived at one of the most beautiful villages I had ever seen. This was Arachova.

We had left Athens early, taking the national road north and then turning off towards the distant mountains. The winding mountain road was dotted with billboards advertising ski equipment and showing cheerful families wearing bobble hats and puffa jackets atop a snowy summit. As we drove into the village, the pine-covered slopes and snowy peaks were reminiscent of Switzerland. The narrow road through Arachova was cobbled, as were the pathways on either side, and all the shops had their wares attractively displayed on hooks outside. Selections of walking sticks, long red salamis, and cheeses bound with twine hung erratically over tables piled with jars of local honey. There were colourful packets of nuts and wild herbs tied up in bunches. Between the shops were bars and restaurants.

Arachova dates back to medieval times and is carved out of the side of Mount Parnassus. As we walked up the hill towards the centre, the mountain was briefly visible to the left, behind the buildings, before disappearing up into the clouds; looking down, the valley vanished into more clouds below. The beauty of the place had overwhelmed me since rounding the bend in the road, and I was still in a dreamlike state of appreciation. The air was chilly and smelled of woodsmoke. But something in my subconscious was nagging at me. Then it clicked. I'd been so busy admiring the quaint shops and inviting restaurants and bars that I'd forgotten why we were there. Now I remembered.

I'd already noticed people wandering around dressed in full snowsuits with skis over their shoulders, but I'd forgotten to notice the most obvious thing. There was no snow.

I turned to Alex. 'This is a ski resort, right?'

'Yes. Look, he's got skis,' she said, pointing to a boyish man sitting outside a cafeteria with all the kit leaning against a spare chair.

'Where's the snow then?'

She waved her hand in the direction of the mountain. 'Up there somewhere, but let's have breakfast first.'

We selected a cafeteria and walked out to the balcony at the rear. The view was spectacular. Our table looked over the valley and in the distance we could see the village of Delphi. A grove of olive trees was bathed in sunshine, and beyond that the seaside resort of Itea met the distant Gulf of Corinth.

Replete after a traditional Greek breakfast of coffee, cheese pies (teropitas) and yogurt with honey, we booked into a hotel and changed into warm clothes, ready for our skiing adventure. We drove on up the mountain, in search of snow. At the edge of a pine forest, a police officer flagged down the car, pointed to my front wheels and demanded we fit snow chains, even though the snow itself was still proving elusive. Back down the mountain we went, to find a garage and buy a set of new chains, which we duly brought back to the officer. He'd gone to sit in his car by now, with the heater blowing, but he emerged as we approached and gave me a quick lesson in fitting chains.

Just a few metres further on, snowdrifts appeared along the banks of the road. These became deeper and deeper as we continued up the mountain, until the snow now covered the entire road and we were driving in the tyre tracks of other vehicles. It soon got considerably thicker. The snow that had been ploughed the previous day was banked up along the roadside, in places to a height of more than three metres, leaving a narrow passage for us to pass along. Eventually we emerged at a sign welcoming us to Parnassus Ski Resort.

A row of compact cable cars was steadily inching along on wires between large pylons, some rising into the clouds, others coming towards us and disappearing into the building ahead. Inside the cable-car station, the gigantic metal wheel was grinding and whirring as the cars turned to let people off and then admit more skiers. The relentless passage back up the mountain continued.

Once fitted out with hired boots and skis, we jumped into the next car and began the next part of our mountain ascent.

'Have you ever skied before?' Alex asked.

'No. You?'

'Me neither,' she replied.

So there we were, on our way up a mountain, fully kitted out with warm puffa jackets, skis and bobble hats, our only experience with snow being the building of a snowman. At the terminus, we jumped out, with our skis over our shoulders, and stared up at the chairlifts rising to the peak of the mountain. The chairlifts were empty, as were the slopes. Nobody seemed to be skiing. Alex dragged me towards the one advertising 'Red Run'.

I pulled back. 'Don't you think we should try skiing before we go up there?'

'No, it looks easy,' she replied and continued her attempt to drag me towards the moving chair.

I pulled back again. 'I think we should at least put our skis on and try walking,' I said, pleadingly.

We both fumbled with our skis and with a satisfying click fitted them onto our boots. I tried to walk. My legs wouldn't work. I tried to walk sideways, lost my balance and fell over. Alex tried; she also lost her balance and landed on top of me. There was a slight gradient between us and the restaurant 150 metres away. I suggested we get up, point the skis in the direction of the building and try to ski to it. After a few metres, we picked up speed.

Alex laughed. 'See, this is easy,' she said.

We accelerated and were now going at quite a fast rate.

'How do we stop?' I yelled.

'No idea,' Alex yelled back.

The front stone wall of the restaurant was approaching fast. Neither of us had any idea how to turn or stop, and we were going to crash. I had to think fast. So I reached out, grabbed Alex's sleeve and sat down. My reasoning was that I could use my backside as a brake. As I sat down, I pulled Alex, who tumbled over on top of me as we slid down the mountain. Our skis snapped off and flew in different directions. We reached out for anything we could grip onto to slow our progress. By now we were being watched: people sitting on the terrace were excitedly pointing at us and laughing. We finally came to a stop close to the wall. A line of bobble-hatted heads peered down at us.

We were intact. No wounds, and all arms and legs unbroken. We gathered our skis and walked up the few steps to the terrace. A few people were applauding our efforts, others were smirking at each other. We ignored them and found a free table. The waitress appeared; she was also trying to hide a grin. We ordered a hot chocolate each and agreed that skiing was a little more difficult than we'd thought.

As we sat there enjoying our drinks, I looked around. There were no skiers on the slopes at all. The chairlifts continued rolling up and down the mountain, still empty. The entire population of this ski resort was sitting on this terrace drinking coffee, smoking and talking. Men in top-of-the-range Lycra suits sat chatting with women dressed the same way. Their skis were unused and smooth. These people were not here for skiing; they had obviously seen photographs of cool, laid-back jet-setters in exotic resorts like St Moritz and wanted to look the same. They were only here for a photograph to send to their friends and had absolutely no intention of skiing or ever getting wet or injuring themselves. It was all for show.

Alex and I decided that skiing was definitely not for us either. We took the cable car back to base, handed in our skis and drove down the mountain in search of a good taverna for lunch.

A rusty old metal sign led us to a small log cabin with a few parking spaces dug into the side of the mountain and an alluring aroma of woodsmoke, charcoal and roasting meat. A puppy was tied to the doorframe. He was cute, but there was something different about him. Alex stroked his head and looked into his eyes. 'He's a wolf,' she said.

The warmth from the raging log fire heated our faces as we entered and we chose a table a safe distance away. Only two items were on the menu: goat and snails. Alex wrinkled her nose at the suggestion of snails. We ordered a kilo of the goat and as neither of us had ever tried snails, we ordered a portion of those, together with a carafe of local wine. The mandatory Greek salad arrived first – tomato, cucumber, onions and peppers with a slab of feta cheese on top, olive oil drizzled over the entire thing and a sprinkling of oregano to finish. Warm baked bread appeared and then a vast bowl of black-and-white-striped snails. I sniffed them. They smelled of garlic and fish. This local cuisine had not impressed me. Alex had a disgusted look on her face as she picked up the aroma.

'We have to eat at least one,' I said.

We reached into the bowl, trying to find a couple of small ones, extracted the slimy black creatures from their shells, popped them into our mouths and chewed. They were horrible! I looked at Alex, who had already spat hers back into the bowl. As a polite English gentleman, I resisted the urge to follow her example and swallowed. I felt sick and quickly swigged the rough white wine to take away the flavour.

The owner grinned at us. 'I knew you'd hate them,' he said. 'Most people do. I only cook them for the locals – they adore them.'

'I love your wolf,' Alex said.

'It's not a wolf, it's a dog,' he replied.

'It looks like a wolf, and it's got yellow eyes,' she said.

The owner thought for a moment. 'I found him last week near the mountain. I thought he was a stray puppy.'

'He might be just a puppy,' Alex said, 'but if he howls at the moon, I suggest you set him free before he eats you. Meanwhile, he looks hungry. Perhaps he would like some snails.'

It was getting dark when we arrived back at Arachova. The air smelled strongly of woodsmoke now, and the cold air nipped at our faces as we meandered along the street, gazing into shop windows and browsing the attractive displays outside. There was a tremendous variety of produce for sale. As well as the salamis, cheeses and local honey, there were strings of village sausages and fresh nougat, and bags of dried pasta hung from nails or were arranged in a pile on tables below. Among the tourist memorabilia, shopkeepers had spread cured animal skins over walls next to cuckoo clocks. It was a delightful mix.

Every restaurant and cafe had its windows steamed up and a roaring wood fire to ward off the cold. We were still wearing our skiing coats and were warm enough, so we made for the village square, which was set back between two restaurants and lined with cafes whose tables and chairs filled the space. As our two steaming mugs of hot chocolate appeared, so did the snow. White flakes danced in the glow of the streetlights and settled onto the ground and tables. It was gorgeous. When we walked back to our hotel, we left footprints in the thickening snow.

We awoke the next morning to find Arachova blanketed in white. Snowdrifts had massed against the sides of the stone buildings and were hanging off roofs, ready to drop on passing pedestrians and slow-moving vehicles.

As we descended the mountain and headed for Delphi, the snow thinned out and black tarmac became visible, and once we'd entered the village, the snow disappeared, leaving a view of green olive trees and ancient monuments on both sides of the road. We stopped outside the museum. It was still early, but a series of coaches had already parked along the road, and tourists were filing out of them.

Delphi is an ancient religious site dating back to around 800 BC, famous for its oracle, the priestess Pythia, who was known throughout the ancient world for predicting the future. Kings consulted her, and later Roman emperors too, in the hope of receiving good news on the outcome of future wars. Pythia was said to have predicted the Trojan War and to have made countless other prophecies too. Some came true, others didn't.

Originally, when one oracle died, another would be selected from one of the priestesses at the temple. At first, women with epilepsy were chosen, as seizures were taken as a sign that she was in touch with the gods. After falling into a trance, Pythia would mumble words that were said to be incomprehensible to mortals (probably because she was high on the intoxicating gases that emanated from the ground under her shrine). These were then interpreted by the priests and delivered to those who had requested them.

The prophecies were always open to different translations and were often ascribed opposing meanings. Sometimes the priests would have their own agenda and would make a little extra cash by interpreting the prophecy in the most profitable way. It was traditional for the person seeking an audience with the oracle to bring an offering of a sheep or a goat. The priest would sprinkle warm water onto the neck of the animal. If it flinched, this was considered inauspicious, and the person would be turned away with the order to return the next day. Sometimes the cunning priest would sprinkle ice-cold water onto the animal, knowing that it would react, thereby entering into further negotiations with the supplicant.

In ancient times, Delphi was believed to be the centre of the universe. The god Zeus let loose two eagles to fly around the world in opposite directions; they met over Mount Parnassus, which was then determined to be the navel of the earth. Zeus decreed that a sanctuary should be constructed – Delphi – which he then dedicated to his son, the god Apollo.

Alex and I joined the tourists and spent an enjoyable hour walking around the site and imagining the time when Delphi was a fully functioning shrine visited by the most famous kings in history. I stared across the valley, over the remnants of its majestic stone and marble pillars, while deep in thought, envisaging the long-ago activities of this now silent place. A distant shout echoed off the mountainside. Several tourists stopped and turned their heads to listen. I looked to my side; Alex had disappeared. I glanced up the slope. There she was, standing on the shrine to Pythia, her hands cupped around her mouth, calling 'Apollo! Apollo!' at the top of her voice. She was asking the ancient gods to take care of our families and to guide us in our future endeavours.

'It worked for kings and emperors,' she said, 'so why not us? We need all the help we can get.'

I thought seriously of joining her and adding my prayers to hers. Under my breath, I asked Apollo to protect us from dodgy builders.

We left Delphi behind us, feeling that the ancient gods were on our side, and continued down through a vast tract of olive trees towards the harbour at Itea, some twenty-five kilometres away, which used to serve as the landing point for dignitaries visiting the shrine. It was scorching down there, and we both stripped off our warm outer clothing and sat on the sunny beach in our T-shirts. It was strange to think that only two hours earlier we'd been digging our car out of a snowdrift.

From here we decided to take the long way back to Glyfada. We would follow the coast road along the side of the mountain, cross the Gulf of Corinth at the new suspension bridge near Patras and continue up the coast road to Athens. It would be a five-hour trip, but we didn't mind and were looking forward to a scenic drive.

We contoured the mountain, with the sea below us, and headed towards the bridge an hour ahead of us. The road took us inland, and further up into the mountains, before landing us at a crossroads. There were no signs and both directions looked similar. Logically, the sea had to be on our left, I thought, so we chose that way.

We passed several turnoffs and then the road narrowed.

Grit replaced the tarmac. A herd of goats stood in the middle of the track obstructing our progress and refused to move. We'd obviously taken a wrong turn and were now lost. Alex pointed to the top of a nearby hill. A goatherd was standing there with a dog by his side, watching us impassively. She got out of the car and beckoned him towards us to ask the way back to the main road. He ambled over as Alex went to meet him halfway. They were just out of earshot, but I could see that they were having a pleasant conversation. A few moments later, Alex arrived back at the car. She put on her seatbelt as I turned us back in the direction we'd come.

'So which way?' I asked.

'No idea,' she replied. 'But he had a hilarious nose, and his dog's name is Woof.' She had asked for and received instructions on our route but had become so engrossed in his strange facial features and the 'very sweet' dog, she'd forgotten the directions.

The goatherd was now far behind us. We were still hopelessly lost and continued exploring for another half hour, taking a series of promising-looking side roads only to discover that they were either dead-ends or petered out into shingle paths. Eventually we rounded a bend to see a scruffy old man striding into the road ahead of us. He lifted one hand in a gesture for us to stop. In the other hand he was holding a stick with a tatty red handkerchief tied to the end.

I stopped the car. Satisfied, he returned to the side of the road, sat down on a rock, took out a bag of tobacco and rolled a cigarette. We didn't understand why he'd stopped us, so I took my foot off the clutch, revved the engine and crept forward.

He stood up and waved the stick at us. We stopped again. He returned to his rock to continue rolling his cigarette.

I was still a little confused when an almighty explosion rocked the ground. Dust and stones flew into the air ahead of us, creating a thick white cloud. Out of nowhere, a bulldozer appeared, ploughing the debris off the road.

The old man stood up and waved at us to continue. They'd been using dynamite to blow up the side of the mountain as part of a road-widening programme, and our only warning had been a tatty red handkerchief.

I drove off, but Alex called for me to stop. She walked over to the man to ask for directions.

A conversation ensued, and after a while she returned. This time I didn't start the engine until I was sure she'd retained the information. 'Which way?' I asked.

'His teeth are so funny, and he has a strange accent,' she informed me.

'But did you remember the directions this time?'

'Next left.'

Back on the main road, we crossed the bridge and turned onto the Patras to Athens motorway. We had been driving for a while and had passed two toll booths and paid the charges. Just after the second toll station, the road became a gravel track. No more smooth tarmac or white lines. Traffic cones diverted us up several steep hills full of mud and potholes. We navigated around the obstructions and slipped and slid over the loose gravel until after a few kilometres the cones directed us back onto an even stretch. In front of us was a toll station. I stopped at the window, ready to pass a few coins to the operator.

Alex yelled for me to stop. 'Don't pay!' she shouted.

She jumped out of the car, marched past the bonnet, tapped on the window of the booth and sweetly asked the operator to lift the barrier. He replied that we should pay first.

'For what?' she asked. 'We have not used a road since the last toll station. We've been driving up and down the mountains on gravel.' She folded her arms and demanded he open the barrier.

By this time there was a queue of cars behind us; the drivers now left their vehicles to support the protest. After a while, more than fifteen angry motorists had joined in and were assisting Alex in haranguing the operator, demanding the barrier be opened. The poor chap had closed his window and was now on the phone, obviously to report the potential riot brewing. He put the phone down, pressed a button, and the barrier swung open. He looked at Alex and waved us through. It impressed me. This was democracy at work, in the country that invented it. I was pleased to observe first-hand that there were some places where public opinion still carried weight.

We arrived back in Glyfada late that afternoon and decided to take a last look at our old house. We returned to our street. Our house had gone. Stavros had clearly been busy. He'd completely demolished it, leaving only a gigantic pile of rubble and broken stones. 'He was probably in a hurry,' Alex said, 'in case we hated his horrible temporary apartment so much that we decided to move back in.'

# 7

# DESTINY WOULD NOT DENY ME AGAIN

J ust as Alex's grandfather managed the building of the original house remotely while he was away at sea, we were living and working mostly in the UK during the building process. I remembered that Jannis's dodgy builder had fleeced the family with inflated bills, so, using this lesson from history, I was determined that we would not make the same mistake. Now that building consent had been granted, we could begin. We made sure to keep in daily communication with Stavros. We bombarded him with emails. If a reply didn't come back quickly, we telephoned and made a nuisance of ourselves.

We had insisted on design rights, which meant we could choose the look of the building from the outside. As Jannis had built the old house with two curved bays to resemble the bridge of a ship, we echoed this by designing our new balconies as a curve, in his honour. I kept asking Stavros for the final designs and kept being told that they were not ready yet and that this had something to do with planning permission. I persisted, but with no success, so we flew to Athens to see for ourselves. Stavros had assured us that all was well and that the first phase of the structure was in place. Our neighbours, the elderly, cat-loving Stella, who'd been the first on our street to have her house redeveloped into an apartment block, and nosey Pandelis, were watching the progress and reporting back, and they confirmed what Stavros was telling us.

It was six months since the old house had been demolished. In its place was now a massive skeletal concrete structure with a concrete staircase leading from the ground, zigzagging all the way to the roof level five storeys up. It was enormous. Looking down into the basement level, there was a concrete floor and what looked like a large swimming pool five metres below with water accumulating in the corners and concrete columns rising towards the sky. I could never have imagined that something so big would fit on our small piece of land twenty metres by thirty metres. But there it was. A skyscraper almost touching the clouds.

As soon as we pulled up outside the site, Alex jumped out

of the car, scrambled over the piles of builders' rubble, ran across a plank over the basement excavation and raced up the concrete stairs. Stavros was already halfway across the road by the time Alex reached the second floor. She continued to climb. He shouted for her to stop, but she just kept on going and was almost at the top by the time he started up the stairs to follow her.

I was still standing outside at ground level admiring the structure when I heard loud voices from the top. Stavros had caught up with Alex and was busy telling her in a loud voice to get down. Alex, having expended all her energy getting up there, was in no hurry to take orders and remained where she was, shouting back at him. So there were Alex and Stavros, standing on a tiny concrete platform twenty metres up in the air, having a heated conversation.

The first word I made out from Alex's distant voice was *malaka*. She calls all her friends *malaka*, and until I knew better I thought this was a common Greek name. People she doesn't like are also called *malaka*, but in a different tone, which they seem to understand. *Malaka* is the most common word in the Greek language. Tourists learn it before they learn to say good morning. It's used with a variety of different meanings by men and women, but it literally translates as 'man who masturbates'. While people typically use it as an insult, with its equivalent in English being 'wanker', the meaning alters depending on the context. It can be an exclamation of pleasure, an expression of horror, a cry of anger, a declaration of affection, or something else entirely. This was not a friendly '*malaka*'.

I waved frantically at Alex and eventually caught her attention; I beckoned her to come down and argue at ground level. She finally relented and started down with the relieved architect following closely behind in case she turned around and went back up.

Once she was safely on the ground, I asked her what all the fuss was about. She told me that Stavros was intending to have the lift open into a small lobby area on the top floor rather than directly into our apartment as we'd agreed. The steps up to the roof terrace would therefore be accessed from the main stair-case and not from within our apartment as we'd specified. The terrace would no longer be part of our home; it would be freely accessible to everyone in the building. I understood the reason for the argument now. I joined in.

This would be the first of many squabbles with Stavros, and we would not establish a precedent by stepping down now. I took the drawings out of my bag. These were only interim designs and showed little detail. After a few minutes, Stavros realised he would not win this one, but still he kept on trying. He hopefully mentioned fire regulations. This didn't work. He tried suggesting that it was a security risk. Again, we blocked that one. By this time Alex was red with rage and I was relieved that we were at ground level as I felt for the safety of this man while Alex was emphasising her point by repeatedly poking him in his chest in sync with each carefully pronounced word. He finally agreed to our demands. We suspected he was plan-ning to keep the terrace legally in his name, which would have allowed him to build another floor if permitted by local building regulations. This is when we realised we were defi-nitely dealing with a shark and needed to be extra cautious.

We told Stavros to cease all further work until he'd completed the detailed designs. We wanted nothing more done without our approval as the trust was fading fast. He looked at us, seemed to sag, and asked us to wait a moment. He crossed the road and returned in a few seconds with a full set of draw-ings. It was clear that he'd been keeping them from us until he'd got far enough into the construction to make it too troublesome for us to change anything.

We set another appointment for the following day. Meanwhile, Alex and I studied the drawings. We had the right to change the internal design on our three apartments and shop only, as the remaining portion of the building would belong to Stavros. There was no illustration of the lift position, and there was a large area blocked out on the drawings to the rear of the building.

At the meeting, Alex wanted to go into more detail about the positioning of the internal walls, but Stavros suggested we speak to the bricklayer, who would deal with that later in the project. I then asked about the blocked-out area at the back of the building. Stavros's eyes narrowed. He looked at us and winked. 'This will be a little off-plan, but we can't talk about it now.' I asked if this area would be the plant room to house the water tanks and boiler. He avoided my question. I tried persisting, but he tapped the side of his nose and told me not to worry. I assumed that this had something to do with the planning regulations and would become clearer later. It didn't seem too big an issue, so we left it and asked him to update us when he could.

There was nothing more to see on site, so we decided to while away a few hours at Moonshine, a neighbourhood bar a short walk away. It was popular with expats and Greeks alike, the conversation was always lively, and there was invariably someone there that we knew.

Sure enough, sitting outside on a small wooden bench was our local defrocked priest, Pater John. He had never got over being sacked by the Church for drunkenness and had refused to defrock himself, so continued to wear the black cassock. This had faded over the many years since and routinely showed evidence of his last meal in stains both fresh and old. He was permanently drunk but always smiling. Everyone that entered the bar would stand him a drink, and he would bless them by making the sign of a cross before downing the gift. We would usually buy him a cheese pie and a sweet pastry from the bakery next door and leave it in his lap as we passed. He would have preferred whisky, but we thought he needed to eat too. He would still give us a blessing, but less enthusiastically than if we'd presented him with a glass of ouzo.

The bar was modern, and instead of tables there were high wooden benches with lines of stools. Soft pop music played in the background as we took our seats. An unsmiling thirty-something Englishwoman called Susan ran the bar on behalf of the owners, who were rarely around. She spoke Greek fluently and demonstrated her skills frequently with her choice of language when she was in a grim mood or angry, which was most days. Susan would complain about the heat in the summer and the cold in the winter. She disliked most of her customers and always had something scathing to say to anyone that would listen. Baiting Susan was a local hobby and the regulars held daily competitions to see who could cause her to lose her temper first. The Greeks and the English would form opposing teams and take bets on who she would swear at first. The winner earned themselves a beer.

We, however, were not there for the Susan-baiting. We were there to play chess.

Alex plays chess well. Although chess for me is a game, to Alex it's a contact sport. Anything she does, she must do well. And that includes chess. She has to win, regardless of the cost, the possibility of blood being spilled or the chance that she might outdo Susan as the most unpopular person in the bar.

I went to the corner, picked out a chessboard and placed it on the bench between us. The more experienced bar locals slid away along the bench, leaving a little more room between Alex and themselves.

We set up the pieces and Alex made her first move. After a few moments of rapid moves, I saw an opportunity and unwisely took it. I captured her queen.

She looked at the board, looked up at me and yelled, 'Give it back, *malaka!*'

'No,' I replied. I had taken her queen. The game would be mine. I called over to Susan for another beer to celebrate my prowess, while Alex continued to stare at me.

Then she lowered her voice and smiled. This was worrying. I could cope with Alex shouting at the top of her voice, but whenever she smiled and spoke softly I knew I was in trouble.

Again, I bravely refused to return her queen. And that was it.

'You have swollen my balls!' she yelled.

The chessboard flew into the air and its pieces rained down on nearby drinkers; one piece narrowly missed my eye.

Living with Alex has taught me all sorts of commonly used Greek expressions that cannot be found in dictionaries or phrasebooks, and this was by no means the first time I'd been accused of making her testicles sore. We'd been having a conversation one day about British history. She was happy to listen to the stuff about wars and invasions, but when I began citing dates, she lost interest and said the same thing: 'Mou eprikse t'arxidia' (my balls are now swollen). Greeks say this when they've had enough of a subject, been nagged, received complaints or when they're just generally irritated by too much information. Similarly, when Alex loses patience with someone, she won't say 'I don't care' but rather 'I have written it on my balls' or 'I write you on my balls' (sta arxidia mou).

'Okay, it's a draw,' she said. 'Set the pieces up again.'

I was quite used to my wife's high spirits. It's one of the

things I love about her. She has always been sparky and slightly unpredictable, which makes our lives interesting. She has a kindness that rivals her mother's, and she is sexy and beautiful, the dream of any man. But you have to be honest with her at all times. I couldn't believe my luck when she agreed to go out with me. She was the most magnificent creature that I had ever seen and I considered her to be well out of my league.

After we had lost contact as teenagers, it was more than twenty years before we met again, and that came about entirely by chance. Also fortuitously, we were both free agents at that point, Alex having got married young and divorced not so long after, and me having suddenly lost my wife to illness.

It was a cold, frosty morning and I'd just left my house in Watford, Hertfordshire. I rounded a corner and drove into a narrow residential street to find a white car marooned in the middle of the tarmac. The driver was leaning against the open door, one hand on the steering wheel, trying to get it going by pushing it along the road. I stopped and asked if he needed any help. He gratefully accepted and together we pushed the car forwards until it jump-started. He then pulled into a space, left the engine running and got out to thank me. He shook my hand and introduced himself as Christos.

We talked for a while as his engine ticked over and the frost melted from the windows. I suggested that he try turning off the engine to see if it would restart. It did. Christos invited me to come into his house for a quick coffee. I looked at my watch. I was already a little late, but I really liked this chap and agreed. He led me through the small terraced house to the kitchen at the rear. A large, smiling lady dressed in a blue and white flowery dress was sitting at the kitchen table, her chubby hands wrapped around a steaming coffee mug. I immediately recognised her! It was Alexandra's mother, the Greek lady that I'd met at that birthday party all those years ago.

'Are you Alexandra's mother?' I asked.

'Yes,' she replied. 'Have we met?'

I proceeded to tell her about the red-faced sixteen-year-old that had come to a party at their house once in Northwood, about eight kilometres from where we were now standing. A big smile of recognition spread across her face. 'You were the butcher's boy,' she exclaimed. 'My name is Debbie. I see you have met my son Christos, Alex's brother.'

'So how is Alexandra?' I asked. 'Is she still in Greece?'

'No, she's upstairs. Wait, I'll get her.'

My heart was thumping. This was the girl who had invaded my dreams. I was panic-stricken. My face was getting hot and I knew that I was blushing. I was going to meet her again. I doubted she would remember me, so I tried to control my breathing while Debbie disappeared upstairs to find her daughter. Christos put a coffee in front of me, but I resisted the urge to pick it up in case my hands trembled.

Over the last two decades, my memories of Alex had not faded. I remembered her as the most beautiful girl I'd ever seen. But she had only spoken to me once, to introduce herself and ask my name, and that had been in Greek, which had to be translated by her mother.

A perfect English accent now woke me from my thoughts. She was there, standing in front of me. 'Hello, Peter, how are you after so many years?'

She remembered me! I held out my hand in greeting. She ignored it, put her arms around my neck and kissed my cheek. She was even more dazzling than I remembered. The young girl had blossomed into an exquisite woman. Her long brown hair hung over her shoulders. Her brown eyes were sparkling with curiosity and wisdom, making her look mature beyond her years. She was lovely. Debbie and Christos left us to talk at the kitchen table. We reminisced about our former lives and similar experiences growing up. She told me about her marriage, I told her about mine, and slowly and for the first time we got to know each other. I had missed work, but I didn't care. Destiny would not deny me again.

The next day we met at a local Italian restaurant. Alex was currently living and working in Greece and had her own beauty therapy business. She was in England only for a couple of weeks to visit Debbie, who was staying with Christos during his studies at the local college. Then she broke the news: she was going back to Greece in two days' time.

By the end of the meal, I quietly knew that this was the person I wanted to spend the rest of my life with. Alex seemed to feel the same as we were both so comfortable in each other's company. I asked her when she'd be returning to the UK, but she didn't know as she'd already used her savings to get there and needed to return to work again now.

I had to check myself to make sure this was not just a teenager's infatuation. After all, she'd been in my thoughts since our first meeting more than twenty years ago, and all we'd ever done then was wave at each other as she passed the butcher's shop every morning on her way to school. We both had to be certain.

Alex has always been upfront and direct. She suggested I come to Greece and stay with her for a while so we could get to know each other properly. She must have seen some potential in me worth the risk. I agreed immediately. I had my own business as a chartered surveyor, so I'd have no trouble taking a few days off. And as I hadn't had a holiday that year, I was due for a break. It was all decided. Alex would go back to Glyfada in a couple of days' time, and I would join her as soon as I'd organised cover for my business.

A week later, I was in Greece, where, on that first evening, Alex took me to the club in Piraeus and showed me how Greek women really danced. The relationship blossomed over the next few months as we became closer. I changed my work schedule in England to allow me to spend more time in Glyfada with Alex.

Christos, meanwhile, went on to gain his degree in electrical engineering. He and I became very close and discovered that we share a sense of humour that is foreign to other people. I think he is the most intelligent person I've ever met. He can solve the most intricate electrical problems and the most complicated mechanical conundrums. Indeed, his early career was in robotics and inventing. But he has difficulties tying his shoelaces, lacks any sense of direction and usually hasn't got a clue what day it is. The family call him the absent-minded professor. While he was still in England, he owned a series of old bangers that never seemed to function. Most days I would have to pass by his house to give him a push start on my way to work until after three months he discovered the starter button. He went on to marry a Dutch woman and now lives and works in Amsterdam. Whenever we get together, we spend our time laughing until our faces ache and have to keep mopping tears from our eyes.

But I am jumping ahead. As far as I was concerned, I had found in Alex a wonderful person who made me laugh every time we met. I prayed that our relationship would continue. She is deeply philosophical and would listen intently to my life story. She wanted to understand me, as I did her. After a few months we were not only a couple but best friends. I was still slightly in awe of her, but things were going well and we were happy.

Alex was also showing me in her own way that this was going to be a long-term relationship. She did this by wittingly or unwittingly presenting me with certain challenges. This must be a Greek thing. They required Hercules to perform seven labours to prove himself. If I wanted to be accepted into Greek culture, I would be expected to do the same.

I had already passed my first labour, which was to steer my way out of a handbrake skid on a mountain road in the Peloponnesus. My next labour was to learn the Greek language.

# 8

# THANK YOU AND HOLD MY DICK

I was struggling to speak or understand Greek. The pile of phrasebooks I had accumulated didn't seem to be much good, as a lot of the words I was hearing in normal conversation were nowhere in their pages. As with most novices trying to learn a language, I understood the swear words, and there were many. I already knew about the different interpretations for '*malaka*', depending on the context, but there were countless others. In Greek, such words can be used as an insult, a compliment, an expression of surprise, a term of endearment and so on, and the meaning will entirely depend on the tone used. This was really confusing for me as before I used a tone, I would have to have at least some clue about what I was saying.

I knew how to ask for a coffee and I was getting the hang of ordering in restaurants, but everyday conversations still eluded me. I would study my phrasebook, learn a sentence and go out to find an opportunity to use it. I would walk around the supermarket repeating under my breath the Greek for 'Can I have a carrier bag?', but then the checkout operator would just look at me blankly or, even more embarrassing, ask me a question. I might have practised a particular phrase, but this did not prepare me for an actual question-and-answer exchange. It was tough, but if I were to join a Greek family, I needed to be able to talk to them rather than sit in a corner and avoid all conversation, or, worse still, have them stop their flow of chatter to translate for me.

I asked Alex if she would help me. She assured me that the language would come naturally, so not to worry. But I persisted. I suggested she should write a new phrase for me phonetically once a day, so I could start to communicate outside the home with native Greek speakers. Writing it down in Greek letters was pointless as I still couldn't read the written characters, which just looked to me like strange shapes and squiggles.

I planned a trip to the petrol station. It would only be a one-way conversation as, if they talked back to me, I'd have no idea what they were saying, but I had to begin somewhere. Alex wrote the Greek sentence using the English alphabet. I studied the writing, learned it off by heart and set out. I arrived at the petrol station and the attendant walked over and unscrewed the cap. I proudly recited my learned sentence. 'Cali mera, gamista to, parakalo.' (Good morning, please fill it up, thank you.)

The attendant smiled at me, then a big grin spread across his face. He called over to his co-worker and repeated my order. He also had a wide smile. By the time my attendant screwed back the filler cap, he was trying to stifle his amusement and his shoulders were shaking. I paid for the fuel and left. In the rearview mirror I watched as they finally let go of their repressed laughter while I drove away.

I arrived home to find Alex and Debbie standing on the steps of the house. They were both smiling and keen to hear how I'd got on with my lesson. I explained that I thought I'd done okay. I got the petrol, though the attendant had been a little strange. Debbie asked me to repeat what I'd said. When I did so, she collapsed with giggles and Alex ran away to hide. It turned out that I'd asked the attendant for sex, requesting that he fill *me* up rather than the car.

A few days later, after spending hours with my nose in several Greek-language books, I had learned the alphabet, but only the capital letters. I could now at least read those shop signs and posters that used only uppercase letters. I was struggling with the lowercase letters, which still looked like meaningless squiggles, but I was working on that. To my delight, I could also now count up to twenty. I was ready to try out my new language skills.

Alex had been monitoring my progress and would throw the odd Greek word at me and ask for a translation, which mostly I was getting correct. My confidence had suffered a minor setback with the petrol attendant, but I was getting over that now. I was ready to try again. I would go to the baker's and buy two loaves of bread and four cheese pies. I knew the word for bread (psomi) and cheese pie (teropita) and with my newfound numeracy I felt ready. I practised out loud to myself. 'Kalimera (Good day), thelo (I want) theo (two) psomi (loaves of bread) ke (and) tessara (four) teropitas (cheese pies) parakalo (thank you).' This sounded good, but I felt the need to pass it by Alex for final approval. I recited the entire sentence.

'Kalimera, thelo theo psomi ke tessara teropitas parakalo.'

She smiled and clapped her hands in delight. This was the first full sentence she'd heard me speak in her language. There was just one minor detail. She preferred a different bread to the one I would order and asked for psoli instead. I agreed to change the word; after all, there would be lots of different varieties, so I wanted to get the right one. She also suggested that I ask for it to be wrapped as I shouldn't really carry bread all the way home without some paper around it. This would just require adding: 'Piase tin psoli mou.' Otherwise, my Greek was perfect.

Off I went to the local bakery. Most Greek bakeries are also sweet shops. Although bread is sold in the morning, warm from the oven, through the rest of the day and evening they serve a variety of sticky cakes and puddings, as well as sculptured ice-cream cakes and chocolate-covered lollies from the freezer. Also available are bottles of whisky, local brandy and assorted spirits, all beautifully gift-wrapped. It is traditional when visiting someone to take a cake as a present. These are always professionally wrapped with multi-coloured ribbons and lace.

The bakery was busy. Several assistants were furiously serving the mass of customers crowded into the small shop. My turn came, and I proudly recited in my best Greek: 'Kalimera, thelo theo psoli ke tessara teropitas parakalo. Ke piase tin psoli mou.'

The shop went silent. Customers and staff all turned in my direction. One of the women behind the counter grinned. Another laughed. The customers staring at me realised I was a foreigner and assumed that I had a pronunciation problem. One kindly older gentleman even tried to translate for me. He suggested I might have it slightly wrong and asked me in English what I actually wanted. I thought I must have messed up the words between home and the shop or mispronounced a key part of the sentence. I looked at my saviour and told him. He laughed and told me what I'd said, which was: 'Good morning, I want two penises and four cheese pies, thank you and hold my dick.'

I paid for the bread and cheese pies, left the shop and went to hunt for Alex to hit her with the bread and tell her what to do with her Greek lessons.

The Greeks have a different temperament to the English. We English tend to be reserved and don't express our feelings too much. Our culture teaches us to be calm and to not show our emotions – 'big boys don't cry', as they say.

Alex is more fiery; she shows herself for who she is. I can tell what mood she's in from a hundred metres away, just from how she walks towards me. Based on the body language, I know if I need to run.

Although Alex attended university in England and had a few English friends, she never got to grips with the temperamental differences. So when we became a couple, she made it her mission to change my outlook on life and soften my British stiff upper lip. I have always been a calm person and I'm not easily fazed. I don't lose my temper and I am generally happy with life, but perhaps I wasn't showing this enough.

In Alex's opinion, I needed to open up, lose some of my Englishness and become more Greek. I already felt more

Greek. I loved the country, the people and the food. It thrilled me to be there, and with such a wonderful woman beside me I was completely content. But when Alex gets an idea in her head, she will not shift it. Accordingly, she launched a one-woman project to broaden my horizons and, in her words, 'open up' my mind.

This was early in our relationship and I was still commuting from the UK. My usual cycle was to spend ten days working in England and five days in Greece before flying back to London again. Alex lived in Greece permanently as her job as a beauty therapist required her to be in Glyfada. It was tough being apart, but we accepted this as we both had to continue earning a living. At the time, this arrangement was manageable, but nowadays we spend every day together. I can't imagine being apart for more than a few hours.

My education was about to continue.

At the start of one particular visit in those early days, I arrived as usual at Athens airport around noon and was looking forward to a relaxing time with Alex and the family. Perhaps we would go to the beach, or we might make a quick visit to Athens for some shopping or a mooch around one of the many markets. I didn't really mind what we did; I was happy to let Alex organise our itinerary.

After a light lunch at a local taverna, she suggested that we should have a brief rest as she had planned a night out, so I needed to be fresh.

'Where are we going?' I asked.

Alex looked cagey and said it was nothing special, just a nearby nightclub. 'And we're going to an island tomorrow,' she added.

This sounded good. I loved to visit different islands and was keen to explore another one so was happy to agree.

During the summer, Greeks will sleep in the afternoon

when the sun is hottest and will rarely leave home for a night out before 11 p.m. Most nightclubs open at midnight. We arrived at ours just after midnight. The sign outside read 'Diamonds and Pearls', and fixed to the wall above it were a series of flashing neon silhouettes of slim women in provocative poses.

A bleak reception area led to a darker room with tables spread around the perimeter, all of them facing a large circular platform with a pole in the middle. We ordered drinks.

'Will there be a band?' I asked Alex.

'No. But there will be music.'

With that, loud saxophone music started. A naked woman appeared from behind a curtain, jumped up onto the platform and gyrated in time to the music while doing suggestive things with the pole. I looked at Alex with incredulity. Alex was just giggling. As the first part of her mission to open up my mind, she had brought me to a lap-dancing club.

As the evening went on, the music became louder, and more and more naked girls arrived to take their turn writhing around the pole. Once they'd finished their routine, they mingled with the customers at the tables. Pretty soon, there were lots of naked and scantily clad women mixing with us and offering lap dances. Alex called over one of the girls, whispered in her ear and grinned at me. The girl then approached me, swung a naked leg over my lap, sat down on me and wriggled in time with the music.

This was really embarrassing. I glanced over at Alex. She had slid down in her chair and was laughing at my obvious discomfort. I was trying not to look at the girl gyrating her groin onto mine and was grateful when the music stopped and she went off to assault another victim. I picked Alex up off the floor and pulled her towards the door.

Outside, she was still giggling, and I was still feeling embarrassed.

'You must have enjoyed that,' she said.

As I wasn't thinking too clearly, I didn't really know if I had or not. The only emotion I felt was confusion. 'Why did you do that to me?' I asked.

'You have to feel free,' she said. 'It's okay to look, it's okay to feel things. You will not have an affair with her. So where is the harm? Just enjoy life.'

Her logic was sound. But it was not something I needed. I was more than happy being with Alex and no one else. Even so, she had taught me to relax a bit and not take things too seriously. I was on the way to being more Greek. Alex felt she had opened me up just a little. But that was by no means the end of it. She had lots more ideas on how to complete the process.

The day after my uncomfortable experience in the strip club, we took a taxi to Piraeus and boarded a ferry. Alex refused to tell me where we were going, and the timetable wasn't much help because the ferry was due to call at several islands. So we just sat on the deck and drank coffee as it left the harbour and headed for the open sea.

After pulling in at several idyllic-looking little islands, the ferry approached our mystery destination. The front ramp was lowered as we edged nearer to the concrete pier. We stepped off and walked towards the narrow street visible ahead. It was beautiful. The road had been freshly whitewashed and the kerbs were picked out in light blue to match both the shutters and the window boxes, the latter planted with red geraniums that tumbled down the walls of the whitewashed houses. Small blue metal balconies were almost invisible against the blue, blue sky.

Every street was equally pretty. As we made our way along them, at first we could hear nothing but the sound of canaries singing from inside the glinting cages that hung from ornate hooks outside people's homes. Soon a deep, throbbing beat replaced the birdsong. We turned a bend between the blue and white houses, and the street opened into an enormous square. The music was now deafening, and there were hundreds of people squeezed together, some with drinks in their hands, others just waving their arms in time with the music.

There was no way around, so we began pushing through the crowd as we tried to reach the street on the other side of the square. About halfway across, I glanced at Alex, who was giggling. I looked for the source of her amusement. At first I saw nothing out of the ordinary, but then I realised that the revellers were all men. The only woman in that enormous square was a sniggering Alex. She had brought me to Pierros, the world-famous gay bar. This was Mykonos, the world-famous gay island, and it was Gay Week.

We made it to the other side of the square. There was a small bar with a few empty chairs in a line overlooking the festivities. Alex beckoned for me to take a seat, and we sat down on either side of a little table. The waitress came over and I ordered us a beer and a coke. She returned very swiftly, placed the drinks on the table and sat down beside me.

'Have you seen her tattoo?' Alex whispered to me.

I looked round at the waitress. She was a pretty girl with ebony hair, dressed only in a bikini top and a pair of revealing shorts. Across her belly there was a tattoo of a colourful snake; its tail was hidden behind her bikini top, and the head was presumably down the front of her shorts.

Alex leaned over to me. 'Ask her about her tattoo,' she said softly.

I was still in the process of being 'opened up'. I was hesitant and felt a little embarrassed to ask. But Alex persisted, so I turned to the attractive young woman and complimented her on the design.

She smiled and thanked me, then added, 'Would you like to see the rest?'

'Yes, please,' Alex said from across the table.

The waitress immediately pulled her top up to reveal a tail wrapped around a nipple. Then the shorts came down to reveal the head of the snake. My eyes, previously focused on the tail and the nipple, refocused and followed the snake over her belly, down towards her pubic region and onto her penis.

So there was the waitress with her/his legs in the air, pointing to the snake; and there was Alex, now lying on her back on the ground, hysterical with laughter and with tears streaming down her face; and there were some of the crowd from the square, who'd turned towards us from their dancing and were applauding; and there was me, in the middle, trying unsuccessfully to look unfazed and cool.

I bought the waitress a beer, and we sat for a while chatting about the island. I asked about recommended hotels, but Alex dipped into her bag and produced a set of keys. 'No need for a hotel. We have a friend's house to stay in.'

Her friend had a summer house on Mykonos and had offered us the use of it for as long as we wanted. So we said goodbye to the bar and set off to hire a car. With the aid of a hand-drawn map, we went looking for Olga's house. Her instructions led us up a hill and into a large complex of around a hundred apartments arranged in blocks across the hillside overlooking the sea. It was obviously a recently built development as the roads were not yet fully finished and loose kerbstones were lying near the road ready to be fixed into place. When we drew into the parking area, I asked Alex which flat belonged to Olga.

'No idea.' Then, helpfully, 'Olga said it has a blue door.'

We pulled our bag out of the car and went in search of the blue door. We soon realised that every apartment had a blue door as this was the colour of Mykonos and the developer had obviously been keen to maintain the tradition. He had also not bothered to put numbers on the apartments. It was now late afternoon. As the sun threw lengthening shadows onto the ground from the identical blue-doored apartments, we continued to try the keys in random doors. But most of the properties were owned by Athenians as summer houses, and as it was now late summer, they were no longer on Mykonos, so there was nobody to ask. We tried to call Olga, but there was no answer. We tried a few more doors, but still no success. After another hour the sun had set and it was getting dark. We were both tired after a long day, so we returned to the car, reclined the seats and went to sleep.

Next morning Olga called. 'Do you like the flat?' she asked.

Alex explained the saga. Phone in hand, we followed Olga's directions to the furthest block, ascended a flight of stairs, tried the key in the blue door, and opened it.

Although Alex lived in Greece and I was now spending a lot of time there, swimming in the sea was a rare experience for both of us. We were often too busy to relax, as there was always something else that needed doing. So we decided to make the most of being on Mykonos, beginning with a morning on Paradise Beach. With its golden sand and the bath-like temperature of the water, it really did live up to its name.

From our sunbeds, we watched as a water taxi shuttled bathers back and forth between Paradise Beach and another cove just out of sight around some rocks. We decided to try it. As the little boat chugged around the coast, a small sandy bay was revealed. It was packed with people, some wandering around, some lying on sunbeds, and others swimming in the clear water. As we neared the shore, I noticed that everyone seemed to be wearing the same colour bathing costume. Nearer still, and I realised they were not wearing bathing costumes at all. This was Super Paradise Beach – for nudists.

Alex was already laughing out loud at the expression on my face; yet again, her eyes were wet with tears.

'I'm not going nude,' I yelled over the droning of the boat's engine.

She told me it didn't matter if you were nude or not; everyone was free to do what they liked there.

As we walked up the beach towards a restaurant at the top, we picked our way between sunbeds and naked bodies sprawled on the sand exposing themselves without a care. I was trying so hard to avoid looking at the display of private bits scattered around the beach that I trod on someone's water bottle, slipped over, and buried my face in the sand. I lifted my head and was confronted by a large tanned penis wearing a gold ring piercing; it was attached to an equally well-tanned man, who smiled at me and offered to help me get up. I didn't need any help – I had to escape from the decorated penis as soon as possible, so I rolled away from it, sprang up and ran off, with Alex following close behind, still trying to suppress her giggles.

We spent a wonderful afternoon there. The beach was lively thanks to the twenty-four-hour nightclub which occupied one corner of it. People danced, stretched out in the sun, and enjoyed the balmy Aegean Sea. It didn't matter if you were gay or straight, black or white, rich or poor. The Greeks don't care about that as long as everyone has an excellent time.

The island of Tinos is only about eight kilometres from Mykonos, and Alex was keen to visit its famous church, Panagia Evangelistria, on our way back to Piraeus. All the ferries stopped there en route. The church is celebrated throughout Greece and the hundreds of pilgrims who visit daily feed most of the economy on the island.

Before walking into the little town, we lingered at Tinos's harbour and strolled along the sea wall, gazing down into the clear shallows at the fish darting around in shoals and leaving V-shapes in the calm surface. The town is dominated by the church, which stands at the top of a hill. I was surprised to see a long length of carpet running the entire kilometre up the hill, all the way to the base of the church steps. I was even more surprised when I heard a shuffling sound behind me and turned to see a woman, dressed in a long skirt and headscarf, on her hands and knees, crawling along the carpet towards the church.

This was an act of penance, Alex explained. Some faithful devotees crawl all the way up to Panagia Evangelistria from the harbour; others start at the top of the hill and crawl only the last few metres.

As we walked up towards the church, Alex stopped at a small shop to buy four two-metre-long candles wrapped in brown paper and an empty plastic pot in which to collect holy water. We started our climb. On approaching the white marble steps leading to the church, Alex handed me the long candles, reached into her bag and took out a headscarf and a long skirt. She dressed, fell to her knees, and crawled up the steps. At the church courtyard, we diverted to the right and into a small outbuilding. A church worker took our candles from us, unwrapped them and trimmed the wicks before handing them back. We then placed them on special racks under a large brass chimney and lit them from the other candles burning in a row.

I followed as Alex continued her penance and crawled up the final white staircase to the church door. There was a short queue of people, who stood aside to let Alex pass. Priority is given to those serving their penance; they are never required to wait in line. I waited my turn and went in. Alex was there, kneeling before the icon of Mother Mary, hands together in prayer and with tears flowing. I wanted to hug her to assure her that everything was fine, but thought it best to keep my distance as this was a personal thing between her and her faith.

She finally rose to her feet, came over to me and smiled. We spent a few minutes exploring the ornate interior. It was a treasure trove of gold and silver offerings left by pilgrims over the years in thanks for miracles or in the hope that their prayers would be answered. Glass display cases stood around the perimeter, and there were more in the middle of the church. They contained all manner of precious items: diamond rings and necklaces, other items of jewellery, and golden sculptures, mostly in the form of fishing boats or ships. The majority had a maritime theme; after all, Tinos was an island of fishermen, a dangerous occupation.

We filled our container with holy water from the font and descended the hill towards the harbour. The primary reason most people visit Tinos is to make a pilgrimage to Panagia Evangelistria. The road from the port to the church was long and straight, with just a few shops spread up the hill, selling candles and containers for holy water. There were no other distractions. This allowed the faithful to climb the hill in quiet contemplation and remember their own personal reason for visiting. The road back down to the port, however, was completely different. Having completed their visit to the church and done their penance, refreshed pilgrims were now ready to relax and linger in the many tourist shops. Hundreds such establishments lined the road to the port. They all sold similar products – religious icons, wooden crosses and costume jewellery, and assorted mugs, plates and memorabilia with the name of the island proudly displayed.

We spent an hour browsing our way down to the ferry port. At the bottom of the hill, just before the harbour, was a small pedestrian walkway leading off the main road. From the corner we could make out the unmistakable sound of live music. We still had two hours before our ferry to Athens, so, being in no hurry, we followed the soft melody along the cobbled path.

The path narrowed as we got further from the main road. Vines full of fat, dark red grapes were growing up the walls and across wire mesh above our heads. The music became louder and the gentle strains of someone playing a bouzouki drifted on the warm breeze. The path opened out into a small square containing the brightly coloured facade of a little restaurant and a few outdoor tables. In the corner was an old man sitting on a stool, with an ornately decorated bouzouki resting on his knees. He was plucking at the strings and playing beautifully. He continued to play until we took our seats at one of the empty tables. Then he rested his instrument against the wall and came over to us. He was the owner of the small taverna and the music was his way of attracting clients. It worked for us. Without it, we would likely have just continued our walk to the port and missed this little gem.

The old man introduced himself as Petros and recited the special food available that day. He pressed his forefinger and thumb together and kissed the digits of his hand when he mentioned the wonderful calamari that his brother had caught just that morning. He suggested we try them stuffed with peppers, cream cheese and breadcrumbs. 'It's our speciality, and my brother makes the cheese,' he said proudly. I asked if he had any local white wine. He looked offended. 'Of course I have wine,' he replied. 'The best on the island. My brother makes it.'

I already liked his brother and looked forward to sampling his efforts. We ordered the recommended calamari, a salad, some green beans in tomato sauce, and a kilo of his brother's wine. Petros took our order to the kitchen and quickly returned with a large tin jug filled to the brim with the amber liquid. I poured us each a glass and sipped. It was delicious and refreshing.

Petros returned to his stool and continued to play music. Alex and I had assumed that as Petros was the owner, he would also be the cook. But there he was, strumming on his bouzouki while wonderful smells emanated from the kitchen. Maybe his wife was the cook. Alex called over to him and asked who the chef was.

'It's my brother,' he replied.

A moment later, a bell sounded in the kitchen. Petros paused his recital, disappeared into the kitchen, emerged with steaming plates of food, placed them in front of us and retook his seat. We turned to look into the dark restaurant, hoping to glimpse his productive bother. We couldn't see him, and he clearly had no intention of coming out to introduce himself, so his identity remained a mystery. But his food was perfect and the wine was heavenly.

A couple of hours later, as I sat back in my aircraft-style seat on the ferry to Piraeus, watching the sea splash by, I replayed the weekend in my mind. It had started with a naked girl wriggling on my lap and ended with a pilgrimage to one of the most famous places of worship in Greece. In between we had whiled away an afternoon on a nudist beach, joined in the celebration of Gay Week and spent a night sleeping in the car because we couldn't find the right blue door. It had been great.

Was my mind opening up? I certainly thought so. Alex had shown me a different side to her. She knew she was beautiful, she knew that I loved her, and she had the confidence to show me it was okay to be human. It was okay to feel passion; it was fine to be myself, to talk to people and point at strange tattoos and sit with pretty women without the burn of jealousy and misinterpretation that plagues most relationships. I felt free and I knew that Alex was with me as a best friend, confidante and wife. What was I going to do with this newfound freedom? Nothing. It was enough to know I had it; there was no need to prove it.

# 9

## FACE CONTROL

No longer was our new apartment block a skeleton; it now had red-brick walls in-filled between the columns, and spaces for the doors and balconies. It was looking like a building at last. As we walked up the concrete stairs, it pleased us to see that we also had floors, so we could wander around the apartments and take a proper look. We wasted no time climbing to the top floor, which would be our private home. Alex's parents would be on the first floor and much closer to the ground.

Our apartment seemed huge. The lift shaft was in place and the staircase ascended to the roof, which we were now reassured would also be part of our home. There were no internal walls or ironwork yet, so we carefully picked our way up the last flight of stairs and stood on our roof terrace. The view was incredible. Our building was now the highest in the area, and whereas in the last few years we'd been living in the shade, we were now casting shadows over others while standing in bright sunshine ourselves.

From our lofty perch, we could look out over the blue Aegean Sea and gaze down at the beach and harbour a few streets away; further out, there was the island of Aegina luxuriating in the sun. To our right we could see the port of Piraeus and the white tracks in the sea that followed the dozens of ferries sailing in and out. Oil tankers and container ships sat at anchor waiting to unload their cargo or take on more goods and depart for ports around the globe, keeping the world provisioned. Greece has been a maritime nation since ancient times. Because the mountainous landscape of the mainland wasn't good for farming, the Greeks took to shipping instead. The country's position was ideal for trade, being at the crossroads of ancient sea routes across the eastern Mediterranean, and the proximity to other advanced civilisations shaped the seafaring character of the Greek nation. Most of Alex's ancestors were ship's captains, so the sea is in her blood.

The coastline between Piraeus, the country's principal port, and Glyfada to the south is graced with several natural shallow bays, and the flatness of the land around Glyfada made this area an ideal access point for these protected harbours. The fishing fleet grew, and the village of Glyfada expanded in response. Much more recently, the land was found to be also perfect for Greece's first airport. Ellinikon served as Athens's international airport for six decades, until its replacement was built twenty-five kilometres away in Sparta, just before the 2004 Olympics.

Glyfada's fishing fleet had since been reduced to just a few privately owned wooden boats. Debbie assured me that this was because the fish stocks had been so depleted by modern fishing methods. When she was a girl, boats would tie up at the dock in Castella overflowing with huge multi-coloured fish. Now, the fishermen's tables were filled with small specimens of baboonia (red mullet) and tiny silver fish similar to whitebait.

I had heard that there were sharks in the Mediterranean, so one day, when I was thinking of going to the beach to swim, I asked Debbie if they were a problem in Greece. 'What would the sharks come here for?' she said. 'There are no fish. Nothing for them to eat.' When she was younger, the only time she ever saw sharks was after the Second World War, when the British and American fleets came to Piraeus. The sailors would throw scraps into the sea during their voyage, and the sharks would follow. Only tourists would swim when the fleet was in; the Greeks stayed at home.

Turning our backs to the sea, from our terrace vantage point we had an unobstructed view of the thousand-metre-high Hymettus mountain range. The range is also known as Trellós (Crazy) or Trellóvouno (Crazy Mountain), from the French 'très long' (very long), because it runs sixteen kilometres from Voula in the south all the way to Athens. When the wind blows from that direction in the summer, it brings the perfume of mountain herbs wafting down to us. The thyme up there is especially popular with bees, so the slopes are dotted with thousands of little beehives that produce deliciously aromatic thyme honey. Also up there on the mountainside, about halfway up, is the little church of Profitis Elias, known locally as a place of healing for any sick person who can make it that far up the slope.

In between us and the hillside church we could see the chimney of George's Taverna on Meat Street. The mouth-watering smells of barbecued meat invaded our nostrils and reminded us it was lunchtime. We headed off to eat.

As usual, the McDonald's on the corner was busy. A crowd of youngsters were sitting outside, their mopeds leaning against the wall. The local council was building tracks up the middle of the road for the new tram system; this would connect Glyfada with Piraeus and central Athens and was due to be ready the following year, in time for the Olympics. In Athens itself, the tracks were almost complete and the trams were being tested. This was causing a problem as motorists had found the unused stretches of concrete to be convenient places on which to park their cars. The government responded by putting out a fake news alert that the tracks were going to be electrified. But by the time the motorists caught onto this, it was too late and the trams were running.

Preparations for the Games were in full swing. Roads had been marked up with special lanes for the exclusive use of officials, which drivers also ignored. New stadiums were under construction and the authorities had cleared our local beach area of any unsightly huts or buildings, ready for the arrival of the world's media.

We turned right and walked past yet another parade of fashionable coffee houses and upmarket shops selling expensive shoes, designer dresses and accessories. Glyfada was now very much an upscale coastal suburb, complete with private beaches boasting their own pools and waiter service. Gone were the dusty dirt tracks of Alex's 1960s childhood, and gone too were most of the tiny fishing boats; in their place were multimillion-pound yachts with crews that never seemed to take them out. The few fishing boats that remained were confined to a small pontoon, and this was where locals now came every morning to buy their fish, fresh from the night's catch.

When Alex was a girl, Glyfada was like one enormous family. There were no multi-storey apartments then, and people did most of their domestic chores outside, in the gardens in front of their ramshackle homes. This meant that everyone knew everyone, and, more importantly, they all knew each other's business.

No one's home had an oven back then, so people did most of their cooking on bottled gas. If you needed to bake something, you took it to the local forno, which doubled as the bread bakery. The bread was baked early in the morning, and after that the ovens were repurposed for the cooking of family meals through the rest of the day. If Debbie had something to bake, Alex would take it to the forno for her and hand it over to George the baker. George always wore a white smock, white apron and matching beret. He limped because he'd had his leg blown off in the war and now used a wooden one.

At the appointed time later in the morning, Alex would return to collect her dish. George always wrapped newspaper around the tray's hot handles so she could carry it home without burning her fingers. The smells emanating from the ovens were wonderful, and Alex always had to resist the temptation to nibble her mother's food on the way home – Debbie would definitely have noticed. All the families used these fornos. At lunchtime there'd be a stream of people carrying trays of food past the gardens so the entire village would know what you were having for lunch.

The bakery had long since closed, to be replaced by Everest, another type of bakery selling pies, coffee and sandwiches.

Just as no one had ovens back then, only rich people had refrigerators. Everyone else, including Alex's family, bought ice from vendors who trundled through the neighbourhood with huge blocks of ice on their horse-drawn carts. The ice men wore white aprons and caps, and filled householders' buckets with ice flakes chipped off the big block. The buckets were then taken home and placed in an insulated lead box.

Every day assorted vendors would visit, some of them on carts led by a horse or donkey. They'd plod up the unmade road, flogging their tomatoes, watermelons or whatever else was in season. Others sold fruit preserved in syrup, usually grapes, segments of orange or green quince. This fruit in a jar has long been an essential part of Greek culture. Whenever a friend or neighbour visits, Greeks will offer them coffee, a glass of cold water, a small bowl of this preserved fruit and a shot glass of homemade cherry brandy. If the guest stays a little longer, a meal is always served. Every family makes their own cherry brandy: fresh cherries are dropped into a large bottle with an equal amount of sugar and this is then left in the sun for several weeks to liquefy. It's strained and then a bottle of Greek brandy, Metaxa, is added.

Before our local cat-woman, Stella, had her house demolished and replaced with a shiny new apartment block, she was the egg and chicken supplier to the street. Debbie used to send Alex over to buy eggs. Alex always hated this chore because Stella would chatter away to her while wringing the neck of an unfortunate fowl and eviscerating it, making her wait for the eggs.

The chickens had gone now, so like everyone else in Glyfada we bought our eggs from the supermarket. The gardens and tiny houses had gone too. Life was now hidden from view behind concrete blocks and double-glazed windows. The hum of air conditioners had replaced the fresh afternoon breeze blowing through countless little yards. Many of the original villagers had sold up and moved, taking advantage of the prime property prices. Most had family homes elsewhere in mainland Greece, but a few preferred to go back to their islands and resume a simpler way of life. Others, like us, had decided to knock down their little houses and replace them with towering blocks that would also generate a rental income.

Although the village atmosphere of old was hard to discern in what was now a lively and wealthy suburb of Athens, we could not walk more than a few metres in Glyfada before meeting a long-lost friend or neighbour still living there. These people, although richer now, had not changed; where once they'd greeted each other from their gardens or from chairs set out in the road outside their homes, nowadays they simply yelled at each other from their new balconies, high above the ground. Stella was the neighbourhood champion at this.

One neighbour Alex was never very comfortable bumping into was nosey Pandelis, the man who'd been so quick off the mark in carting Debbie's abandoned piano away to the flea market. He was the local plumber and handyman, though, like many tradespeople who claim they can fix anything, his botched attempts usually resulted in having to bring someone else in to put right whatever he'd mangled.

Pandelis was the village gossip and knew everything about everyone. He knew who was having relations with who, how much everyone earned and how much tax they paid. When Alex was younger, he used to monitor her clandestine nocturnal activities, recording to the minute her time of departure from the house and her time of return, and taking great delight in assuring Debbie that he 'knew things' about her daughter. When pressed for more information, he just tapped his finger to his nose and told her he was watching. This caused bad feeling with the family as he would disclose no details to Debbie, but used to spread the word to others in the neighbourhood that Alex was up to no good. Alex hated him and retaliated by picking on his daughter. That poor woman grew up strange and now spends the summer nights watering her balcony in the nude.

Meat Street was one of the few places in Glyfada that hadn't been gentrified. The narrow road was still lined with its original tavernas. They had resisted the many tempting offers from developers and continued to stand side by side, large silver chimneys protruding from their roofs, traditional wooden tables and chairs filling the entire street out front. This was the place to come for traditional Greek food, and we loved it. The tavernas cooked mostly on charcoal and the smell of meat was continually wafting along the street, reminding everyone that authentic Greek food was the best. Some enterprising people had tried to compete by opening smart sushi bars and fashionable Chinese restaurants, but these were short-lived, being no match for the Greeks' favourite fare of souvlaki, spit-roasted meat and good Greek salad.

We were hungry so we opted for a traditional souvlaki. This is the classic street food of Greece, like a Friday-night kebab in the UK but far better. Every village has several of these establishments and the food is always good. Whole chunks of meat are pressed down onto a skewer which is rotated vertically near a heated element. It bears no relation to the minced doner meat found in British kebab shops, and nor indeed does the bread. The meat is sliced and laid onto a freshly cooked circular flatbread; tomatoes, cucumber, onion and tzatziki are added, then everything is wrapped in the bread and served in a greaseproof paper cone. You wash it down with a glass of local white wine.

We know most of the local wine sold in these traditional tavernas as retsina. This is wine which contains pine resin. The practice originated in ancient Greece when animal skins were used to hold wine. Corks were unknown and it was usual to make stoppers from rolled-up pine resin to keep the wine fresh. The flavour of the resin infused the wine and people developed a taste for it. So now resin is added as a flavouring.

In Greece wine is rarely drunk neat because alcohol causes dehydration in the hot climate, so a small amount of water is always added. I always drop in some ice, which both dilutes the wine and keeps it cool. We sat and watched the ice melt into the wine while we waited for our food to arrive. We were both still in shock, having just seen our new building, and impressed at the speed of its progress.

We discussed the interior layout. Alex didn't want any walls in our apartment. We had already agreed on large patio doors stretching along the entire front of the apartment, so this would just be a wall of glass leading to the balcony. We chatted about the furnishings and agreed to go with an ancient Greece theme.

Alex picked up her souvlaki, took a bite and chewed thoughtfully while staring into the distance. 'I want columns,' she suddenly announced.

'What sort?'

'The same as the Parthenon – you know, on top of the Acropolis.'

I suggested we didn't need them as the structure was already in place and they would have nothing to support. Undeterred, she replied that they would only be a feature and didn't have to support anything. It would be in keeping with the ancient Greece theme, she said. I liked the idea. By now, the wine was running low and I was getting merry. As Alex rarely drank alcohol, she would be fine to drive, so I ordered a little more. I was now warming to her proposal and in my wine-induced haze wondered aloud whether, in addition to the two columns inside the apartment, we might build a replica Parthenon on our roof as well?

Alex clapped her hands in joy. 'You are a *poústis*,' she told me.

Directly translated, *poústis* means homosexual. This is one of the highest compliments that a man can receive from a woman. They use it for a really smart suggestion, a great idea or being a lucky person. For example, if you were lucky at cards or gambling and won consistently, not only would you be a *poústis* but in this case you would also have a big arse. The latter is usually emphasised by holding out both hands with extended fingers forming a ring to represent a large anus.

However, as with *malaka*, the meaning entirely changes with the tone and context. *Poústis* can also be a strong insult.

Ancient Greek culture did not have any problem with homosexuality. The discrimination came with Christianity. They did not talk about sexual desire or behaviour in terms of the gender of the participants, but rather in terms of the roles played in the sex act: that of giver or receiver. They associated the giver with masculinity and the receiver with femininity. This is still generally the case in Greece today.

Alex loved the idea of building a mini Parthenon on our roof terrace. A scaled-down version of the elegant rectangle of columns that sat atop the Acropolis and was dedicated to the goddess Athena would be the crowning glory of our new apartment block. I had a nagging thought in the back of my head that Stavros would never go for that, so if we were to go ahead with this, we would have to pay for it ourselves. Not having any money didn't deter us. The souvlaki was excellent and the wine even better, so we continued to plan as the afternoon darkened into evening.

We must have been more exhausted than we realised, as we woke up early the next morning with the birds outside the window struggling to make themselves heard over the roar of the traffic heading into Athens. We had slept right through from the evening – not surprising, given that our day had started at 3 a.m. in the UK. In the dawn light, I began recalling yesterday's conversation in the souvlaki taverna, where I'd agreed to have twenty Corinthian columns in our new home. What had I been thinking? It was hard enough trying to make sufficient money in England to survive and fund our monthly trips to Athens to check on the building. This new expense would stretch our finances to the limit. But I had committed to it, and being a man of my word, I would do it.

We set off in search of a company that sold Parthenons and soon found a builder's merchant whose front yard displayed an assortment of samples from classical Greek architecture. We sat down with the owner to explain our plans.

'You want what?' he exclaimed.

We repeated ourselves.

At last he smiled; we could see that he was coming round to the idea. He was probably picturing a nice advertising campaign complete with glossy brochure featuring a newly built Acropolis Parthenon on a rooftop in Glyfada.

He began doing his calculations. Unlike the original Athenians, we didn't have an army of slaves to carry the columns up to our roof, so we agreed to add on the cost of a crane to lift the concrete pillars five storeys up and fit them in place. The quotation was eye-watering, but I had promised Alex, so I went ahead with the purchase. The building wouldn't be ready for this new structure for another year and we would have to wait until Stavros had finished his work, so there was no real hurry. At least that would give me some breathing space to earn enough money in England to pay for it.

We thought it best not to discuss our plan to re-create a little corner of ancient Greece on our roof with Stavros. He already had enough to worry about, so we temporarily avoided sharing that little gem.

Back at the site, we climbed the long staircase to the new apartment. Having recovered from the joyful surprise of yesterday, we could now look at the property with cooler heads. Stavros was red-faced and puffing when he arrived at our floor, so we let him catch his breath before pulling out our list and starting on our queries.

Now that the outline was in place, we needed to discuss details. We started with the balcony design. Alex wanted small columns and a handrail, but Stavros was proposing simple railings instead; he said that if he agreed to columns for our apartment, he'd have to do the same for the balconies on all the other floors as well. Neither of them would back down. 'It's my house, and I want columns,' Alex reiterated to the back of Stavros's head.

The squabbling got more and more heated until eventually I requested that they both stop for a moment. Once the shouting had ceased, I asked Stavros why he was denying Alex her columns. It would cost more, he said, and he would not spend any more than necessary. 'How much more?' I asked.

'About £150 more per apartment.'

I nodded but didn't commit to anything. I didn't want to set a dangerous precedent, as once Stavros realised we were willing to pay for certain amendments, where would it end? So I stood back and let them carry on attacking each other while I wandered up to the terrace to admire the view.

As I stared down from my high vantage point, admiring the

luxury yachts in the harbour below, I could still hear muffled shouting from the floor beneath. I felt a bit sorry for Stavros and was tempted to go back down and offer to pay the extra, but I knew that Alex would likely then turn her fury on me, so I stayed put. A short while later, Alex joined me on the terrace and announced that Stavros had finally agreed that we could have columns instead of railings.

Alex was in the mood to celebrate, so that evening we went to a nightclub. As with most Greek nightclubs, there would be live music from the in-house band and then some guest singers too. We call these clubs bouzoukias. They are free to enter and have no dress code, but the young men who guard the door – the equivalent of bouncers in the UK – do turn away anyone that they consider to be inappropriate for the venue, which is why these chaps are referred to as 'face control'. As there's almost never any trouble at bouzoukias, the face-control guys don't do any bouncing but instead simply assist people into the club.

Athens is one of the safest cities in Europe and young people flock to Glyfada every night to enjoy its famous nightlife, filling its many bars, beach restaurants and night-clubs. Many times, Alex and I have strolled the streets around midnight. The bars are always packed with both the young and the elderly, and sometimes even with young children. Rowdy behaviour is rare, and drink-fuelled violence just does not occur. Greek youngsters are happy to sit in a cafeteria or bar drinking coffee; if alcoholic drinks are consumed, it's always in moderation. The only time we've ever felt uncomfortable was when there was a football match due to be played. This was the final of the European Cup, and Athens was hosting the match as a neutral ground. Swarms of England fans and opposing Italy supporters came to Glyfada to get tanked up prior to the match. Even then, it was not a violent scene, but it was unusually threatening for our village.

Once past the face control, we settled at a table in front of the stage. In the middle of the table was an unopened bottle of whisky. For this, it's normal to pay around a hundred euros, to cover the entrance fee and your drink for the evening. Included in that will be any mixers for the whisky, and selections of nuts dished out regularly to the table throughout the show. Other alcoholic drinks have to paid for, so most people just stick with the whisky. For a small surcharge, you can ask for the whisky to be sealed at the end of the evening and stored until your next visit.

The tables were slowly filling, and a warm-up band appeared on stage. Two bouzouki players and a bass guitarist were accompanied by a drummer, and a girl blowing on a clarinet. It was traditional Greek music, and I loved it. As the night went on, the music got louder. By the time the band got to their last number, the tables were vibrating. Now it was time for the featured artists, the reason we were there. On the bill were A-list singers who were some of the biggest celebrities in Greece.

Greeks have an eclectic taste in music. Traditional will always be popular, as will well-known names like Nana Mouskouri and Vangelis, but modern pop is very big too, and musicians have no trouble mixing the two, sometimes within one song. It is a popular format and seems to appeal to everyone.

First of the stars to appear was Anna Vissi. She's sold more than ten million albums worldwide, is famous in America as well as Greece, and has now represented Greece twice in the Eurovision Song Contest, in 1980 and 2006. She is a household name. As she performed her first few songs, the volume got steadily louder. People began stepping up from their chairs and dancing on the tables, while others clapped in time with the music. Soon every table in the club had one or two women dancing on it. Anna continued her set. As one song ended, she started another, this time gesturing to the audience to come and join her on stage. Some of the women did just that, clambering down off their tabletops and up onto the stage alongside Anna; others remained where they were and just carried on dancing.

It amazed me. Anna Vissi was one of the top superstars in the country and had invited anyone who felt like it to share the stage while she continued to sing. All the celebrities that followed her that night did likewise. Everyone was welcomed up on to the stage alongside the artiste.

Finally, after many hours of exuberant dancing, the house band reappeared, signalling the end of the evening. People began drifting away.

We filed out through the door and into bright sunshine. It was after 6 a.m. and a new day had begun. We'd had a glorious time. The lack of formality fascinated me. I could compare this to an Elton John concert: instead of banks of security men stopping people from invading the stage, in Greece it was actively encouraged and was very much part of the show, with performers exhorting the participation of their fans.

# 10

# BURNING RUBBER ON SANTORINI

The plane banked over the volcano as we dipped towards the airport on Santorini. I could make out the island's capital, Fira, with its miniature white buildings spread along a high ridge. It looked as though God had sprinkled the crest with icing sugar. The sea beneath us was dark and inky, unlike the rest of the Aegean, which is normally an inviting light blue. The blackness within the caldera seemed appropriate, for under the silver-capped waves lay the remains of the most destructive explosion in human history. Around the year 1646 BC, the eruption of this volcano wiped out an entire civilisation, on Santorini as well as on the island of Crete more than 150 kilometres away.

Down at ground level, blackened hills of lava were everywhere as we picked up our hire car – a nice red convertible with the hood tucked away – and drove across the island to our hotel in Oia, a tiny village to the far north. Dark, jagged rocks and ancient olive trees dominated the landscape as far as we could see, but we didn't linger because we'd heard that Oia had the best sunsets in Greece and we were keen not to miss out.

Oia proved to be a delightful village. The smooth, brilliant white walls of the buildings made a striking contrast to the deep-blue paintwork of their window frames, archways and church domes. They'd painted the pathways between these charming homes in grey, picking out the lines in white and blue to match.

Alex pointed at the light blue sign displaying the name of our hotel. There was no building visible, just an arched gateway leading us off the road and down a stone staircase. At the bottom was the hotel reception, located alongside a kidney-shaped swimming pool that had been cut out of the rocky hillside.

In fact the entire hotel had been gouged out of the hillside. We followed the owner down more steps to our room, more accurately a cave, which had been lined and converted into a snug apartment. The ceiling had been moulded around the uneven contours of the cave roof and plaster coving hid a selection of uplighters which illuminated the hand-painted ceiling depicting puffy white clouds on a sky-blue background. To the rear was a door leading to a light-blue-tiled bathroom with a white marble floor.

The room was luxurious, but the view was better. All the hotel's rooms had been cut out of the mountain at different levels, creating a series of stepped terraces, so we had an unobstructed panorama before us. Much of the semi-circular caldera was in shadow now, from the surrounding mountains, but the little black volcanic island in the centre was bathing in the late-afternoon sunshine. 'Is that an active volcano?' Alex asked.

The owner confirmed that it was. 'It's called Nea Kameni (Young Burned Island),' he said. 'It rumbles and smokes sometimes. You can take a boat trip there and walk around it.'

Alex clapped delightedly. She'd always had a fascination for volcanoes, and now we would walk on one. This would be first on our list of activities tomorrow. Meanwhile, we had to find a vantage point from which to watch the world-famous sunset.

We walked into the village centre. If you were to close your eyes and picture the most idyllic Greek island village imaginable, Oia was it and more. It was beautiful. Outside the stunning white and blue houses stood pots of crimson geraniums, placed on steps and windowsills, while creeping blood-red bougainvillea grew up the blindingly white walls. Palm trees along the street swayed gently in the soft breeze and small green cacti nestled along the base of orange trees heavy with ripe fruit. The air was thick with the scent of flowers and fruit trees mingled with the aroma of food cooking in the restaurants scattered around the village square.

We found a spot on a wall next to an old windmill and sat down to enjoy the show. As the golden sun touched the sea, the colours changed from yellow to tangerine. Sea and sun merged and cast rays of gold, orange and purple over the water towards us in a rainbow of rippling colour. Then the sun disappeared below the horizon, leaving a red hue. The famous sunset had matched our expectations.

We made our way up the hill and took a table at a smart-looking fish taverna overlooking the darkening sea. It was a warm evening with little breeze. Beneath the dusky sky, as the stars twinkled above us, we chatted about our new home and made plans for the future while sipping Santorini wine between bites of calamari and salad.

Back at our hotel, the steep pathway down past the pool was now brightly lit, and a vase of newly cut flowers had been placed on the blue metal table on our private terrace. The owner passed by to bid us goodnight as we sat outside our room, appreciating the gorgeous environment. It was a lovely place, and we were happy to be there.

At breakfast the next morning, we watched a helicopter hovering over a fleet of small boats in the caldera, about three kilometres away. 'They're making another movie,' the hotel owner told us. 'It's called *Tomb Raider*, I think.' Little figures were jumping into the sea from the boats, making tiny white splashes in the deep blue water. The boats were buzzing around in circles, being followed by the helicopter; then the helicopter flew away and the boats parted and motored off in opposite directions.

We set off in the car for the old port of Fira, at the bottom of the mountain, departure point for boats to Nea Kameni. The day was scorching, and I was regretting having hired a convertible; the sun was already beating down on our heads. Being blond and blue-eyed, I'm not very good with heat. I need shade and cool drinks to keep me from melting. But that would be in short supply today. The temperature was already nudging thirty-five degrees and it was still only ten in the morning.

In Fira, we parked the car and started the lengthy walk down the winding mountain path to the dock whence the boat would ferry us across to the island of the active volcano Nea Kameni. I was armed against the sun with a straw hat, cool shorts, a loose cotton shirt and sandals. Alex, being a native, did not suffer with the heat and was wearing tight leggings and a T-shirt, with a cardigan over her shoulder in case it got cold.

As the boat drew closer to the dark, barren-looking island, we could see smoke rising from the low summit ahead. There were no trees or plants visible, just steaming rocks. A grey gravel path took us towards the interior, through a landscape of charred black rock, piles of enormous lumps of grey pumice stone, and sandy red deposits that looked like iron. The air had a whiff of heat and rotten eggs. There was not a green shoot in the earth nor a bird in the sky, just rocky deposits and heat. The heat was coming at us in all directions – from beneath my feet as well as from above my head. The sun continued to beat down on me, but now there was also an unconformable warmth under my toes and radiating up my legs. Within just a few paces, I was wet with perspiration.

I looked at Alex, who skipped away from the path, leapt over the razor-sharp rocks and pointed excitedly at a jet of steam pushing up from the ground. She was entirely unaffected by the temperature. I, on the other hand, felt as if I were in a sauna with one of those enthusiasts that continue to pour water over the coals to make it hotter.

After twenty minutes I had stopped taking an interest in my surroundings and was now wholly consumed with finding ways to cool down. I remembered that Alex had told me I'd be able to swim on the island. I brightened at this thought and looked for a route down to the cool sea. I was disappointed. Large, sharp rocks encircled the entire perimeter of the island.

There was no way of entering the water other than via the pontoon far behind us, where we'd landed.

'Can I have the bottle of water?' I said.

'I haven't got it. I thought you brought it,' Alex replied.

We'd left our supply of water in the car. Realising that I had nothing with which to quench my thirst made me long for a drink even more. I recalled scenes from old movies about people who got lost in the desert and died of thirst. I wondered how long it would take before my lips cracked and my tongue swelled. I needed to get off this island.

Alex, meanwhile, was having a lovely time jumping from rock to rock, a piece of pumice stone in one hand and an interesting chunk of bright yellow sulphur in the other.

I was grateful when we reached the summit as this meant we could now start on our way back to the boat. But Alex had other ideas. She was already halfway down the other side, crouched, her knees level with her ears, examining a stream of steaming water bubbling up from the ground and leaving bright, sunshine-coloured sulphur deposits on the adjacent rocks.

'Can we go now?' I pleaded.

'A few more minutes.'

Searching for somewhere to sit while Alex continued her hunt for volcanic artefacts, I found a smooth rock. Within moments, my bottom got warmer, then painfully hot. I stood up quickly. I had sat on a hotplate and my bottom was burning as if it had caught fire. My feet seemed even hotter than before. I checked the soles of my sandals; they had melted and were emitting an aroma of burning rubber. 'I really think we need to go now,' I said.

Fortunately, Alex had finished rummaging through the interesting rocks and agreed.

By the time we got back to the boat, I was perspiring less.

This was a dangerous sign. I assumed that the heat had dehydrated me, and I began to get panicky. It seemed like I was walking on jelly. Was I hallucinating now? Not quite – it was just that my sandals had continued to melt. They were now nothing but wobbling, misshapen blobs attached to my feet by a leather strap.

I asked the boat captain if he had any water. He didn't but assured me it was only a fifteen-minute trip back to Fira, where there was a cafeteria on the dock. I stared down at the clear sea. It looked good. How many sailors cast adrift on the ocean had given in to the temptation and taken a drink to quench their raging thirst? I was already minded to have a sip and I'd only been dying of thirst for an hour.

Before I had a chance to join those desperate mariners, we arrived at the port. We jumped off the boat and headed straight for the welcoming cafe with tables set under a rocky overhang. The icy water tasted magnificent. After gulping down three bottles, I was feeling better. We were in the shade away from the direct sunlight, a cool breeze was caressing us, and my body temperature had returned to normal. My next concern was the impending hike back up the mountain path to the car. Coming down had been okay, as it required little effort, but climbing the six hundred steps back up to the peak without shade and in temperatures that were hitting forty degrees would be a challenge.

We looked across at the other side of the little port to a long string of cable cars swinging in the breeze. They were stationary, however; undergoing maintenance, apparently, and therefore out of action. That left us with two options. We could either climb the mountain ourselves – Alex, being young, fit, and immune to the heat, thought this would be a pleasant stroll, whereas I was wondering if I could carry enough water to avoid getting heatstroke – or we could go by mule.

We had seen these sturdy creatures during our descent earlier. They wandered up and down the mountain with no supervision, carrying tourists to the port at the bottom or the town at the top. They were aware of what was needed from them and seemed content to plod up and down for the reward of a carrot or two. That would solve my problem.

As a child, I'd taken a few horse-riding lessons and had a fair idea of how to do it. Alex was a little worried as she had never sat on a horse before, and these mules looked rather large and powerful. I assured her that it would be fine and that I'd be close by should she get into difficulty. So we followed the signs to a small enclosure where a few happy-looking mules were munching from a basket of hay while using their tails to bat away flies.

The attendant selected a sturdy grey model for me and led it over to the mounting block. I swung my leg over and settled into the saddle. As it was quite rotund, I had trouble getting my feet into the stirrups. When I managed it, my legs stuck out either side at an angle of forty-five degrees. I tried to tuck them in as we set off. The mule walked three paces and stopped. I looked behind me to see Alex grinning at me from the top of her chestnut transport. I tapped the side of my animal with my heels and shook the reins while telling it to 'giddy up'. It didn't move. I tried again. I kicked it a little harder. Still no movement. A roadblock was forming as mules queued to our rear. Perhaps it didn't understand English, so I changed to Greek. 'Griara!' I yelled.

It moved.

This was not an auspicious beginning.

The pathway up the mountain was a series of shallow zigzags, so we were continually turning back on ourselves. At the first turn, my mule saw a black bin bag on the ground and stopped to investigate its contents. No amount of pulling at the reins or jabbing of heels into its flanks could distract it. It continued to pay no heed as the line of mules behind us continued to lengthen. Eventually it lost interest and we plodded on. The path widened, allowing mules coming in the other direction plenty of room to pass on our right, but when we approached an overhanging tree branch, my mule headed straight for it. It would pass under the low branch with centimetres to spare, but I would not. I had no time to flatten myself against the mule's back, so I grabbed the branch, lifted it briefly to avoid getting hit, then let it go with a twang – a twang that, unfortunately, slapped the rear end of my transport, which bucked, leapt forward and ran towards an oncoming mule. I gripped the reins tightly, trying to pull it back, and we slowed just before we collided.

The mule's plan to scrape me off its back had been unsuccessful, but it hadn't given up yet. For its next attempt it decided to rub along the white wall, trapping my left leg and grazing my knee. I tried to move my leg, but it jammed in the stirrup. I had to endure the pain until the wall came to an end. I pulled my foot out of the restraint in case it tried that again.

The next opportunity to get rid of me came in the shape of two grey mules that were coming down the slope towards us, carrying tourists with floppy hats and flowered shirts. Rather than keeping to the left to avoid them, my nag ploughed straight between them, forcing the two mules apart and squeezing through the gap. This caused my sandal buckles to scrape the flanks of the poor creatures and cut into the legs of the unfortunate riders, who screamed in pain as they yelled abuse at me in some strange language.

At this point I turned around to see that Alex had almost dismounted herself with laughter. While my mule was attempting to make my day as difficult as possible, hers was obediently walking up the slope without incident.

Another overhanging branch loomed, but I had warning this time and pulled the reins to the right. The mule pulled back to the left. I tried again, yanking harder this time. To no avail. The mule headed straight for the branch as I flattened myself against its back and put my arms around its neck. The leaves brushed my head first; then came the prickles of small branches. Now the major branch came into view. I would not avoid it. With one arm still holding onto the mule's neck, I rolled over until I was suspended over its flank, my head level with its chest and my leg pointing up into the air. The leg caught the branch and the pain was intense, but I had survived. I rubbed my sore skin and noticed red lines running from above my knee to my shoes.

My straw hat was in tatters, my cotton shirt was ripped and stained green from the foliage, my shorts had split up the side, and I felt a suspicious draught around my crotch region. To top this off, I was having trouble walking as my melted sandals had now cooked down into a blob so it felt like I was balancing on tennis balls. As I hobbled away from the mule, it turned its head and watched me suspiciously. I stopped, went closer and held out a hand towards its nose in a gesture of friendship, to show that there were no hard feelings on my part. The mule clearly felt otherwise, however. I withdrew my hand quickly as it tried to bite my fingers.

I needed a beer to calm my nerves, and Alex needed to wash the tears of laughter from her face. A few steps above the mule station was a bar with tables set out on a balcony over-looking the caldera. As I took my first sips of a frothy amber beer served in a glass fresh from the freezer, I looked across at the black volcanic island. It didn't look so threatening from here. But I knew better.

We had by now realised that Stavros was slipperier than we'd hoped. It was obvious that he would try and save as much money as possible on the build and that he would likely snaffle the odd metre here and there, so we had to be on the alert.

He was waiting for us at the site with a worried look on his face. He hated our visits, which always either caused him trouble or cost him money. He had arranged for the bricklayer to meet with us to discuss the position of the internal walls to divide the rooms. We all climbed the stairs to our apartment. The bricklayer asked Alex to draw out where the walls would be. Alex said she didn't want any apart from for the bedrooms and bathroom.

'Don't you want to divide the living area into rooms?' the brickie asked. 'And what about a hallway or a kitchen?'

Alex shook her head. She wanted the kitchen to be part of the overall living space, and the lift would open directly into the apartment, so no hall either. Stavros looked pleased as the bricklayer would cost him much less than he thought. But Alex was now focusing on the rear balcony. She called Stavros over. 'I don't want a balcony there; I want to continue the living room into that space,' she said.

'No way,' replied Stavros, his face reddening. 'We've already agreed this with the planning office. It cannot be changed.'

Alex insisted. Again, the argument got heated. Stavros would concede nothing without a fight and carried on protesting and throwing in various reasons why he couldn't do it. I stepped in. I knew a way to change his mind.

'How much will a patio door cost as designed?' I asked.

He quoted a figure.

'So is a window cheaper than a patio door?'

'Yes,' he replied.

'So, if you're not putting in a patio door, just a window, you've saved money, right?'

His eyes brightened. The rear balcony was history.

Debbie and Zissis's apartments were much smaller than ours. Our property occupied the entire floor, whereas their floor was divided into two apartments, one to live in, the other to rent out. They looked good. The kitchen had been incorporated into the living area, which led onto an ample balcony overlooking the street. It was cooler down there as it was not in direct sun and was also in the shade of other buildings in the road. Debbie and Zissis preferred it that way. If they wanted some sunshine, it was only a quick elevator ride up to our place to sit on the roof.

We continued our inspection to the ground floor. Outside the building, I stood back and looked at where the shops would be. This was currently just an enormous space with no walls yet to divide the shops. I looked to the right, at where Stavros's shop would be, then to the left, at ours, and realised something I hadn't noticed on the drawings. The elevator shaft and concrete staircase were on our side and would be behind our shop. This would make our shop half the size of his. We'd been so enthusiastic on seeing the built-up shell and preoccupied with minor details that we hadn't noticed that the biggest issue was right in front of us.

Alex was furious. But before she had time to confront him, Stavros jumped in. 'It's in the contract,' he said. 'Your shop will be forty square metres, and that's what you agreed to.'

Unfortunately, he was correct. He just hadn't told us that his shop would be double the size of ours at more than eighty square metres. It was difficult to vent our anger at him as he was technically within the law, even though his behaviour was deceptive and immoral. A quick glance at the drawings revealed that the empty space that he had previously told us not to worry about had now been incorporated into his part of the building.

All of our happiness evaporated. We felt let down and ripped off.

# 11

# THE CUTTLEFISH AND THE SHRIMP

We decided to spend a night away from the overpowering heat of the city. The island of Hydra was only a short boat trip away, and I had never been there. We left the site, collected our overnight bag from our temporary apartment and drove the short distance to Piraeus. This would be a fresh experience as we were travelling not by ferry but by Flying Dolphin, effectively a yellow cigar tube that looked more like an aeroplane than a boat, with a line of windows along each flank.

The engine started and the floor rumbled under our feet. Once out in the open sea, the noise increased as we rose above the water; we were now skiing on hydrofoils. Although it was exciting, it was like being in a washing machine on a spin cycle. We were buffeted to and fro, and shaken all the way to our destination.

On disembarking, we dragged our overnight bag around the harbour as we went in search of the tourist office. Every Greek island has its tourist office close to the port as this is where you go to find accommodation. Staff keep a list of rooms for rent and will contact the owners on your behalf. The owners will usually come and collect you and your bags to get you settled in. We found a nice, clean, airy room in a stone house with blue shutters. It had one window and a single-glazed door leading out to a small balcony over the harbour. It was very basic, as most rooms in Greece are. There was a bed, a small table and a doorway leading through to a tiny bathroom. It was perfect.

Hydra is exceptional as the only inhabited Greek island that has no motorised vehicles. Most of the commuting is by donkey. By now I knew that Greek donkeys didn't like me, so I vowed that whenever we came within kicking distance of one on Hydra, I would ensure that Alex was between me and it. If a mule did take the chance to attack me, I would likely be the only visitor to Hydra ever to be savaged by one.

Another thing Hydra is famous for is its association with the late Canadian singer-songwriter Leonard Cohen. He appreciated the peace and tranquillity of the island so much that he bought a house there in the 1960s. It cost him just US $1500. Cohen and his long-term girlfriend and muse Marianne

Ihlen spent many years together on Hydra, and it was here that he wrote his poem to her, 'Days of Kindness'. We could see the terrace he described in the poem not far from our room. The scenery he wrote about will be familiar to anyone who hangs around after all the tourists have gone – the deep blue sky and sea with fog rising from it. After his death, the locals decorated his house with flowers as a tribute to one they accepted as their own.

Wandering around the harbour later, we stopped and spoke to some local fishermen sitting in the shade, mending their nets. Conversation was easy and consisted mostly of recommendations for the best restaurants around: 'You must try that one as they buy my fish.' We settled on a small taverna at the end of the bay with old fishing boats tied to the railings and tables overlooking the clear water.

As I gazed into the shallows, I spotted a colour-changing cuttlefish stalking a shrimp. I felt sorry for the shrimp; in fact, I empathised with it. I knew how the poor creature felt. Although our architect was turning out to be a shark, he probably had cuttlefish somewhere in his ancestry. He seemed to continually change his colour and in the latest episode of our building drama had shown us that, yet again, he'd been lining us up as a lucrative snack.

I was relieved to observe that the shrimp had now realised it was in imminent danger. With a flick of its tail, it disappeared into a cloud of sand. For Alex and me, this minibreak to Hydra was our cloud of sand.

We had been away from Athens for more than a month and had been keen to see the progress of our building. We'd tried to communicate with Stavros by email and phone, but he always seemed evasive and did not want to get too involved in a conversation about the details. He kept telling us he would talk to us when we got there. Yesterday, that day had finally come.

We'd already notified Stavros of our arrival time and asked him to make himself available. As we drove into our street, the structure was there ahead of us. No longer was it a pile of concrete beams. Since our last visit, the windows and patio doors had been installed, and they gleamed in the sunlight. It looked at last like a building.

We walked around to the entrance and climbed the stairs to our apartment. It looked wonderful. True to his promise, he had incorporated the rear balcony into the living room, creating a nice L-shaped feature. A stone fireplace sat proudly in the corner and curved from wall to wall with a chimney disappearing through the ceiling, ready to burn logs during the winter months. The floor was still a dusty concrete surface. Beautiful, enormous windows had been fitted, together with patio doors, stretching the entire length of the living room. So why was Stavros being so evasive?

We went up to check the roof. Nothing had altered there apart from the chimney for the new fireplace. We stood and admired the view but avoided going too near the edge as the perimeter barriers hadn't been built yet and it was a sheer drop.

Stavros appeared. We greeted each other, and we complimented him on all the advancements. He smiled but looked uneasy. He told us his plans for completion of the electrical system. We discussed the radiator positions and chose a colour scheme for the bathroom tiles and kitchen units. It all went smoothly, without arguments or heated discussion. I was surprised and felt like we were at last beginning to communicate amicably. We still felt raw about our shop being half the size of his, but it was too late to continue that squabble. We had decided to let it go.

We descended the staircase and took a quick look at Debbie's first-floor apartment before continuing down to the shops. Stavros had now built the dividing wall between his shop and ours. The lift shaft and staircase were behind and due to be closed off. We noticed that he had now extended the concrete staircase to the basement level, so we followed it down to inspect the rest of our property. There was a decent-sized space below our shop, which continued below the driveway and compensated in part for the space lost on the ground floor. But there was a wall to the other side of the lift shaft and a dark, unlit space beyond it. With the aid of a flashlight, we went in to look around.

Stavros had stolen most of our basement! Four storerooms had been constructed, one for each floor, and they were all in our half of the basement, not his. Also in our half was the room for the building's boilers and the giant water tanks. This explained his evasiveness. We had been ripped off yet again.

Alex was looking for blood. She raced up the stairs two at a time to find Stavros and confront him. He'd obviously realised that Alex would be after him as soon as she saw the basement, so now he was nowhere to be seen. We stormed into his office. The receptionist claimed not to have set eyes on him since that morning. Alex insisted that she call his mobile. No answer.

Alex was now glowing a furious red; she was on the rampage. We left his office, hoping to track down his hiding place. His car was still in the driveway, so he couldn't have gone far. We searched three coffee shops before we found him lurking behind the door of the fourth, a coffee in one hand, a smoking cigarette in the other. His face drained of colour when he spotted us.

'I want a word with you, *malaka*,' Alex screamed.

'Okay, but not here,' he said. 'I'll see you back at the site in ten minutes.'

I took Alex's arm and physically led her away. She was furious and had no intention of holding her anger for a moment longer.

Fifteen minutes passed. I tried to calm Alex down, and I pleaded with her to be logical. It wasn't working; she just wanted to kill him in a painful manner and bury his body in the pile of rubble on the road outside. We watched him amble up the road towards us in the way that a naughty dog slinks home on its belly after having been caught eating the family cat.

We had the advantage here. The basement plans and design drawings had shown no walls apart from the one dividing his basement from ours. This space was part of our property and he had taken it.

He tried to defend himself by reminding us that two of the storerooms would be ours and that some of the water tanks were also for us.

This was not acceptable to Alex. She demanded to see his shop and his basement. He reluctantly agreed and led us up the stairs, around the front and into his shop. It was huge compared to ours. We descended the stairs and entered what would become an enormous commercial kitchen, already being prepared. He had rented this property out as a restaurant and had taken a large cash deposit to fit it out to the client's specification.

As he had broken our contract, we now needed to think about our next step. Alex's fury slowly turned to sadness and disappointment. We had trusted this man with our only asset and felt that our home was being taken from us piece by piece.

We had signed the contract and agreed to a shop of forty square metres. That was what we were getting. Regardless of Stavros's games, this was on paper and confirmed. We had made the mistake of not being persistent in discovering the reason for the blocked-out area on the plans; we had wrongly expected this would hold the plant room, whereas it had now become part of Stavros's shop. We hadn't really thought about the storage rooms for each apartment, nor the location of the boiler room. We'd just assumed that they would be spread between our properties. He had already taken advantage of us by positioning the lift shaft and the staircase on our side, thus maximising his retail space. Now he had taken most of our basement.

Alex and I took some time out to regroup. I suggested to her that rather than resort to the law, which would mean a delay with the construction, we should see if he would change his mind.

Alex opened the next round of our discussion with Stavros by expressing her disappointment. We had chosen him as our architect because he was a local man. She had hoped that this would at least enable us to work together as friends. For Stavros, however, business was paramount; he had no interest in friendship. Profit was king in his eyes. But we were legally in the right and we had him. He knew that we could stop the work and delay the project while we sought legal advice.

Stavros slipped into cuttlefish mode. He agreed that he should have consulted us on the basement rooms, but it had slipped his mind. In recompense he was going to offer us 'a good deal'. His proposal was to build a mezzanine level above our shop, extending it over the driveway. In addition, he would install a spiral staircase leading up to the mezzanine and continuing down into the basement. This would no longer be a storage space but would become part of the shop.

We did some calculations. This arrangement would give our shop a new mezzanine of sixty square metres and a new basement of sixty square metres in addition to the original forty square metres, increasing our retail space to 160 square metres in all. Our anger dissolved.

Stavros saw that this had worked and pressed his newfound advantage. 'I am having problems getting columns for the balconies,' he said hastily, 'so I'll need to install wrought-iron railings instead.' We were absorbing the prospect of having a much bigger shop, so Alex quickly agreed. We left feeling elated and pleased with our victory. (We found out later that the mezzanine level and basement could not be used for retail space as these would not comply with fire regulations. But it made us happy then.)

Like the shrimp I'd been watching from our Hydra restaurant, Alex and I had deflected this latest attempt by our predator to devour us bit by bit. It was late afternoon and the sun was just setting as the owner of the taverna appeared, spread a plastic tablecloth and clipped it in place with small metal clamps to stop it from blowing away in the warm island breeze. A while later, he reappeared bearing our drinks, then left us in peace and wandered off to sit on a chair outside his restaurant and gaze out to sea. In Greece, nothing happens fast. Realising we were in no hurry, he was content to let us relax, drink a glass or two and settle in to admire the view.

We sat looking across the calm water as the sun sank below the distant horizon. The moon crept up over the mountain. Lights from the village were reflected in the bay and seemed to dance in time with the soft bouzouki music coming from a bar not far away.

Alex and I always made our plans while in a taverna. Today was no exception. Although we'd won the last argument with Stavros, we both felt uneasy. He had proved himself to be slippery and seemed intent on stretching our agreement to the limit to claim as much of our property as possible. The family had signed the contract in good faith and were expecting us to take the responsibility of protecting their interests; we needed to recharge our batteries for the next round.

We called the taverna owner over and confirmed that we were ready to eat. As we were undecided, he suggested we follow him into his kitchen to see the options for ourselves. He directed us to a large tin tray of multi-coloured fish arranged on a bed of ice. Small silver whitebait and fresh sardines sat next to some larger pink fish; fresh calamari and shrimps were piled up alongside two clawless lobsters. It all looked fresh and appetising. We chose a selection of sardines and red mullet. I avoided the shrimps, out of kinship, so just added a portion of calamari.

The sweet aroma of fish roasting on charcoal wafted over to our table from the kitchen as the owner set a traditional Greek salad in front of us, along with bread and a bottle of olive oil. The lights flickered over the calm water as we enjoyed a wonderful meal.

The next day I woke up feeling ill. My head was aching and my throat felt like I'd swallowed a razor blade. My head thumped as I eased my feet out of bed and tried to rise. By the time I'd made it the short distance from my bed to the bathroom, I was sweaty and feverish. I really wasn't well. I tried to remember the previous night. Had I drunk too much? No, I'd had just a few glasses of wine with our meal, so it wasn't a hangover.

Alex looked at me and with confidence told me that I wasn't ill but had caught the evil eye. The evil eye (to kako mati) is the most feared affliction in Greece. You can catch it if others are jealous of you, if you receive excessive compliments, or even by just being told your hair looks good today. If I wear a new shirt and it looks nice, Alex will spit on me three times and using three fingers make a sign of the cross to ward off the eye. If you feel poorly or tired, it's unlikely to be an illness; rather it's a sign that you have caught the eye.

The only way to get rid of this affliction is by having a special prayer offered on your behalf by an older woman. The prayer for the eye is a closely guarded secret; it is told to a daughter by her mother, using her last breath as she lies on her deathbed.

One day a while back, I'd woken up late after a night out with some friends at a local bar in Glyfada. We'd been celebrating our win at a cricket match, the British expats having beaten the British Embassy team. We'd spent most of the evening trying to explain the rules of cricket to some Greeks, who eventually gave up trying to understand and suggested getting drunk instead. Not being a big drinker, I was now suffering the effects of having overdone it.

As I lifted my thumping head from the pillow, I was reminded of the enormous quantities of ouzo I'd consumed. I staggered into the bathroom and looked in the mirror. My face was pale, I had bags under my eyes and my teeth felt hairy. I went downstairs to the terrace to get some coffee and an aspirin. Debbie was at the table peeling potatoes. When she glanced up at me, a sympathetic expression spread across her face.

'Oh, you poor thing, you have the eye,' she said.

Not wishing to admit to my drunkenness of the night before, this seemed like a good excuse, so I readily agreed with her diagnosis. She went inside and returned with a mug of coffee.

'Just sit there, drink your coffee, and I will deal with the eye.'

She then sat down beside me and prayed. After a few moments, tears began rolling down her face and dripping onto the plastic tablecloth. For some reason, I started to yawn. Seconds later, she finished, and I felt better. I was well into my second coffee when Alex came home wheeling her trolleybag.

She had been to the local market for some fruit and vegetables. She appraised my face and immediately ratted on me. 'I expected you to look a lot worse after coming home so drunk last night,' she scolded.

Debbie leapt to my defence. 'He may have had a little to drink,' she said, 'but he must have got the eye at that bar. I did the prayer, and he had a lot of eye, but he's fine now.'

Alex's face softened as she sat down beside me. I could see I might yet get away with this. 'When Mum did the eye for you, did you yawn?' she asked.

'Yes, many times.'

She was convinced. This had nothing to do with the vast quantity of booze consumed; I had been afflicted by the evil eye. She took my hand and with a look of concern assured me that I would start feeling better now that Debbie had done the prayer. Strangely, I did feel better.

This Hydra affliction, however, was not the evil eye, and I knew it. This was more likely to be full-blown flu. After feeling my forehead and burning her hand, Alex finally agreed. She knew exactly what I needed to put me right.

Greeks have a fascination with medical matters. In England, if you ask someone how they are, the reply will usually be 'fine'. In Greece, they will answer with a full medical history and graphic details of any current complaint. There seems to be a pharmacy on every corner and they are always busy. Most prescription drugs are freely available over the counter and, with the aid of a pharmacist, most people self-medicate. Until recently, you could purchase antibiotics along with a packet of aspirin or paracetamol. Although Greece does have a functioning national health service, accessing it usually involves vast amounts of bureaucracy and queuing in order to actually get to see a doctor. GPs are almost unknown here. However, just about every village has a variety of private medical specialists, from cardiologists to neurologists and everything in between. They advertise their services via large signs over their premises, which are usually either above a shop or outside an apartment block.

Alex duly disappeared off to the nearest pharmacy on Hydra while I sat in a cafe staring at a cup of tea and feeling sorry for myself. She returned with a carrier bag full of brown medicine bottles and assorted tablets. She insisted that I take a sip from each bottle and swallow two of each tablet. Even though I was struggling to drink my cup of tea, Alex decided that I should follow this with a large glass of Metaxa, the strong Greek brandy that can also be used for lighting barbecues.

Having downed this concoction of tablets, potions and half a pint of brandy, I felt well enough to walk to the hydrofoil for our return journey to Piraeus. The trip aboard the long yellow washing machine passed in a blur, but by the time we'd reached the car back on the mainland, I had taken a turn for the worse. I was now coughing up nails, my fever was worse, and all I wanted was my nice soft bed back home and a long sleep. Alex had other ideas.

She was on a mission to cure me and announced that we had to go to church. 'The saint will heal you.'

'Is it on the way home?' I asked optimistically.

'Well, we have to go home first,' she replied.

I was too ill to argue and knew there was no point. No amount of protest would deflect her. So I lay back in the seat and fell asleep as she drove us home to our rental flat. I woke up as she slammed the car door and disappeared inside. Minutes later, she'd returned, carrying two walking sticks, which she threw onto the back seat before getting in the car and driving us away.

'I don't need a walking stick,' I protested. 'I'm not that ill.'

She ignored me and carried on driving for a few minutes

until the road came to a dead end. We were now at the foot of the Trellóvouno, the Crazy Mountain, the range that looms over Glyfada and could be clearly seen from our new roof terrace.

I looked around. There was no church visible. Alex by this time had got out of the car, picked up both walking sticks and opened my door to usher me out.

'So where is the church?' I asked

'Up there.' She pointed.

I followed the line of her finger up the mountain. Hundreds of metres away, just about apparent between the rocks on the side of the mountain, was a little bell tower nestling among the green shrubs. 'I'm not climbing up there,' I yelled.

She smiled sweetly and assured me that it might look a long way but was in fact a simple walk. I really was feeling poorly, but my pride kicked in. I had no wish to show weakness. So I grabbed one of the sticks and followed as she led me from the base of the mountain towards the church of Profitis Elias.

Prophet Elias, also known as Elijah, is revered for his many miracles, including curing a leper. He told the sick man to bathe in the River Jordan seven times. It cured him. Most of his miracles involved healing the sick, so all the churches devoted to him throughout Greece gained this reputation.

The church was built in the 1950s by a man who'd dreamed that he would find the icon of the Prophet Elias on the mountain. After some searching, he did find the icon and duly set about erecting a church on that very spot. He had no help from anyone but his donkey. There were no roads or paths up there, just a steep mountainside that was thick with brambles on the lower slopes and treacherously unstable higher up, prone to rockfalls from the ledges above. It was a dangerous climb, and all tools and building materials had to be laboriously carried up the mountain.

It is said that a hermit also used to live there, looking down on the sea and islands below. Being a wise and good man, he was likened to the saint. Food and water were taken up the mountain daily and exchanged for blessings.

Every year, for the name day of Prophet Elias on 20 July, the pathway up to the church is illuminated with strings of lights after dark, forming a long white snake from the base of the mountain to the church. Pilgrims climb the mountain on this night to pay their respects to the saint. From our terrace, the church is just about discernible as a small white dot on the green mountain.

After the first hundred metres of the ascent, I felt exhausted. I was aching all over, it hurt to breathe, and sweat was dripping into my eyes, rendering the rocky path a blur. As we got further up the mountain, I started looking for the bones of other ill people that had failed in their attempt to climb it and get cured.

By now we were above the clouds. I turned around. From here I could see aircraft on their final descent into Athens airport, and they were below me. Beyond the airport stretched the blue Aegean, and the island of Aegina. Other further away islands were just visible through the haze. We gazed down on Athens, followed the coastline to Piraeus and the many ships anchored in the bay. The view was incredible. Without realising, I was getting better. The breeze was cooling my hot skin and my headache was fading as we approached the little church on the rocky outcrop just ahead.

It was no larger than a shrine, with just one tiny window and a small terrace leading to an iron door. The key was hanging on a nail. Nearby was a whitewashed bell tower and a rope hanging down, moving in the breeze. Alex rushed over and swung on the rope to announce our arrival. The sound of the bell reverberated across the mountain and echoed back after a few seconds.

We took the key off the rusty nail and unlocked the door. The church was so small that we only just fitted inside together. The smell of incense filled our nostrils. Oil lamps fed by olive oil were burning on the shrine. Ornate icons in gold frames had been placed around the walls and there were smudges on the saints' feet, where countless pilgrims had kissed them in devotion over so many years. In pride of place was the icon of Prophet Elias. There was also an icon portraying the Virgin Mary with the infant Jesus on her lap, both with golden halos; pictures of other saints hung in frames behind the small altar.

We put a few coins into the box, took two candles and lit them from the oil burner. We both said a quick prayer before stepping out of the door, locking up and returning the key to the nail.

We stood outside the church holding hands, looking across the mountain and down to the sea. I could see the island of Hydra, where only a few hours ago I had woken up feeling poorly. Now, however, I felt fully restored to health. The little white church had taken away all trace of my illness. For me, this was a miracle. I would never have believed that I could be healed by walking up a mountain to visit a small building. Was it divine intervention, the handful of pills and potions, or the love of my wife? Either way, I was grateful as my family were arriving from the UK the following day for a holiday and I needed to be up and about to take care of them.

# 12

## ALEX'S EXORCISM

Having a lamb's head complete with horns plonked on your restaurant table is not every tourist's idea of an appetising centrepiece. Especially when you've literally just stepped off the plane from England. And so it proved for my mum and sister, who had come to Greece for their summer holiday. My nephews and niece, on the other hand, were intrigued.

It was a lovely warm day, and as usual the sun was shining. We hadn't seen a cloud for more than a week, in contrast to the UK, where it had been cold and wet for the last few days, which, being July, was normal. We decided it was the perfect excuse for a leisurely lunch at our favourite taverna in Kalyvia, a village in the hills between the airport and Cape Sounion.

The village stands alone on a mountainside, isolated and off the tourist track, but Greeks know where it is as it's famous for serving the best grilled meat in Greece; almost the entire village is taken up by a single taverna. Originally just one compact restaurant, the taverna became so successful that it spread to occupy five buildings and the entire square, closing off the road.

Although vast and usually an evening venue, it was already packed. Large glass cases in each of the four corners displayed a profusion of meat being slowly turned on spits over charcoal, with masses of tables and chairs spread out in between. We estimated there were around two hundred tables in all, each seating up to six diners, meaning that the taverna could accommodate more than a thousand customers at a time. Waiters were running in all directions, all wearing white shirts and aprons, taking piled-up plates of food to tables and returning with empty dishes.

We walked over to one of the large display ovens and watched as the meat turned. The top spit contained five whole lambs, the next one down was the traditional kokoretsi, there was a long row of whole chickens, then a row of suckling pigs and at the very base nearest the charcoal was a row of lambs' heads, a regional delicacy. It fascinated the kids as the only time they had ever seen anything remotely like this was a few chickens cooking in a glass oven in their local supermarket.

This was vastly bigger, and the choice was enormous in comparison.

My mother and sister were focusing on the rotating lambs' heads and their faces betrayed their distaste. I picked up on their fear and told them it was not compulsory to eat them, or any of the meat, if they didn't want it; the restaurant also served a good selection of vegetable dishes and various types of pasta and rice. They both relaxed visibly as we were led to an empty table in the middle of the square.

Balloon sellers were wandering between tables, their wares floating above their heads in an enormous gathering of inflated Tweety Pies, cars, hearts and multi-coloured dogs and other animals. I called over one of the merchants and the kids were spellbound as I invited them to choose one each. We ended up with two Tweety Pie balloons, a yellow racing car and a big red shiny heart, the latter requested by Alex, all of them tied to the backs of their chairs.

Alex ordered our food in rapid Greek. I only caught a few of the words but got the gist. She also ordered a kilo of the local white wine. My mum and sister pounced on this and attacked it with appreciation.

They were already halfway through the carafe when the food arrived. A Greek salad on a plate the size of a dustbin lid was brought out first, accompanied by two loaves of bread and some dips. We had started to munch through this when the meat dishes arrived. A plate holding a kilo of sliced barbecued lamb was placed on the table together with another tray holding pork chops and a T-bone steak with a plate of kokoretsi for Alex. Then piles of chips and plates of vegetables, fried cheese and battered aubergines.

The table was already groaning beneath the weight of so much food, but the waiter hadn't finished yet. He reappeared with a small plate of small, deep-fried battered items which looked like cod balls. I took a bite. They were balls, but not from a cod! They were lambs' balls. The table erupted in laughter. Alex had ordered a selection of testicles and battered lambs' brains to see how Greek I had become. Obviously not Greek enough yet, as I hated them. Whether it was the taste or just the idea, I wasn't sure; either way, I decided to avoid these in the future.

The last dish arrived and was set in the centre of the table. It was a lamb's head, and it still had horns. Alex had ordered this as a joke. My mother and sister dropped their cutlery and looked at it with a mix of repulsion and curiosity. It fascinated the kids, who were poking the horns. Alex again was giggling as she asked the waiter to take it away, which he did with a knowing smile.

We finished as much of the food as we could, and Alex asked for the leftovers to be collected for the local dogs, as she didn't want it going to waste. Meat restaurants do not serve desserts but will always give you natural yogurt and honey to help with your digestion. A light-brown glazed ceramic dish arrived full of local homemade yogurt. On a separate plate were containers filled with syrupy preserves and the all-important honey. We each took a large dollop and added a spoonful of multi-coloured preserves.

The whole family spent the next couple of days on the small, friendly island of Aegina, an hour's ferry ride from Piraeus and with a pace of life far slower than the capital's. We could sense the relaxed atmosphere as soon as we arrived.

Aegina is famous for pistachio nuts, whose flavour and aroma are considered among the best in the world. As we drove around the island, we could see them heaped up in piles along the roadsides, drying in the sun. The cultivation of pistachios started there in around 1860 and most of the fields are on the western side of the island, which is more fertile and less mountainous than the eastern side.

We stopped the car at the top of a hill beside a field of pistachio trees, picked a few nuts and chewed while we wandered across to admire the view. Alex pointed towards a distant monastery further down the valley. It was dedicated to St Nectarios, she said. 'When I was a girl,' she continued enigmatically, 'my mother took me there to be exorcised.'

Of course we were intrigued by this and keen to find out more. So we left the warm grass, the smell of wild oregano and the chatter of crickets to drop my sister and the kids off at the beach. Then Alex and I took my mother to the monastery for a guided tour and to learn more about Alex's demonic possession.

St Nectarios is well known for his healing powers and is considered to be particularly effective in the curing of madness. When Alex was young, she was a rebellious child. She was always in trouble, and there was concern that her unusual, sparky character might be a sign that she was possessed by the devil. So Debbie sent her to the Monastery of St Nectarios to find out.

As a girl, Alex was responsible for a lot of the mischief in her street. If a cat ran past with a tin tied to its tail, it was her. If a neighbour's fence had mysteriously disappeared, she had moved it to make a ramp for her bike so she could jump over things – usually her brother, Christos, who she forced to lie on the road at the end of the ramp. Whenever the parents of the local bully came to the house to complain about his injuries, Alex would hide her bruised knuckles behind her back and wear her cutest expression; they invariably left convinced of her innocence and now swearing at their own child for telling lies.

Debbie grew so worried about Alex's naughtiness that she took her to the local doctor, who declared that there was nothing physically wrong with her and suggested a priest. The priest diagnosed demonic possession and suggested a visit to the tomb of St Nectarios of Aegina.

Alex, more than happy to take time off school to visit the island, spent the day picking flowers from the grounds and being fussed over by the monastery's nuns and monks. She was taken into the chapel for the exorcism. She was quite content as she had armfuls of flowers from the gardens by now and needed to sit down for a while to arrange them in her hair and make flowery designs on her clothes. She just concentrated on the flowers while two priests read from a book and sprinkled her with holy water and oil. But when they brought out the smoking incense burners, these made her cough. This was taken as a sign the exorcism had been a success and the demon expelled.

Debbie, however, suspected the demon was still hanging around. As Alex got older, her attention turned to her appearance and she began taking an interest in her mother's best clothes, which she wore with pride while parading up and down the street distributing fresh flowers taken from vases in the house. This dressing-up phase took a temporary pause when she raided all the jewellery boxes in the house and went out to play adorned with diamond rings and pearl necklaces. Her parents recovered most of them, but a few never came back.

Some of Debbie's approaches to child-rearing would be frowned on today. As well as sanctioning an exorcism on her daughter, she also arranged a visit to a strange old man to cure Alex of an illness. Alex was nine years old and had been feeling unwell, so Debbie took her off to a doctor, who diagnosed the liver infection hepatitis. He told her to go home and burn all of Alex's clothes and blankets, and to boil all the cups, plates and cutlery. He sent them away with a packet of aspirin and said that Alex should get better in two or three months.

Debbie was worried by this and asked around the village. Eventually her neighbour Stella told her of a man who had a reputation as a healer. The first question from Debbie was the obvious one. 'Is he a priest or holy man?' she asked.

'I doubt it,' Stella replied. 'He is fond of communion wine though.'

This didn't sound good, but Debbie was desperate to help her ailing daughter. The doctor hadn't been much use, after all. So she wasted no time in tracking down the healer and eventually found out that he held his surgery at a bar in a seedy district of Piraeus.

The day of the visit arrived. Debbie needed a taxi, but in those days they were rare in Glyfada and had only recently been legalised in Athens. The first taxis appeared in 1964 after a law passed by the government of George Papandreou. The state then gave around 6,500 taxis to drivers with a professional diploma and experience throughout Greece. In Glyfada, however, they still relied on the old way. Debbie would call the tobacco kiosk in the square; the tobacconist would lean out of his window and yell at the unlicensed drivers sitting around. These chaps used their private cars to run a makeshift taxi service, and it worked. Soon, an unmarked car would arrive outside the house and honk.

Alex was so happy that day because Debbie hadn't sent her to school; she thought she was going on an excursion with her mother and was looking forward to it. When they reached their destination, Debbie asked the taxi to wait while she took Alex into a dark bar that smelled of stale wine and strong pipe tobacco. An elderly grey-haired man was sitting at a table holding a smoking cigarette in one hand and nursing a glass of red wine in the other. Debbie introduced herself and Alex, and explained the problem. The old man thought for a moment and then announced that he could cure her but that it might be a little painful. Not knowing where else to turn for help, Debbie agreed.

The old man cleared the glasses and ashtrays off the table and asked Debbie to lay Alex on the table face up. He reached into his pocket and extracted an old darning needle and a length of thick cotton. He threaded the needle. Then he pulled out a stained handkerchief and gave it to Debbie. 'Hold this under her chin,' he said.

She complied.

The man stuck his nicotine-stained fingers into Alex's mouth and wriggled them around until he located her labial frenulum, the thin piece of tissue that connects the gums to the upper lip. He then pierced it with the darning needle. Alex squirmed and screamed as he proceeded to saw through the membrane with the thick cotton until her top lip and gums were partially separated and the procedure was complete. Blood ran down her throat and some spilt onto the dirty bar table. The old man kept his grip on her as he took a handful of coarse salt from a bowl and rubbed it onto her bleeding gums.

'Take her home,' he said. 'She's cured now.'

Alex was still screaming, and Debbie was in shock as they got back into the taxi for the ride home. Luckily, the old man hadn't completely separated the membrane, so it would eventually grow back, but this was no comfort to a distressed Alex, who was still bleeding in the back of the taxi and being told off by the driver for making a mess in his car.

Two days later, Alex's symptoms were gone. Her temperature was back to normal and she felt physically well. Debbie was a loving mother, and in her eyes she was doing the best for her daughter, but for Alex the psychological scars from that episode endure to this day.

Fortunately, the exorcism had no such detrimental effect on Alex. She was quite happy to return to the monastery and show me and my mother around. We entered its gardens via an arbour of roses in full bloom. The perfume was almost over-powering and enticed us further in, to a paved area surrounded by more arched trellises of aromatic flowers. We wandered around the gardens in the cool shade and felt the power of the beautiful place. It was wonderfully peaceful.

Nectarios is perhaps the best-known saint in the Orthodox Church and his remains are enshrined within the yellow sand-stone church of the monastery, beneath its three red-tiled Byzantine domes. He was born in Turkey in 1846 and spent time in Cairo and Athens as a monk, priest and preacher before establishing the monastery on Aegina in 1904. In 1920 he became ill and was moved from the monastery to a hospital in Athens, where he was diagnosed with terminal cancer and placed in a ward for men who were destitute and dying. He passed away on the evening of 8 November 1920, at the age of seventy-four. As his body was being prepared for its final journey back to Aegina, Nectarios's shirt was put on the adja-cent bed, in which lay a man long paralysed. The man quickly stood up and walked. The room was filled with a sweet fragrance for many days. That ward in the Athens hospital has since become a chapel.

Nectarios's corpse was placed in his tomb within the monastery walls. Thirty years later, when the tomb was opened, his body was fully intact and smelled of perfume. The branches of lemon blossom interred with him were still fresh, but wilted shortly after the casket was opened. Nectarios was recognised as a saint a few years later. Pilgrims to the monastery put their ear to the tomb to listen. If tapping or scratching is heard, it means they have received a blessing and their prayers will be answered.

For my own part, I had no need of St Nectarios for this. My prayers had already been answered.

As a small boy in the north London suburbs, every weekend I would go to the local cinema. My favourite movies were about ancient Greece. The legend of Hercules enthralled me, as did the adventures of the three hundred Spartans, but my very favourite was Jason and the Argonauts. When I was a child, the cinema would keep the film running throughout the day, so when the first showing ended, it would immediately begin again. I watched that film at least five times every Saturday it was on and got to know every scene and character; I even remembered the script.

I would leave the picture house and walk home under drizzly grey skies dreaming of the clear blue Aegean Sea, dry mountains dotted with green shrubs, and heroes doing battle with one-eyed monsters while rescuing white-clad priestesses from evil, toga-wearing kings. As I grew up, I kept that picture in my mind, secretly wishing that someday I might be part of that imaginary world.

And now here I was, sitting in the garden of the Monastery of St Nectarios under an umbrella of blood-red bougainvillea, listening to the peal of bells from the church tower while gazing across the valley at the bright blue Aegean, as my beautiful Greek wife wandered the courtyard smelling the flowers. She turned and smiled, with love in her eyes. My dreams had become real.

# 13

# PHILOXENIA ON AEGINA

STUFF WE NICKED

On our way back to the beach from the Monastery of St
Nectarios, Alex suggested a quick diversion to the
Temple of Aphasia. It's been a place of worship since the Stone

Age and stands in a beautiful spot in the hills above the pine forests with fabulous views across the Saronic Gulf.

I perched on a chunk of marble in the middle of the nicely restored temple and stared at the thirty-two huge, white, ornately carved sandstone columns. My mind drifted back to that dark London picture house all those years ago. I recalled the flying harpies who tormented King Phineus until he was rescued by the Argonauts from within a Parthenon structure similar to the temple I was now sitting in.

I was awoken from my daydream by a trickle of sweat running into my eyes. My head was starting to bake in the hot sun. Alex, entirely immune to the heat as always, was skipping over the fallen columns, pulling my mother by the hand and picking out interesting designs. I pointed out Glyfada across the sea; my mother strained her eyes, trying to make out our building far away, but it was just an indistinct blur of houses.

Back at the beach, my sister and the kids were nowhere to be found. We paced up and down between sunbeds, peered under straw parasols and scanned the sea, but still we couldn't spot them. Then a distant shout made me glance up. Overlooking the beach was a series of buildings, all with balconies. My sister Gill was leaning over one, waving frantically to get our attention and beckoning us to join her.

We followed her directions and entered the building from the rear. This was an old taverna which had been converted into a summer house. The recent residents had kept the commercial kitchen and divided the dining area into bedrooms and a living space. Loud bouzouki music was blaring from a speaker on the balcony, and Gill and the children were dancing the sirtaki with the owner of the apartment, an older man who looked to be more than slightly drunk.

Gill had been walking around the beach looking for a toilet for her daughter and had asked the old man, who was sitting on his balcony, for directions. He had waved away her request and told her to bring the children up to use his bathroom. This was two hours ago, and in that brief time they had become firm friends. Gill now introduced us to Panagiotis, her newfound pal, who invited us to join the party. We thanked him, but we were hungry and wanted to find a restaurant for lunch. Panagiotis was having none of it. 'I will cook for you all,' he slurred and left to go into the kitchen to prepare lunch.

A few moments later, hearing no further noise from the kitchen, I went to investigate. Panagiotis was fast asleep on a chair in the corner, snoring gently. He was obviously a friendly person and eager to please his new guests, but he had consumed a little too much wine. I returned to the balcony, explained the situation and suggested that we leave him to sleep it off.

Alex disagreed. Panagiotis had been kind enough to offer his hospitality, and she felt it would be rude to just disappear. We understood her point. She and I gently woke him and led him to the living room, settled him into an armchair and made him comfortable. Rather than allow him to cook for us, we decided that we would prepare the meal.

I looked in the fridge and found a few bits and pieces, but not enough for a meal for six. So we left Gill to monitor the old man while Alex and I headed to the supermarket. Having stocked up with provisions, I set about frying some lamb chops, steaks and sausages while Alex prepared a salad, got the fryer going and peeled the potatoes. Gill, meanwhile, had located plates, cutlery and glasses, and had set the table.

Within half an hour we had a small banquet ready and woke Panagiotis. A smile spread across his face as he eyed the loaded table. He jumped up, walked to the fridge and took out two bottles of wine. He was refreshed and raring to go again.

We relaxed and enjoyed the meal while chatting into the afternoon and beyond, until the sun sank below the horizon.

Our experience with Panagiotis was a typical example of philoxenia: the art of expressing love and friendship to strangers. Though it's a word that tourists never hear, all visitors will have first-hand experience of philoxenia. It is the rock on which Greek culture was built.

In ancient Greece, hospitality was a sacred duty. Any stranger could be a god in disguise, on a mission to test your generosity as a home-owning mortal. If hospitality was not offered, the wrath of Zeus could be brought down upon you. Regardless of a guest's identity, you had to welcome them with food, drink and shelter before asking questions. You might also be expected to entertain them and to offer them a bath and anything else they needed. The guest was required to be equally respectful, listening attentively to their host and returning the favour by entertaining them with their own stories. They undertook to not be a burden in any way. It was also traditional for the guest to offer a parting gift. The most famous example of someone abusing Greek hospitality led to the Trojan War.

Visitors continue to always be treated as honoured guests and Greece is well known as a welcoming destination. The spirit of Greek hospitality is found across the country, in every person who is or feels Greek. Philoxenia literally translates as 'friend to the stranger'.

Whenever someone came to our old house in Glyfada, they were always treated with kindness and generosity. There would be a glass of cool water and some spoon sweets, followed by coffee and cake and a glass of homemade cherry brandy. If they stayed, they would always be fed. If they declined the food, it was packed and given to them as they left to eat later.

Alex was raised to observe the traditions of philoxenia. My

sister once commented on a bracelet that Alex was wearing. Alex immediately removed it from her wrist and clipped it onto Gill's. If my mother admired a lamp on the shelf in our house, there was a real possibility that it would be in her bag when she left. It soon got to the point where, when my family came to visit, I had to ask them not to admire anything in the house and to refrain from lingering over anything of value, for if they complimented Alex on any of her possessions, it would be given to them.

Greeks measure their worth and honour by how well they treat their guests. This is not only at home but also at a restaurant, a nightclub or a bar. In England, it's common for bills to be split. In Greece, when taking a foreigner to a restaurant, it is unthinkable to allow them to pay. When I first came to Greece, I felt continually embarrassed that I never paid for a meal. The family would have made an agreement with the owner to not take any money from me as they were the hosts. I had to become more inventive and used to try sneaking off to the toilet as a pretence, then asking for the bill. This rarely worked as the taverna owner, being Greek, fully understood philoxenia and knew that he would offend his customers if he accepted money from me.

This is also common if Greeks go for a meal together. It's an honour to pay for everyone. Frequently, good-natured arguments will flare up in tavernas as an individual tries to pay for the entire party, thus becoming the host.

While the family was with us, it was an excellent opportunity to show them some of the impressive sights of Athens, the birthplace of democracy. We began our tour in Constitution Square.

The soldiers were there, wearing their national-dress uniform of white skirts, red shoes with black pompoms, and red hats. These chaps were enormous and marched in formation, holding their rifles. Gathered tourists watched and took photographs.

The area outside the parliament building is the favoured location for Greek riots and protests. Greeks have a deep distrust of officials, and especially politicians, and are quick to vent their anger if they suspect injustice in any form.

Public disturbance is relatively civilised here and is almost a spectator sport. A demonstration will begin peacefully, with a march through Athens that terminates at the parliament building, but then something invariably sparks the violence. Usually, it's the hundreds of armed police trying to break up the crowd with the aid of shields and batons. This then develops into the next act of what is a well-rehearsed dance, in which protesters attack the police with kicks while trying to penetrate the line of Perspex shields. When this proves unsuccessful, petrol bombs and red fireworks are lobbed towards the officials. This continues until one or other side is either pushed back or gets tired. The police will change shifts, and the protesters will often wander off to one of the pavement cafes and sip a coffee while they take a rest. If any of them are being chased by the police, they just head for the sanctuary of the university, which, under Greek law, the police are not allowed to enter.

Protests are usually organised in disapproval of a government policy, but they rarely happen during the tourist season. Firstly, because Greeks don't like to offend their guests, and secondly, the tourist season is in the summer, and it's far too hot.

It is possible to take a ringside seat at a pavement cafe safe in the knowledge that the protests will be confined to the square outside the parliament building. Greeks do not rampage through the streets causing chaos as in other less organised riots such as the ones in London. I was in the area one day, watching the goings-on from an outdoor cafe, when one rioter smelling of petrol came over and sat on the next table. A police officer was also taking a rest there, so they just had a coffee together and chatted amiably before returning to re-join the confrontation on opposing sides.

We descended the long, pedestrianised street towards Monastiraki. On both sides of this road were outlets for well-known international brands alongside stores selling tourist memorabilia and postcards. The centre of the street was full of small market stalls, street performers, and bands of musicians, some of them playing traditional Greek music, others playing classical music on violins. An old man pushing a brightly coloured barrel organ on wheels passed us while turning the handle and singing out of tune in a reedy voice. It was a fantastic and entertaining mix.

At the base of the hill stood the small monastery, literally Monastiraki, from which the area took its name. Alex ducked through the small doorway to light a candle and reappeared a moment later. Crossing the road to the main square outside the station, we lingered to admire the performance of a school choir who had set up outside the station entrance. This was the central point between Monastiraki and the old town of Plaka.

We turned right into a warren of pedestrian passages leading towards the flea market. These were too narrow for any vehicle bigger than a bicycle, and the closeness of the shops made it superb for browsing. The shops were tourist-oriented and sold everything from traditional Greek cotton dresses and local football shirts to copies of classical statues, pots and vases. In between were antiques stores, each with its own theme. One sold maritime memorabilia such as antique ships' bells, brass horns and ships' wheels. Another specialised in old dentists' chairs, complete with pedal-operated drills. My teeth ached even at the thought of going near one of those instruments of torture; who would buy one, I wondered, and what for? They obviously sold some, as the shop had been here for years.

In a little square nearby, army-surplus stores were filled with all kinds of collectables, including old swords and broken guns, Nazi helmets, medals and Victorian cannons. One shop had a machine gun on a tripod for sale next to a table piled with Second World War hand grenades.

At the flea market itself, the wares were spread out on the ground on lining sheets or tarpaulins, and we had to be careful where we trod. Goods seemed mainly to comprise thrown-away items that people had picked out of dustbins and were hoping to sell on. It was an interesting variety, and they seemed to be doing a brisk trade.

We reached the end of the market and turned onto a pavement packed with the outdoor tables of cafeterias, bars and restaurants; waiters were buzzing around serving their many customers. A few traders were selling homemade costume jewellery and small trinkets. We found a free table and sipped at our drinks while being accosted by street sellers trying to talk us into buying everything from fine lace to lumps of green jelly on sticks. Some were just beggars with children on their hips; others were playing musical instruments. One scruffy and particularly enterprising child came to our table and banged a drum incessantly until it drove us so nuts that we paid him to go away. One euro did the trick, but he only moved one table across and continued to beat his drum until a waiter came out and shooed him away.

Alex meanwhile had become most interested in a small crowd gathered nearby. A shabby-looking man with a dirty green T-shirt was dealing cards on top of an upturned cardboard box. Six men had gathered to the front and were taking it in turns to pass money to the dealer, selecting one of the upturned cards and receiving back double their investment in winnings.

Alex left the table to watch more closely. She turned to me and said, 'Give me ten euros.'

I tried to explain to her that this was a con and well known throughout the world as the three-card trick or Find the Lady. She would have none of it and pushed her way through the growing crowd. She laid the note on the table, looked at the back of the three playing cards and chose wrongly, just as I'd expected she would. Her money disappeared into the pocket of the card shark. He continued to deal to one of his accomplices, who, not surprisingly won.

'Give me another ten euros,' Alex insisted.

I took her arm and pulled her away from the group, then sat her down to explain the scam. She still didn't look convinced and assured me we could make a lot of money here. I just asked her to watch for a while.

Suddenly, the dealer grabbed the cardboard box and ran off, closely followed by his six winners. A few moments later, two police officers wandered past and disappeared into the nearby flea market. Soon after, the scruffy man in the green T-shirt reappeared and set up his box once more. The other six men left their hiding place too and joined him to start the deception all over again.

Now at last Alex realised that they had robbed her. She wanted to go back and recover her money, but there were at least seven of them and likely to be additional lookouts, and I considered ten euros was a small price to pay for the experience.

Within sight of our cafe table were several buildings with immense marble columns, ancient remnants of classical-era Athens. Together, these comprised the agora, the city's large central square and associated civic buildings, where citizens might assemble for a market or for an election, a dramatic performance, a religious procession, a military drill or an athletics competition. Most importantly, this was where democracy was first practised before being shared with the world. It was also the place where Socrates, Plato and Aristotle discussed philosophical ideas and instructed their pupils. The square had a line of columns all along one side, in two tiers. This building now housed a museum with relics dating back to the Stone Age.

Casting our eyes higher, we could see the Acropolis and the majestic Parthenon sitting proudly atop it, towering over the city in the sunshine. I wondered if by constructing our very own replica Parthenon on the roof of our new apartment block we might compensate in some tiny way for the fact that the real structure had lost some of its treasures to London's British Museum. Might it be taken as one Englishman's apology for his countryman's abuse of Greek hospitality?

This is a sore subject for Greeks, who claim that Lord Elgin stole pieces of their revered monuments during his service as ambassador to the court of the Ottoman sultan. The British say that they were purchased; the Greeks prefer to use the term looted. Between 1801 and 1812, Lord Elgin snaffled half the surviving marbles and spirited them out of Greece. The British Government insists he bought them from their legal owners. The problem is that the legal owners at the time were the occupying Turks.

During our last trip to England, Alex had expressed an interest in going to the British Museum, saying she wanted to see the Tutankhamun exhibition. I was also keen to see it and innocently agreed to accompany her. As we entered the museum, we were confronted with an enormous sign that read 'Elgin Marbles: This Way', with a large arrow pointing to the left. Alex pulled me towards it. I pulled back, in the direction of the Egyptian hall. I then realised that she had duped me. Alex had no interest in dead pharaohs. She was there to reclaim her stolen property.

We stepped into the hall and onto the white marble floor. There ahead of us were the beautiful relics. An ornately carved frieze stretched the length of an entire wall. The sculpture known as the Horse of Selene had pride of place, together with an abundance of precious artefacts under careful lighting designed to show them in their full glory. My eye was immediately drawn to a carving of a bearded centaur holding a young man by the throat. The poor man had lost his penis, which seemed to have been snapped off. By the look on Alex's face, I was likely to be the next person to suffer that indignation. She was not impressed. She turned to me and said, 'You are a fucking pirate.'

I was shocked. She'd never sworn at me in English before, and she obviously thought I was somehow personally responsible for the theft of her heritage. I tried to comfort her by pointing out how well cared for the sculptures were, mumbling something about the nice presentation. But she was getting angrier. Alex has a temper, though thankfully it rarely burns hot for long. Concerned that she would make a fuss in the middle of the hall, I searched for ways to defuse it. I settled on an attack strategy. I took her arm and looked into her eyes. 'How dare you swear at me?' I said. 'And I'm not a pirate either.'

This seemed to work. She had in her anger misdirected her rage towards me and was now feeling sorry about that. So before her fury reignited, I led her out of the hall, suggesting we look at something else. We walked around some other areas of the museum, but she was uninterested in the displays. 'So which part of this massive museum houses the British exhibits?' she asked sarcastically.

I fumbled to answer that question. Obviously, the Egyptian relics were not British, nor were the Elgin Marbles. After peeking into hall after hall, I did eventually find a small section on ancient Britain, but this was dwarfed by the huge displays from China, Africa and the Americas. I realised I was not going to win this one. I had suddenly become personally responsible for my country's avarice and its looting of the world for treasures that were now sitting in glass cases, staring accusingly at me.

As we sat outside the modest pavement cafe in Athens, relishing what had to be one of the best views in the world, I felt both privileged and a little guilty. I did feel sorry for Alex. As a true-blooded Greek, she could not simply look at this wonder of the world and appreciate the beauty and magnificence of this incredible piece of history; as she gazed at it, all she could think about was that her heritage had been stolen away and was currently residing in a faraway country that had claimed Greece's precious artefacts as its own.

# 14

## YOU ARE IN BIG TROUBLE NOW

We were now more than a year into the building of our new apartment and were feeling the strain. Alex and I were both working eighteen-hour days in England to make ends meet, so on our trips to Glyfada we tried to include some time for relaxation as well. But events routinely conspired to scupper such plans, not least when bureaucratic housekeeping was involved. This meant paying visits to various government offices, which was not to be taken lightly. The Greek government has an infuriating preoccupation with bureaucracy and engages a vast number of people as civil servants. A recent study put this at around ten per cent of the working population, whereas in the UK it's 1.5 per cent. That's a lot of people who need to be kept busy, not least in the traffic management department.

On one occasion, I went to the airport to collect my father-in-law, Zissis, who was flying in from Turkey for a brief break before returning to his cruise ship. I checked that the plane had landed and parked outside the terminal to wait for him to come out. I was getting thirsty and he still hadn't appeared, so I left the car, walked over to a small kiosk and bought an iced coffee. As I returned to the car, I noticed that my front number plate had disappeared. I walked around the back; no number plate there either. As I stood there wondering why anyone would steal my plates, Zissis walked out of the terminal. I made a mental note to pop down to the car component store to have an extra set made. I thought nothing more of this and drove the short distance home.

Back at the house, I mentioned that my number plates had been stolen.

Alex looked at me and smiled. 'You are in big trouble now,' she said.

'Why?' I asked. 'It wasn't me that removed them.'

'The police took them,' she said.

Why would the police take my number plates? I'd done nothing wrong. I was not part of a criminal network or a terrorist. I would have understood it if Alex had been driving the car, but me? I was squeaky clean. Perhaps they thought me suspicious by association, being married to her.

'So why would they steal my number plates?' I asked.

'You must have been parked illegally,' she replied with a gleam in her eye.

'But there was no ticket on the windscreen,' I protested.

She explained the procedure. In Greece, parking restrictions are difficult for a foreigner to understand. There don't appear to be any single or double yellow lines. Parking regulations are unclear and the police have little idea either. They will decide if we have broken the law. The definition of an illegally parked vehicle is based on whether they're in a grim mood. If a police officer is having a particularly unpleasant day, he or she will share their misfortune with you. They will take their screwdriver out of their pocket and remove your number plates and take them to a mystery location in order to ruin your day too. They offer no official documentation and leave no parking ticket in a little plastic envelope glued to your windscreen. They have their hands full, with your number plates in one and a screwdriver in the other. So they just sneak off, leaving you unable to drive your car away. Even I know it's illegal to drive a car anywhere in the world without number plates unless you're the queen.

A while ago, the local council in Glyfada had the bright idea of introducing a pay and display system, but they didn't bother to tell anyone. Pay stations appeared overnight, and lines for parking bays were drawn on some roads. The job of enforcing these new parking regulations was given to a new breed of government employee: the traffic warden. These hapless stooges were dressed in nice new uniforms and hats, and wore an official-looking badge pinned to their jacket. This did not impress the car owners of Glyfada. They were used to fighting for parking spots and putting their vehicle wherever there was a space. The wardens became unpopular when they slapped sticky tickets on windscreens. Not only did this leave a nasty patch on the glass, but the motorist was also now expected to pay a fine.

Greeks have a certain grudging respect for police officers, mostly because they fear being carted away in handcuffs if they cause a fuss. These new traffic wardens had no such power. They were fair game. After a few days, it became common to see this new breed of tax collectors being chased along roads by angry car owners. Some even pursued them in their cars, if they couldn't run fast enough to catch them. The traffic wardens quickly got wise to these antics. They began to be described as phantoms because of their newfound practice of approaching illegally parked cars on their bellies. They literally crawled up to the offending vehicle. A hand would rise and sneakily attach a ticket to the car before ducking down again and withdrawing.

The average Greek male has a hierarchy of priorities in life. Their first love is their mother, the second is their car. Wives and other family members come further down the list, after coffee, food and football. So having some stranger interfere with their cherished car is like a stranger meddling with their mother and cannot be tolerated. Glyfada's new parking system lasted a month before the ticket machines disappeared and the traffic wardens were redeployed to another government office to make people's lives difficult in a different way.

We had to get our number plates back but had no clue where they were. We walked around the corner to ask at our local police station. A scruffy Albanian man was sitting on a bench inside the door, bound by a pair of handcuffs. A middle-aged police officer was lounging on a chair opposite, drinking iced coffee through a straw, out of a plastic cup. He looked bored as Alex tried to explain about our number plates.

'So where would they be?' she asked.

'How do I know?' he replied. 'In Athens somewhere. Try the central courts.'

The issuing of number plates is the job of the ministry of transport and requires an official stamp. Plates are not available from car accessory shops like in the UK. We could not use our car without plates, so we hailed a taxi and went to Athens. We arrived at the central courts. I was expecting a building, but this was a village. As we passed through its enormous gates, our possessions were scanned with an airport-style X-ray machine and we had to walk through a metal-detection device. We then joined the lengthy queue at the enquiries desk. One hour later we got to the front of the line.

'What do you want?' demanded the spiteful-looking woman behind the screen.

Alex explained that we'd had our number plates confiscated and needed to pay the fine to get them back.

'Where's the paperwork?' the official demanded.

'They didn't leave any paperwork,' Alex said.

'So go to the police station and get it. They will have your plates. Next,' she called over our shoulders.

Alex flushed red. I could she was getting angry at this person, who was clearly not interested in assisting us. 'Which police station?' she asked.

'The one with your number plates,' the woman said sarcastically.

We were not getting very far here. But Alex was refusing to make way for the next person in the queue until she got an answer. She raised her voice. 'WHICH POLICE STATION WOULD HAVE THEM?'

The obstructive employee finally realised that we wouldn't be leaving any time soon. She picked up her phone, mumbled into the receiver and told us they were likely to be in the central police station in Athens.

The parking infringements section of the central police station was in a dark basement under the car park. A long queue of people was waiting to speak to the fat police officer sitting smoking a cigarette in a cage at the end of the cellar. After thirty minutes it was our turn.

'Paperwork,' he demanded.

'We haven't got any paperwork,' Alex said. 'The police officer that took our plates didn't leave any.'

'Big problem,' he replied. 'Go to the second floor.'

We left his dungeon and climbed the stone stairs to a brightly lit room filled with rows of desks, each with a police officer stabbing away at a computer keyboard. Alex accosted a young-looking chap, thinking he might be more approachable. He smiled, tapped his keyboard, reached to the printer behind him and passed us the paperwork we needed. He was obviously a recent recruit to the police force, as he was nice and obliging. We didn't want to push our luck but needed to know where to take this piece of paper.

'First, you need to go back to the basement. The police officer there will give you a stamp.'

'Are our plates here then?'

'Yes, but you need to pay the fine before you get them back.'

We went back to join the queue in the basement.

'Wow, that was easy,' I said to Alex while we were waiting.

She just looked at me and smiled. After another thirty-minute wait, it was our turn again to see the fat, cigarette-smoking police officer in the cage. We passed the paperwork through the grating. He took it, laid it on the table, rubber-stamped and signed it, and handed it back.

'What next?' asked Alex.

'Go to the courts to pay the fine,' he said. 'Then come back here.'

We took yet another taxi. Back at the central courts, we passed through the metal detectors, got to the enquiries desk, joined the queue, reached the front and passed the paperwork to the spiteful woman behind the screen, who stamped the document and handed it back, then told us to go to building number seven and pay.

At building number seven, we queued up at the cash office for an hour, paid, got the document stamped yet again and had the receipt stapled to it. Then back to the first building to join the queue again. The spiteful-looking woman's mood had not improved. She stamped the paper one more time and sent us back to the central police station. Taxi ride number four. By now we were getting the hang of it. We headed for the basement, queued up for thirty minutes, got to the fat police officer in the cage smoking a cigarette and passed him our paperwork. He took it, stamped it again and sent us up to the fourth floor. We climbed the stone staircase, found the right office, joined another queue, waited thirty minutes, arrived at the desk, and presented our paperwork. The police officer found a small, unmarked corner on the document and applied the last stamp. He then turned away, rummaged in a metal crate and emerged with our number plates.

It had taken us all day. We felt proud of ourselves, as we had at last succeeded. But we'd had to work for it. I resolved to be extra careful to follow the parking rules next time. If only I knew what they were.

Zissis was nearing retirement and as he was away from Athens so much, it was up to Alex and me to deal with the paperwork regarding his pension. We arrived at the pension office, took a numbered ticket from the machine and sat to wait our turn. The number display was on 25; our ticket read 120. I assumed the machine must be out of order. There were nowhere near ninety-five people waiting in that room. A quick count revealed only about twenty.

The office was large and sparse, with walls that had been painted a deliberately dirty white and a line of chairs that stretched along the back. The reception counter was encased in clear Perspex with small holes drilled in it to speak through. Most of the people attending this office were above pension age and some had hearing difficulties so resorted to pressing their mouths to the holes and screaming their requirements. The government officials on the other side of the screen found it equally difficult to hear the requests, so they too were shouting through the holes. This system of communication ensured that everyone in the office could hear both sides of the conversation. We got to know the intimate details of each applicant.

The display buzzed as the number turned to 26. An old man who looked to be at least ninety slowly rose from his chair, shuffled over to the counter and passed a file of paperwork through the slot under the screen.

After scanning the documents, the official shouted through the holes, 'Where is your letter from the priest?'

'I haven't got one,' the old man yelled.

'So how do we know you're alive?' demanded the official.

The old man looked confused. 'I'm here in front of you,' he replied.

'That's not good enough,' shouted the official. 'The law says you must have a letter from your priest to confirm that you are not dead.'

I was having a grand time. I had experienced Greek bureaucracy before, which had amazed me, but this was taking it to another level. I sat and listened. The old man fumbled in his bag, pulled out his ID card, passport and a crumpled-up photograph of himself standing with his wife. He then stuffed them all under the screen to prove that it was him.

The official would not budge. 'I cannot continue your pension until you get a letter from the priest to prove that you are alive.' He then pressed the button, buzzing the number on the screen to 27. The unfortunate man's interview was over, so he left to find a priest for a full medical examination.

I gave Alex a quizzical look. In some circumstances, she told me by way of explanation, the person who determines whether you're alive or dead is not the doctor but the priest. That you are walking and talking is not taken as proof of life. The authorities need an official document stamped, signed and notarised by a priest to confirm it.

We had been waiting more than an hour, and although the goings-on were entertaining, the numbers were not clicking over quickly. In that time, it had only moved to number 30. At this rate we'd be sitting there for nine hours, and the office was due to close in two hours' time.

Alex leaned over and spoke to the old lady beside her. 'What's your number?' she asked.

'32,' the old lady replied. She'd only arrived a few minutes earlier.

'How did you get that ticket?' Alex asked.

'I got it yesterday,' she replied.

All the people in the office except us knew the system. There was no way that you could just arrive and be attended to on the same day. The interview appointment required forward planning. You worked on the assumption that there would be an average of five to seven people seen hourly. The day before you wished to visit, you needed to come and take a ticket. Then you needed to calculate the numbers, dividing this by the hours the office would be open. This would give you a good idea of when to come back.

I suggested to Alex that this might be a deliberate government ploy to keep elderly people's brains active, challenging their mental arithmetic to stop them from going senile. I did a quick calculation. We had ticket number 120 and the screen was still showing number 30, so they would likely see us next Tuesday at 10.30 a.m.

Although watching unfortunate applicants being strangled by red tape was most entertaining, we were not keen to string this out for three days, so we left. I shot Alex an aghast look, expecting a similar expression from her. But she appeared to be her usual happy self.

'Did you actually hear all that?' I asked.

'Yes, of course. This is normal in all government departments. It makes no sense, but we're all used to it.'

As I was making plans to live in Greece and work here, I needed the Greek equivalent of a national insurance number. We know this as an IKA code (Idrima Kinonikon Asfaliseon: Greek social security) and of course we had to go to a government department to apply for it. Luckily, however, the IKA office was nearby, in Glyfada, so we wouldn't need to travel into Athens for once. Even so, it would not be a walk in the park, or so an expat pal of mine warned. A knowing smile crept across his face. 'It will take ages,' he said.

I recalled getting my first national insurance number in the UK many years ago. I just made a phone call and a few days later it came to my house in the post. 'It can't be that hard, can it?' I asked hopefully.

'Take my advice and get a ticket early. About 5 a.m.'

Having experienced this 'come back later' ticketing system recently at the pension office, this wasn't entirely unexpected, but there was a twist.

'If you just turn up when they open at 8 a.m., there'll be no chance of getting seen that day,' my friend said. 'But if you get there at about 5 a.m., the security guard will pass you a ticket through the door. Then you might make it.'

Next morning, I woke up at 4 a.m. and headed to the IKA office. A small crowd had already gathered in the car park and were receiving tickets through a crack in the door, just as my friend had described. I wasn't sure if I had to tip the security guard, but I played it safe and stuffed a five-euro note through the crack, which he accepted and swapped for a ticket.

Although still sleepy, I didn't want to risk going back to bed in case I overslept and missed my slot. So I drove down to the seaside and sat at a beach cafeteria and enjoyed a hot filtered coffee while watching the sunrise.

Around 7 a.m. I left to collect Alex from home. Although my language skills were improving, I wasn't confident that they'd suffice when dealing with government officials. I needed Alex with me.

We arrived at the IKA office at 8 a.m. on the dot. The crowd assembled in the car park were being let in and we followed the flow up the stairs to the primary office. The number monitor read 2 and I had ticket number 25, so not bad. I'd collected my ticket at around 4.30 a.m., so lots of the others must have got up even earlier.

Four hours later, our number came up. We went over to the window. Alex explained our requirements and assured the official that we just needed an IKA number. He reached below his desk and handed us a form. 'Fill that in and come back tomorrow,' he said. This was disappointing. I had been hoping to walk away with the number. Alex asked if we could just fill in the form while we were there and give it back straight away. 'No. Go away, fill it in and come back tomorrow.' He pressed the button to display the next ticket number. Our audience was over.

We returned home to fill in the form. It was written in officially worded Greek, and I understood nothing. Even Alex was having trouble deciphering the formal terms. But eventually she completed it in her best handwritten Greek, in black ink and within the margins. We were being extra careful as we dreaded the form being rejected for some spurious reason. She passed it to me for a signature. We were ready to start again.

Next morning, I woke at 4 a.m., went to the office, passed a five-euro note through the crack in the door and in return received my ticket. I went to the seaside cafeteria, had a coffee, watched the sun rise again, went home, collected Alex, and returned to the IKA office.

This time the wait was extended to five hours. More people had beaten me to the security guard that morning. Finally, our turn came. We approached the desk, handed in our perfectly filled-in form and smiled at the official.

He took one look at it, tore it in half and gave us another blank one. 'In Latin!' he stated. 'Fill it in using Latin and come back tomorrow.'

Alex raised her voice, launching into rapid Greek.

The official responded in kind, none of which I understood.

Alex insisted that we should fill the form in there and then, to avoid us having to come back again tomorrow. He flatly refused to allow this. So we left empty-handed once again.

Alex was red-faced and fuming as we walked down the stairs. I was feeling angry too, but had not fully understood the problem.

'He needs the form written in Latin,' she told me.

'What! I don't speak Latin!' I yelled. 'Do you?' Without waiting for an answer, I asked if he would have preferred the form to be completed in ancient Aramaic or Egyptian hiero-glyphics. 'Would that be better?' I shot back sarcastically.

'No, you're missing the point,' Alex said. 'Because you're English, the form must be filled out in Greek but using the English alphabet. In Greece, we call this Latin.'

This made no sense to me, but if that was the only way that I could live and work in Greece, it had to be done.

Next morning: up at 4 a.m., back to the office, another five euros through the door in exchange for a ticket, coffee by the beach, pick up Alex, back to the IKA office, another five-hour wait. Our turn came at last. We cautiously approached the counter, handed over our form completed in Latin and held our breath while we waited for the next problem to arise. There was none. The official just rubber-stamped the form, reached down to a pad, scribbled out a few numbers and handed it to us. At last, I had an IKA number.

# 15

# RIDING THE GREEK WEAPON OF MASS DESTRUCTION

I f IKA was bad, the tax office was worse. Every year, as in most countries, we needed to complete a tax return. Our accountant compiled the figures and sent our documents off to the government for approval. A few weeks later, the tax demand duly arrived in the post. We had been saving for this, so we had the money ready. I asked Alex if we could just send a cheque. 'No, it's not that simple. We have to go to the tax office to pay.' I didn't like this prospect and was becoming very suspicious of all government departments. Their primary aim was to waste as much of your time as possible and make it really difficult for you to do anything.

No alternative; we had to go. We gathered our papers, made sandwiches in case of a long wait, took two bottles of water to avoid getting dehydrated, and left for the day's adventure.

We climbed the stairs to the first-floor office to be met by a scrum the size of a football crowd, all queuing up to pay their taxes. The office was enormous, with a vast counter that stretched along the side of the room and around the corner before disappearing into the distance. Glass barriers separated us from the line of officials, each of whom had a computer monitor in front of them and was busily tapping on keyboards.

Above each numbered window was a sign showing which tax was being dealt with by that particular official. The signs made little sense to me, or to Alex. So we just joined the shortest queue and hoped for the best. An hour passed and we finally got to the counter. Alex presented our papers. The official took one look and said, 'Wrong line. Go away.' Alex politely apologised and asked which was the correct line. He waved his hand dismissively, muttered, 'Over there,' and went back to staring at his screen.

We still had no idea which line to join, but eventually someone else standing in one of the queues came to our rescue. He was an accountant attending on behalf of a client and knew his way around the maze. The correct queue turned out to be long, but if we left now, we'd have wasted most of the morning. So we stuck it out.

An hour later, screams and shouts began bouncing around the walls of the office. One poor chap had lost his patience and erupted in fury. 'For Christ's sake, all I'm trying to do is give you money,' he bellowed. 'Why are you making it so bloody difficult?'

This was the spark that lit the firework. Other voices chipped in and then more and more people joined. The collective fury was building to a crescendo and it was looking like there might be a riot. By now the queues had dissolved into a crowd that was pushing and shoving its way towards the counter. The press of angry taxpayers screaming through hatches in the glass screen seemed about to turn violent. Although entertaining, we thought it best if we left them to riot without us. There was always next week.

We turned away and headed back out to the car. We were hungry and looking forward to lunch in a scenic spot. As we approached, I noticed that the number plates had gone. Again! The area was so busy with the hordes of people descending on the tax office that parking was at a premium, so we'd squeezed our vehicle onto a small grass verge, which must have constituted illegal parking. For a second time, we would face the odyssey of their retrieval.

It was a Friday. All government offices would be closing for the weekend. We had no chance of getting our plates back until Monday. This clipped our wings. Without a car, our weekend excursion would be impossible, and lunch in the mountains was out of the question. We were even taking a chance by driving the car back to Glyfada, to park it up for the weekend.

Back home, we wandered around the corner to a local taverna. In Glyfada, it's impossible to walk very far without meeting a friend or acquaintance. A mere hundred-metre stroll can take an hour or two, with people stopping to chat and catch up on the gossip. As we turned the first corner, we met a friend of ours, Danos. As the local travel agent, he always booked our ferry tickets and arranged hotels when we needed them. He also rented cars. He listened to our story with a look of sympathy in his eyes. Then he brightened. 'I have a car you can borrow,' he said.

Our plans were back on track. We could go away for the weekend. We followed Danos to the lot at the back of his shop. A row of cars stood gleaming in the sunshine and we waited while he went inside to find the keys. Which one of these beautiful vehicles would be ours for the weekend?

There came a loud grinding and the noise of a throaty exhaust, along with intermittent bangs, as a large car trundled into the car lot. The front wing had been secured with black gaffer tape, contrasting with the rusting, off-white bodywork, and the front windscreen had a long crack running from one side to the other. Something seemed to have come loose underneath and was scraping along the ground, creating sparks.

Danos threw the door open and stepped out proudly, holding the key, which he gave to us with a smile. He assured us the car was legal and mechanically sound. We didn't want to seem ungrateful, so we thanked him for the free loan and drove it away.

The temperature outside was nearing forty degrees. The car had no air conditioning, and the windows stubbornly refused to open. Sweat prickled my scalp and ran into my eyes as I tried to focus on the road ahead. The car veered to the left every time I touched the brakes, and there was still the occasional loud scraping sound from underneath. But we were happy. We were off on an adventure.

We took the national road out of Athens towards Thessaloniki and joined the motorway. This was the first motorway built in Greece. The first time I ever drove on this stretch of road, it terrified me. There were three lanes heading north and three lanes heading south but no central barrier separating the opposite streams. This resulted in drivers using the oncoming fast lane to overtake at high speed, causing crashes at a combined speed of more than 300 km/h. We called this road the Greek weapon of mass destruction.

Driving in Greece is a challenge. You need to remember that you may be the only person on the road who has actually passed a driving test. Until the early 2000s, and perhaps even now, rather than endure the inconvenience of taking a test, it was quite easy to get a permit by paying a friend of a friend that had access to the relevant government department. So a few greased palms in the right department gave you a full driving licence without the bother of learning to drive.

Sharing the road with someone who has no idea of the rules makes driving an interesting experience. Motorbike riders don't even pretend to obey any rules. They only wear crash helmets in the winter to keep their heads warm. They are far too hot to wear in the summer.

In the interests of public safety, I have listed a few rules which will assist you while driving in Greece:

1. Watch out for car owners opening their doors without looking while parked. A Greek driver does not understand that there may be other people on the road and will never look behind them. They only use mirrors for make-up or hair combing.

2. Mountain roads are dangerous. Barriers intended to prevent you from plummeting to your doom are usually missing; in their place will be miniature churches on stilts, reminding you it would be a good idea to slow down. Greek drivers have a habit of parking halfway around a blind bend to admire

the view, relieve themselves or take a selfie with the mountains as a backdrop.

3. Road signs are 'advisory' for Greeks. Obeying a stop sign without checking your mirror will usually result in a motorbike inserting itself into your tailpipe.

4. Greeks dislike seatbelts. Most petrol stations will sell a clip that fits nicely into the belt mechanism to stop the annoying bleeping.

5. Speed limits in Greece are an infringement of civil rights and rarely taken seriously. The government did toy with speed cameras, but the blackened husks of these experimental devices, complete with oily rags around the pole, looked ugly, so they were discontinued in favour of planting some handsome new trees.

6. Be careful where you park. If you park illegally, the police will take your plates and it will cost 150 euros to get them back. Paying the money is the simple part.

7. Driving in Athens at night can be like joining a Formula One starting grid. Young Greek men who've 'borrowed' their father's high-powered Mercedes or turbocharged BMW will weave through the traffic at high speed while holding their mobile phone to their ear with one hand, gripping a frappe with the other, sucking their drink through a straw and steering with their knees. These chaps would think nothing of spending hours in a bar over a single coffee, as though time had no meaning, but get them behind a steering wheel and they have to be first. My advice on driving anywhere in

Athens between the hours of 10 p.m. and 4 a.m. is don't.

8. Transporting your vehicle between islands on the car ferry needs planning. The ferry workers will always try to make it as awkward as they can by insisting you reverse up the ramp into the boat while they shout incoherently at you through the rear window to turn left, right, keep straight, interspersed with 'No, idiot, do it again', until they have successfully directed you into a parking gap so small that you can't open the doors to get out. If you do manage to finally crawl out of the window and escape, the acrobatics have to be repeated when you near your destination as you limbo yourself into the side window. Once you are back in the vehicle, still in open sea and several kilometres from port, the engines around you will start up. They will continue to rev and pump carbon monoxide into the confined, unventilated space and to creep forward, determined to be first off the ramp when the ferry docks. When you eventually disembark, you are likely to have gas poisoning and a headache.

9. Zebra crossings are there for decoration only and not to be trusted. They serve no other purpose. Greeks are fully aware of this, but tourists, assuming they have right of way, take their lives in their hands. Cars seem to speed up as soon as you've placed one foot on the crossing.

10. Hand signals in Greece are different. In England, if we want to say thank you, we hold our hand up. In Greece, it's an insult to show your palm. It doesn't

mean thank you. Irate drivers will return the compliment with other, more graphic hand signals.

11. In the UK, if a driver flashes his lights at you, it means he is giving way to you. In Greece, it means 'Get out of the way. I'm coming through'.

12. Hazard lights do not mean that the vehicle is stopping or is in an emergency parking position. It means the driver is going to do something stupid. Maybe they're rolling a cigarette or just changing the radio channel. When you see a vehicle put on its hazard lights, keep a distance and expect the unexpected.

13. Traffic lights mean different things. The stopping sequence is the same as in the UK. Green to amber, then red. But in Greece, amber means speed up as much as possible. Red means reluctantly stop and rev the engine hard. The start sequence completely omits amber and goes straight from red to green. I defy anyone to get away on a green light before the horns behind you blare to tell you that you've taken too long.

Two hours out of Athens, we arrived at Thermopylae. This is the narrow mountain pass on the east coast between the Kallídhromon massif and the Gulf of Maliakós where the Spartan king Leonidas took his three hundred warriors to face the entire Persian army. Its name, meaning Hot Gates, is derived from its steaming, sulphurous springs. It is said that the god Hephaestus created the springs for Hercules, the great hero of Greek mythology, at the request of the goddess Athena.

Hercules would bathe in the hot springs after each of his famous labours, to regain his strength.

In antiquity, Thermopylae's cliffs were by the sea, but silting has widened the distance to a couple of kilometres. Because of changes in sea levels, it is no longer a narrow pass but a plain. But in 480 BC, the sea came up to the base of the steep hills and the pass was narrow: no more than five metres wide at each end and less than fifteen metres even in the middle. These days it looks nothing like the historical description; it's just another stretch of road. If it wasn't for the monument to the Spartan king placed on the site of the battle, you would drive right by and miss it.

The Battle of Thermopylae was joined because the Persian king Xerxes needed to take the pass before the onset of winter brought a halt to his inexorable advance south. History tells us that Xerxes' invading army numbered more than a million. The defending Greek force was small, with fewer than seven thousand troops, including three hundred Spartans at its core. They were determined to protect this crucial pass with their lives. Their king, Leonidas, refused to accede to the concessions offered by Xerxes, and his army managed to hold on for three days before Xerxes prevailed and the pass was taken. The principle of the few standing up against the many is important in Greek culture. It's part of the Greek spirit. A decade after our visit to Thermopylae, this spirit would be sorely tested following the global economic crisis of 2007. The challenge began with the introduction of the euro.

For the 2004 Athens Olympic Games, Greece was determined to put on a good show, and no expense was spared. This period coincided with the introduction of the euro. On 1 January 2002, the drachma, one of the world's oldest currencies, was replaced. The rate was set at 340.75 drachmas to the euro, and prices rose overnight. Given the introduction of the

new currency, and the massive civil engineering projects that
were happening all over Greece, most Greeks assumed that the
new motorways, airport and other massive building projects
were being paid for with European Union grants allocated for
the upgrading of Greece's infrastructure. Every new motorway
proudly displayed a huge billboard announcing the cost of the
project, emblazoned with the symbol of the European Union.
Following the global financial meltdown of 2007, however, the
European Union asked for the money back. We then found out
it had not been a grant after all, but a loan. Greece's borrowing
costs spiked as credit-rating agencies downgraded the country's
sovereign debt to junk status in early 2010, causing the worst
period of austerity in living memory.

Those challenges were still many years in the future for us,
however, as we sped off from Thermopylae in Dinos's rackety
old car and continued around the Bay of Volos and up Mount
Pelion. It was a hot day at sea level, but as we wound our way
up the narrow mountain roads, the air quickly cooled. We
drove through the clouds and emerged into bright sunshine.
The view was spectacular. Below us was a thick band of white
cloud, above were the bare mountain peaks, far too high to
support vegetation. In the far distance was the shimmering
Aegean Sea. Two hours ago, we'd been rattling along the
motorway in our hermetically sealed car, so hot that we'd had to
pour water over our heads straight from the bottle just to keep
cool. Up here, we needed to switch the car heater on just to
stop our teeth from chattering.

We continued on into the mist. Eventually a small village
appeared, nestled among the pine trees. It seemed to comprise
just one straight street with a few shops and tavernas on either
side and an impromptu stream that gurgled down the middle.
The cobbles and pavements were wet from the moisture-laden
air, and water dripped from shop canopies and windowsills. I

couldn't imagine anything further from the typical perception of Greece. This was more like a Swiss Alpine village.

Having dressed for the roasting forty degrees of Athens, we hadn't considered that we might need to bring a coat. It was August, after all. But we were freezing. Other, wiser people were wandering around in full-length jackets, bobble hats and scarfs. We had to make do by layering on the few T-shirts and towels we'd brought in our overnight bag.

The shops sold local honey, nuts and multi-coloured dried pasta, and the tables groaned under the weight of towering piles of apples and peaches and huge pumpkins and gourds. But it was too cold and damp to linger. We retreated into an attractive little taverna to warm up and dry off in front of its log-burning stove. We selected the table nearest to its welcome warmth and the owner immediately came over and fed two more logs into the slot on the side.

'Is it always so misty here?' Alex asked.

'Always,' he replied. Being in a valley near the top of the mountain, the village was perpetually trapped in cloud that never seemed to move. And in winter it was often snowbound, with snow falling most days and no one able to visit the village or leave it. Apparently, the snow plough had broken down a few years earlier and nobody had bothered to mend it.

We enjoyed a simple meal of homemade cheese pie and a small salad. I avoided the wine and shared Alex's Coca-Cola. I wanted to keep my head clear for the next leg of our journey up these misty mountains.

Back in the car, I turned the heater on full blast and we continued our drive into the clouds. My ears popped with the change in pressure. Soon the mist thinned and then disappeared so that we were now driving in bright sunshine. We were on top of the world. Behind us, the village we'd recently left was hidden by a river of white cloud; the thousands of pines that encircled it were partially visible, dipping their branches into the fog.

Ahead, bathing in the afternoon sunshine, was another village, built into the side of the mountain, its red-tiled roofs and green-slate walls rising like a multi-coloured staircase to meet the blue sky. This village was too high to sustain any substantial tree growth, so the landscape was a patchwork of small heathers and wild herbs sprouting between shiny white rocks spread over the hill and between the buildings.

We took the road past the village and arrived at a plateau where a herd of goats were happily chewing on the sparse vegetation. All traces of mist had gone. The air was clear and fresh. To the north, Mount Olympus, the home of the gods, shimmered in the distance, its bare peak above the clouds. Looking southeast, we could see the islands of Skiathos and Skopelos, deep green emeralds in a sapphire sea. South was the island of Evia with its grey mountains and light green skirt where it met the Aegean Sea.

We stood and watched the sun dip towards the distant horizon, turning the sky a light gold over the far-flung islands. We were getting hungry and remembered passing a small taverna a couple of kilometres back. At the wooden shack with the small rusty Pepsi sign swinging in the breeze, we were greeted by a large smiling lady wearing a pink flowered apron and with a round face of the same colour. She showed us to a table near the window so we could enjoy the last rays of sunshine before night finally descended on the mountains, and introduced herself as Ermophola. 'It means "beautiful",' she proudly told us, then recited the menu, assuring us that she had cooked everything herself using only the best local produce. We ordered a selection of meat and pasta and a small plate of moussaka, a salad and some fried potatoes.

Although we had planned to sleep in the car, Alex and I

were now having second thoughts as it seemed very exposed up this mountain, and Alex had heard stories of bears roaming around at night. But Ermophola told us that the only guest house thereabouts was back down the valley, in the foggy village, and I really didn't like the thought of driving there through the clouds at night. It had been hard enough in the daylight. Ermophola smiled when she heard that we were afraid of the local wildlife. 'There are no bears here anymore,' she told us. 'The wolves have chased them away.' This was not necessarily the assurance we'd been looking for, but when she kindly offered to make a bed for us in the corner of the taverna, we declined, not wanting to abuse her kindness. Alex asked if we could sleep in the car in the car park; being near a building, she would feel safer. Ermophola readily agreed. So, accommodation settled, and with no reason to drive again that day, I ordered a carafe of the local wine.

Back in the car, we reclined the seats and set out the blankets and pillows that we'd brought with us for the purpose. I closed my eyes, but the silence was unnerving. We'd never slept on the top of a mountain before and weren't ready for the complete lack of noise. In Glyfada we would happily sleep through all the normal sounds of the village; car alarms would blare in the middle of the night, and they'd empty the bottle bank at two in the morning, and we'd sleep soundly through all that noise and clatter. But this mountain felt weird, a silent vacuum.

We woke as the sun rose, feeling refreshed. A film of dew had formed on the car, and the air was still and cold. Ermophola had gone home and the taverna was empty.

Yesterday's cloud had cleared a little, and we could see more of the road as we headed back down towards the damp village. Deep ravines, invisible yesterday, were now all too apparent alongside us, sheer drops into the nothingness far below. We had just started on a particularly steep stretch of road when I touched the brakes to slow for a bend ahead. Nothing happened. I tried again, pumping the brakes as our speed increased, as if our lives depended on it. Which they did. Still nothing. I slammed the stick into a lower gear, hoping the engine would help slow us down. No effect. We were still travelling too fast to take the oncoming bend.

Suddenly, the wheels locked, the car veered left and right as I fought with the steering to bring us under control, and we skidded to a halt.

I turned to Alex. 'What happened? How did we stop?'

'I pulled the handbrake.' She smiled. This time it was to save our lives rather than test them.

A mechanic in the village patched up the brakes and we limped back to Athens, more than ready to queue for as many hours as necessary to regain our number plates and get back behind the wheel of our own fully functioning car.

# 16

## BEAR HUGS FROM UNCLE VASILIS

Uncle Vasilis was a bear. Nearly two metres tall and a metre and a half wide, he had no teeth, was never freshly shaved and never wore a beard but had a permanent untidy grey stubble. Like his sister, Debbie, his volume control was stuck on loud. We loved him.

Vasilis was a ship's captain, like his father, Jannis, before him, so he was rarely in Athens, but when he did return to port we looked forward to his visit. His job usually involved flying to a remote corner of the globe to collect a supertanker or a container ship and then transporting its cargo around the world. Only rarely would he collect a ship from Piraeus, which meant he came to Athens just once or twice a year.

Vasilis had been married at least four times (that we were aware of), to women all over the world. We knew about one wife in Spain, another in Greece, and one or two somewhere in the Far East. To our knowledge, he had not divorced any of them; they just seemed to fade into the distance and were replaced by a fresh one every year or two.

When I first met him, he terrified me. I was on the terrace of the old house reading a book when I heard screams and loud voices coming from the garden below. I looked over the parapet to see this enormous man in a uniform of white shirt, golden epaulettes and a captain's hat, swearing at the top of his voice from the gate. Debbie appeared from the side of the house, broke into a run and flung her arms around his neck. Alex raced down from the upper level and jumped on him. He picked her up like a rag doll and kissed her.

Alex glanced up and called to me. 'Come down. This is my uncle.'

I held out my hand, which he ignored. Instead, he simply put his giant arms around me, lifted me off my feet – crushing my ribs and squeezing the breath out of me – and kissed my cheek.

Being a seafaring man, Vasilis was at ease speaking English, so I was grateful when, out of respect for me, the family switched from Greek to include me in the conversation.

At first, Vasilis struck me as an angry man. But I judged him too harshly. He was not angry, he was passionate. Greeks are warm and open people who tend not to hide behind emotional walls. If they are happy, they will show it; likewise with sadness. Anger too must be expressed, not bottled up. I have described Alex as a firework. She is not alone. Anger is vented and forgotten in the blink of an eye here. Everyone accepts this and we take no offence. In Greece, everyone shouts at everyone. It's common to see drivers step out of their cars and give voice to their fury, but after a few brief moments the anger subsides, hands are shaken and then the drivers get back into their vehicles to continue their day. In England, on the other hand, I've seen drivers come to blows over a minor infraction and violence erupt in other contexts over the most insignificant reason. Here in Greece, such incidents never turn violent. Frustration is not allowed to build in this culture; people express it as they feel it and let it out.

In that first conversation, Vasilis criticised the 'stupid government'. He complained about the local police, the traffic laws, the crazy prices in the shops and inflation. The drinking glasses and water jug rose from the table every time he emphasised a point with a bang of his big hairy fist. We listened quietly, and then he moved on to the subject of the latest love of his life. His eyes filled with tears as he told us about Cathy. She was a girl he'd met in Mombasa, less than half his age and eking out a living by granting favours to sailors in a bar near the port. He had seen a venerability in her and she needed protecting. Tears rolled down his cheeks as he told us about her brother, whom she supported and was such an innocent boy. He didn't judge her for her lifestyle, he just fell in love.

Vasilis was a genuine character, and as a seafaring man, he was deeply superstitious. His avoidance of bad luck ruled his life. Whenever we gave him a compliment, he would go through the motions of pretending to spit, to ward off the evil eye. One day he was sitting on our Glyfada terrace, cutting his fingernails and collecting them in a small pot one by one. I watched as he finished trimming one of his hairy paws and counted out the nail fragments before moving on to the next five digits. Suddenly a bit of fingernail pinged off and disappeared behind some plant pots. This sent him into a panic. He ran over to the pots and pushed them away one by one, carefully scanning the ground, looking for the missing nail, but to no avail; he had lost it. Tears brimmed as he sat down with an expression of fear on his face mixed with disappointment at his stupidity.

I looked at Alex for an explanation. She smiled and whispered that he believed that if some evil person were to discover the nail, they could control him, so it had to be found. His soul depended on it.

I had an idea. I suggested that I search for the nail as my eyes were at least twenty years younger, so I might have more success. His expression changed to one of hope as I pretended to rummage around the pots. I hid myself behind a tall shrub, bit off a piece of my own fingernail and surreptitiously dropped it in front of one of the plant containers, then pretended to continue the search. After a respectable period, I stood back, bent over and pointed to my chewed-off nail. 'Is that it?' I asked.

Vasilis jumped up from his chair, crouched down onto his hands and knees and carefully picked it up. He added the nail to the others in his little pot, emptied the contents onto a piece of white paper, counted them out and smiled. They were all there. He carefully took his precious cargo into the house. We heard the toilet flush as he emptied them all away.

The next day, Vasilis announced that he was going to Athens on business. He was sick of taxis – 'they are all bandits' – so he told us he would take our car. This was a little worrying, as he had the reputation of being the worst driver in Athens. As

Athenian drivers are probably the worst in Europe, the competition was stiff.

He was a competent sea captain, used to piloting half-a-mile-long oil tankers with a turning arc of twenty miles and a stopping distance of fifty. Our little white Citroen Saxo should have been a breeze for him. In the event, however, it took him just a couple of hours to cause an impressive amount of damage. When he returned, one wing mirror was missing and the other was dangling on a wire, gently tapping the bodywork in the breeze. The front wing was no longer white but scored with deep scratches and dents, liberally sprinkled with red paint. The other side had similar damage, but the paint was a nice taxi yellow. Number plates were missing, foretelling a wasted day for us tomorrow, trailing around courts and police stations in Athens to retrieve them. We never asked Vasilis what happened, but we agreed to hide the keys on his next visit.

That next visit didn't materialise for more than a year. One afternoon we got a call informing us that he was making a brief stopover in Athens and would drop by that evening to see the progress on the building. Alex suggested we take him out and buy him a meal. Vasilis was not a big drinker, but he was passionate about his food. Many years earlier, he'd lost his teeth and had been given dentures. The day they fitted his new teeth, he instructed the ship's cook to prepare him something soft to eat. The cook presented him with a bowl of soup, a few boiled eggs and a loaf of fresh bread He tried eating with his new teeth, screamed that they didn't work, took them out of his mouth and threw them over the side of the ship. He never wore teeth again. Over the years, his gums hardened so much that he could now crack bones with them.

We had been told about a Lebanese restaurant that had recently opened nearby, so we booked a table. Early that evening, a taxi pulled up outside our house. We heard shouting and what sounded like an argument and tentatively approached the car to find out what the commotion was about. Vasilis had played a joke on the taxi driver by paying him with a fake $50 note that had a pornographic picture on the back, showing a sailor in a compromising position with a mermaid. The driver had not seen the funny side of this joke. A full argument was still raging by the time we got to the cab.

Alex tapped on the driver's window. He stopped shouting, rolled down his window and directed his anger at us. 'Is he anything to do with you?' he yelled.

'He's my uncle,' Alex replied.

'Well, tell him to pay me with actual money. Look what he gave me!' He waved the fake note at us.

Vasilis was still in the back seat, doubled-up with laughter. The taxi driver was red-faced as he thrust the pornographic note towards us. I dipped into my pocket, produced a genuine note, and instructed him to keep the change. At which, Vasilis opened the door, heaved himself out of the back seat, put his bear paw through the open window and shook hands with the taxi driver.

We sat down in the house over coffee to catch up on the news, and Alex told him about our plans for the evening.

'That's very nice, my daughter, but I have no appetite at the moment.' He proceeded to describe his current bout of diarrhoea, listing his symptoms in graphic detail, which included colour, consistency and frequency.

'So shall I cancel the restaurant booking?' I asked.

'No, but I may just nibble a salad.'

The restaurant was a short walk from home. A waiter appeared from nowhere and opened the door for us. Another waiter inside directed us to a table with a freshly ironed tablecloth and napkins folded into a star pattern arranged in front of each chair. The menu arrived with yet another server, who unfolded our napkins and laid them in our laps.

Vasilis jumped up. 'What are you doing?' he yelled.

'Sir, I am assisting you with your napkin,' the waiter replied.

Vasilis, being a sailor, would never go to an upmarket restaurant and did not understand the workings of anything other than a local taverna. He'd thought the poor chap was interfering with him and had been leaping up to defend his honour, and ours.

We tried to explain, but he waved our reassurance away as he studied the menu. He stared at the dishes on offer with a confused look on his face. 'Is this food?' he enquired. He was not used to menus; he would normally just listen to the waiter recite what was best that day and order that. In this place he had to choose from strange items he'd never heard of. The bear was beginning to growl.

Alex took over and chose a selection of meat dishes that she thought might please him, together with couscous, a salad and some pitta bread and dips. The waiter left to get our drinks while Vasilis got busy tucking his napkin under his chin. Fifteen minutes passed. Vasilis had already picked up his knife and fork and was looking towards the kitchen door, waiting for his food to arrive. Another five minutes passed; he was looking angry now and was loudly tapping his knife on the table. We tried to pacify him by changing the subject from the lack of food on the table and asked about his forthcoming trip to China. In return, we just received one-word answers while he continued to stare at the unopened kitchen door.

Seconds later, the table shook and the glasses tumbled as Vasilis stood up, hurled his napkin onto the floor, stormed towards the kitchen door, threw it open and slammed it behind him. From the kitchen, the noise of screams and clattering pans filled the restaurant as he vented his frustration. A terrified waiter ran out into the dining area, closely followed by a flying brass saucepan. Eventually the racket subsided and Vasilis emerged from the kitchen, retrieved his discarded napkin from the floor and tucked it under his chin again while settling back into his chair.

Two minutes later, the chap that had escaped the saucepan reappeared, carrying a large tray containing pitta bread wrapped in napkins, a selection of dips and a large plate with a silver-domed cover which he ceremoniously placed on the table in front of Vasilis. With a practised flourish, the waiter lifted the cover to reveal the food. The plate was enormous; the portion was not. A small meatball sat on top of a tiny bed of couscous with a sprig of parsley laid artistically on top. A drizzle of sauce, carefully swirled around the edge of the plate, completed the design.

Vasilis looked at the plate, looked up at the server. Now he was angrier. He had waited an eternity for his food, and when it finally arrived, it was little more than a mouthful.

'This is not food!' he yelled.

He stood up, pushed the table aside and pursued the fast-retreating waiter back to the kitchen. There came more screams and more clattering of pots, then he strode out of the kitchen and headed straight for the exit.

'We are leaving,' he yelled to us.

The staff looked shocked but relieved to hear this.

By the time we caught up with him, he had already hailed a taxi and was squeezing himself into the front seat beside the driver. We only just got into the back seat before the taxi sped off with the doors still open. A few minutes later we arrived at our destination, with Vasilis still swearing and complaining. It was a meat taverna. Outside, rows of whole, golden lambs were rotating slowly over beds of charcoal, fragrant smoke was rising into the night sky and diners were sitting under awnings at long benches and connecting tables, sharing enormous quantities of meat, salads, and carafes of wine. A bearded chap was sitting in one corner playing a bouzouki, with a cigarette wedged between the strings of the fret, the smoke drifting up in puffs in time to the music.

We found an empty table and settled on our benches. Immediately, the waiter arrived. Vasilis ordered the food and visibly relaxed. Two minutes later, a giant salad appeared, with a tray of chips. A medium-sized whole lamb followed, with the head still attached, along with a selection of fried and fresh vegetables and a carafe of wine. Vasilis tore off a leg and bit off chunks with his gums. The bear was satisfied.

We had tried and failed to give him a special evening. But the failure was our fault, not his. Vasilis was a straightforward man with straightforward tastes. He had never wanted to be anything else. He knew what he wanted in his life and was happy, so why change?

# 17

## HEAD OF THE FAMILY

In 1930s Greece, when Vasilis and Debbie were born, it was normal for parents to announce delightedly that 'we are blessed with a son' and at the same time to state more neutrally simply that 'we have a daughter'. Males carried the family name and therefore the respectability of the family, whereas daughters were expected to marry and change their name, becoming part of another family. A daughter would assist around the house until she was married off, at which point she became the property of someone else. A son, on the other hand, would provide for his family and ensure the continuation of the bloodline. He had a lot to live up to.

As the younger brother of Debbie, Vasilis was therefore the favoured child in their family. So we can imagine the family's reaction when a young Vasilis wrote a letter to his mother announcing that he might be gay.

The letter arrived after Vasilis had been at sea with his father for a year. He was a teenage boy with raging hormones, stuck on a ship populated only by men. With no experience of the opposite sex, he directed his appetites to willing crew members keen to educate him.

Receipt of this letter caused panic. Although Greece was one of the first countries to legalise homosexuality, in 1951, being gay was still viewed with suspicion in the early 1950s and perceived as bringing shame on the family. Vasilis's mother, Bia, was adamant that her son's secret had to be protected. It would be a family disgrace if word spread that the son of the war hero Captain Jannis was a homosexual. Bia resorted to prayer day and night until one morning she looked into the sky and saw a faint vision of Mary, the Mother of God, smiling and waving. As a deeply religious woman, this was all the reassurance Bia needed; after this ethereal visit, she knew that all would be well.

Unknown to Bia, Vasilis's ship had docked at Singapore, leaving him to discover the flesh pits of the port with his wages in his pocket. In a letter to his wife, Jannis described how their son had disappeared for a week before eventually being found in a quiet area of the ship with two local good-time girls. Luckily, antibiotics had recently become available, so most of the interesting diseases acquired during his hormone-led rampage through the red-light zones were swiftly dealt with.

This episode of teenage debauchery was the best news his mother could have received. She celebrated by lighting a candle of thanks in the local church in Castella every day until he returned.

Vasilis's long service in the merchant navy finally ended prematurely, when he was just sixty-two years old. He was quite used to sailing around the coast of Somalia, risking pirate raids, and had once narrowly escaped a boarding party by training the ship's water hoses on a small boat containing armed men trying to jump his vessel. To Vasilis, this was an occupational hazard and just part of his job. But he finally drew the line when he arrived at a distant port to take control of a container ship destined for the Middle East. When studying the manifest, he found that the ship was loaded with missiles, guns and ammunition. Vasilis had seen the effects of war on his travels, had seen the misery caused by conflict, had witnessed the ensuing famines when he'd delivered aid to countries ravaged by hunger and disease. He would not contribute to the deepening plight of such poor, starving people by carrying weapons. And so he refused to captain that ship.

The company flew another ship's master out from Greece to replace him, and Vasilis was recalled to his head office, where he requested early retirement. He returned to Mombasa, settled there, built a house, purchased a share of a shrimp boat and married Cathy.

He was already enjoying his retirement when, during one of his infrequent trips to Athens, I asked him to join me away from the house for a coffee. Vasilis was the most worldly-wise person in the family, and like a second father to Alex, and I needed his advice.

Alex and I had been together for more than two years and

were firmly established as a couple. We were in love and happy. But there was an undercurrent of something which was not quite right and that I couldn't put my finger on.

Whenever I mentioned marriage, Alex became thoughtful and changed the subject. We were both free agents and we were certainly in love, but something was holding her back from even discussing the ultimate commitment. Had her first marriage put her off for good? Was she waiting for me to make a dramatic declaration of love and fall to my knees clutching a diamond ring and a bouquet of her favourite flowers? I would gladly have done exactly that, and more, but I suspected this might not be the answer. Knowing Alex as I did, it was more likely that she was lining up another herculean task for me to accomplish.

Determined to break through this barrier, I decided to go a little deeper. There was no point in asking Alex, as she would just evade the question by assuring me that we were happy and in love and had no need to rush into anything. After all, not being married wasn't making a difference to our relationship.

Vasilis and I chose a coffee house overlooking the village square and close to the big circular church, the centrepiece of Glyfada. It was market day and the breeze carried a vague smell of fish mingled with the heady aroma of fresh coffee. I watched as vendors sold their fresh fish from their artistically arranged displays on beds of crushed ice. We sat down under the wicker parasols and a glass of cold water was placed in front of us by a pretty waitress who took our order and left us to our discussion.

Vasilis was curious to find out why we couldn't have this conversation at the house, where everything was freely discussed. Although he was a big, loud sailor, he was also sensitive. I felt sure that his advice would be valuable and that this would give me an opportunity to measure the opinion of the family.

I broached the subject. I started the conversation by asking how the family felt about our relationship. He looked into my eyes and told me that nothing would make him happier than to see us wed. The family had obviously discussed it and everyone agreed that it would be for the best. Alex being his favourite niece, he would gladly add his blessing.

This was one obstacle overcome. But I still needed Alex to agree. I told him that I really wanted to marry Alex and explained that she seemed distant and a little evasive whenever the subject came up. He listened intently, sipped his coffee and then spoke.

'Have you noticed how Alex speaks to me?' he asked.

As I was by now getting a grasp on the Greek language, I had understood that she spoke to her father and uncle differently than to her mother.

'Yes, I have noticed a difference,' I replied. 'But why?'

'She addresses me with the formal "you", thee-os, as a mark of respect.'

In Greek culture, it is customary for sons and daughters to speak to their older relatives using the second-person plural. Alex would address them as a group. This is a little like the royal 'we'. If she met an auntie in the street, she would ask, 'How are you all today?' instead of 'How are you?' It's not polite to refer to such a person in the singular.

It would also be unthinkable to address an elder by their first name without adding the prefix Mr or Mrs. I'd noticed that Alex had been very uncomfortable addressing my mother and father by their first name alone; she feels the same discomfort even today.

Such traditions have been practised in Greece for more than two thousand years and continue to be passed down through the generations. Although Alex slips easily into modern life, is keen to embrace new ideas and can be rebellious, outspoken and confrontational, her culture goes deep to the bone.

So I had my answer. Currently, Alex and I were friends and lovers. When married, I would become her husband and command her respect and loyalty as a matter of right. Her culture demanded that I, as her husband, would be head of the family, and my will would be law in the household. Not because I wanted it that way, but because Greek culture expected it. Alex would not be required to speak to me in the plural, but all other rules would apply.

Her parents' marriage epitomised the traditional way of doing things. In Debbie and Zissis's generation, the man was in charge and didn't need to discuss anything of importance with his wife. I had observed the dynamics of this relationship at close hand and had seen the difference in Debbie when Zissis was at home. Debbie would always tone down her naturally exuberant behaviour when her husband was around. She'd listen carefully to any orders or instructions given before he left on a work trip. She would nod and seemingly agree. These directives would promptly be forgotten as soon as he left the house. This maintained the happy balance of the home.

I liked Zissis and we got on well together. I would sit with him on the terrace and talk to him over coffee. He was an intelligent man with knowledge of many subjects. He was scrupulously honest and also unfailingly direct, sometimes to the point of rudeness. If Alex had been born with a short fuse, her father had been born with none. He did not see the need for diplomacy.

One day we were all sitting in a restaurant enjoying a nice, relaxed family meal. Zissis asked a passing waitress for a toothpick, and we carried on with our conversation. A few moments later, he stopped talking, turned red in the face, stood up and shouted a stream of abuse at the poor girl. She had not provided the toothpick quickly enough. The whole restaurant turned to watch the commotion until finally a toothpick was supplied, upon which he stormed out, leaving us all behind.

Having been born and raised in Istanbul, Zissis didn't reap the benefits that came from being part of a large Greek family and nor did he absorb the cultural heritage of mainland Greece. His early years in an eastern country did not teach him to respect women. As far as he was concerned, they were second-class citizens and only existed to serve men. He tried to bring this outdated idea with him when he married Debbie.

Debbie's upbringing had taught her that the man was the ruler of the house. Her mother, Bia, had subscribed to the traditional view, which was that daughters – in the words of Xenophon, recognised as one of the greatest writers of antiquity – should be brought up 'to see the least possible, hear the least possible and ask the least possible'. In the parental home, girls learned the basics of child-rearing and housekeeping, to prepare them for their new lives. Bia emphasised that, in any relationship, keeping the peace was more important than having a direct confrontation. This worked to some extent for Debbie and Zissis, until Alex came along and rebelled at such an iniquitous arrangement.

Alex had respect for her elders ingrained within every cell of her body, but she hated injustice. She had inherited the kindness of her mother but also the temper of her father. This led to frequent confrontations and arguments because of his expectations, which were quite out of sync with the way Alex and Debbie normally lived. During the short periods when Zissis was home, the house became a warzone. There were either all-out battles with objects flying through the air or a subdued ceasefire while the warring parties regrouped before the next onslaught. Neighbours would stop calling, and the laughter temporarily ceased.

This was not the sort of married life that Alex wanted to embark on with me, and thanks to Vasilis, my eyes had been opened. Alex and I were happy the way we were. We were equals in everything and made all of our decisions together. If we got married, her upbringing decreed that this must change. I finally understood her reluctance to discuss marriage. She wanted things to remain as they were.

Armed with my new knowledge, I waited until an appropriate time and raised the subject. I explained that by now she knew me better than anyone. She must understand that it wasn't in my nature to take advantage of this newfound power over her. I just wanted her to become my wife and for us to be together forever.

I watched her closely as she considered this. Finally, she looked into my eyes, smiled, and agreed to become my wife.

Once Alex had said yes, her attitude completely changed, and she enthusiastically threw herself into the wedding arrangements. The marriage would be in England, and her relatives would fly in and would need somewhere to stay. As I was not a baptised Orthodox Christian, a church wedding was not permitted, so she set about organising a registry office.

We rented a local hotel for the reception, hired a Greek bouzouki band to play for us, secured a block of rooms for the overnight guests, and arranged the catering, which would be a mix of English and Greek fare. Alex had always had a dream of arriving at her wedding in a white carriage with matching horses, which it delighted me to agree to.

It was a spring wedding. Daffodils were flowering on the lawns around The Bury, a converted Georgian manor house now used as a registry office, and the air was clean and crisp as I arrived to meet our guests. The gardens were perfectly manicured, affording views of sweeping meadows leading down to a lazy river with ducks squabbling and splashing in the March sunshine.

The wedding room had retained its handsome Georgian features. Oak-panelled walls joined Corinthian columns standing proudly around the space, giving an air of formality to this solemn but joyous occasion. The room was full. Too many people had turned up, so the double doors were opened to the rear lawn to allow everyone a look-in.

I was standing at the small table facing away from the seated guests, quietly waiting for my future wife to arrive. We had chosen music to play during the wait for the bride, as well as other songs for the signing of the register. Although the room was busy with friends and family chatting and laughing, I was alone, accompanied only by my thoughts.

My mind drifted back to the first time I met Alex as an adult. She was the most beautiful woman I had ever seen. She'd been in my thoughts since our first encounter, when we were both children. We'd lost contact for years and then a chance meeting had brought us back together. We had forged our relationship in a foreign country, bringing with us our experiences of different places, people and cultures. Already we'd had so many adventures together, and every day we loved each other more. Now she would be my wife.

My eyes filled at this wonderful thought. Tears rolled down my cheeks and dropped onto the table. My shoulders shook as I tried to suppress the sobs. From behind me, a tissue appeared, proffered by Debbie. She had watched as my emotions took hold and fully understood. She put her arm around my shoulders and squeezed as I tried to take back control.

The music changed to announce the bride. Alexandra had arrived. I turned to look at the open doors behind me and to watch her enter. She was a vision of beauty in her white lace wedding dress with a garland of spring flowers as a crown. Her eyes met mine and she smiled.

I held my breath, trying to hold back more tears, but it was too late. We both stumbled through our vows with stifled sobs of happiness and tried to avoid looking at each other in case we broke down completely.

In the wedding photographs, Alex looks magnificent in her fine wedding dress and floral crown, with black stains under her eyes where her tears had mingled with her make-up. Standing next to her in her beauty is her brand-new, blotchy, red-faced husband, with red, tear-filled eyes and a red nose to match. But I look happy.

As husband and wife, we joined the procession of cars to attend our reception at the local hotel. We had hired a function room for over two hundred guests, and they all assembled at the entrance to greet us as we arrived. We entered the hotel to the sound of Greek songs played on a bouzouki.

Food eaten, speeches and toasts made, it was time for the first dance. I took Alex by the hand and led her onto the dance floor. I nodded at the band. A single bouzouki strummed first one chord and then a second. The tune to 'Zorba the Greek' filled the room. Everyone in the room stood and joined us in a vast circle. With arms outstretched and resting on each other's shoulders, we danced, with Alex leading us in the steps.

Alex's delicate arm was resting across my right shoulder as we danced in a circle. Across my left shoulder lay the heavy arm of Uncle Vasilis, with his meaty paw wrapped around the back of my neck. He was formally dressed in his naval uniform together with his captain's cap, which slid down over his eyes as the pace quickened. Stella, our cat-loving Glyfada neighbour, was wearing a pink feathery outfit and matching hat that made her look like a poorly flamingo. She had made a beeline for my mother, pulled her away from the dance floor and squeezed her into a corner for a conversation. My mother didn't speak one word of Greek, but this had never mattered to Stella, who just continued to bombard her. The aunties, all dressed in black, of course, had linked arms and were relying on each other for support as their walking sticks had been discarded so some real dancing could be done. Debbie wore a sparkling blouse and matching leggings as she moved in time with the rapidly quickening pace. Even Zissis seemed to be having fun as the music became so fast it was just a blur of sound.

One by one, people started to drop out and lie on the floor, exhausted, with smiles on their faces. The music finished, and the more energetic guests demanded the song be played again, and then again, until everyone was sitting on the floor sweating and laughing.

It was early evening when we left to head to the airport for our honeymoon. We had planned to visit the most beautiful place on earth. We were going home.

After the wedding, I did notice a difference in Alex. She began asking my permission for things she wanted to do. We argued a little less, and she seemed to give in a bit more easily than before. Our marriage was a blend of cultures. She didn't need to ask my permission for anything. She was equal in every way and superior in many. I kept my vow and refused to let our relationship change, even though her culture demanded it. I was just happy to be married to her. I expected nothing I hadn't earned. Respect should not come automatically with a marriage certificate. I promised myself I would keep proving I was worth it.

# 18

# IN THE PINK ON THE ISLAND OF EVIA

O
ur new apartment now had freshly plastered walls and was beginning to feel like a home. The walls were a nice clean pink with cornices at the top and a few wires poking through here and there, awaiting the last connections. Unbeknown to Stavros, we were going to erect Corinthian columns in the living room. These would be decorative so would not affect his progress. The lift shaft was still a gaping hole with a

plank of wood nailed over the entrance to stop workers from inadvertently falling into it, the floor was a rough concrete screed, ready for the tiles, and the staircase up to the terrace was ready for its marble treads and risers. The skylight was flush with the roof deck and had been fitted with armoured glass so we could walk over it. Staring up at it from inside, we could see nothing but the blue sky.

The whole place was looking like a Hollywood film star's apartment. We were both happy with the progress and wanted to talk about the final elements of the interior decoration. As we always had our best ideas while enjoying a meal, we got in the car and headed for a favourite seaside restaurant.

We took the coast road past Vouliagmeni Lake, driving past the luxury yachts tied up in the natural bay and on until we reached Agia Marina. The restaurant here was a simple ouzeria which served ouzo (a Greek liquor) and mezedes (small finger foods). Ouzo started off as the fierce spirit tsipouro, which is said to have been developed by fourteenth-century monks on Mount Athos; with the addition of anise, this became ouzo. It's usually mixed with water, which turns it a cloudy white, and is served with ice cubes in a small glass. It can also be drunk straight, but that is not for the fainthearted. It tastes similar to absinthe, or Pernod, which is liquorice-like but smoother.

Blue tin tables were spread randomly over the beach. I settled into a blue wicker chair on the water's edge. As it sank into the sand, I reached out and dipped my toes into the sea. It was a beautiful, calm day.

The waiter stepped across the sand with a tray held high containing our barbecued octopus, shrimps and fried cheese. We poured our two miniature bottles of ouzo and Alex started the conversation by asking my thoughts on the floor tiles. I was expecting this. Having now seen our almost completed apartment, I was also concerned about the tiles. We had visions of a wonderful ancient Greek theme. Tiles wouldn't work. We needed marble.

Although once the building was finished we would own three brand-new apartments and a shop in one of the most expensive areas of Greece and would likely be property millionaires, we didn't actually have any money. So buying marble would be a challenge. Neither Alex nor I had any concept of the cost, and Stavros definitely wouldn't assist, so we had to do some research and find some cheap marble. I reasoned that it shouldn't be too expensive as Greece was full of quarries, so it had to be much cheaper than in the UK. Or was I just being hopeful?

I had finished my ouzo and was now onto a second glass. The more sips I took, the more confident I felt. After my third glass of that wonderful cloudy liquid, I had abandoned any worries about cost and vowed to get the best quality marble for our new home, regardless. We just needed to choose a colour.

By now, my head was swimming a little, so I forewent another ouzo and focused on the decor discussion. We decided against white marble, as it would look cold. Alex suggested pink. We both considered this. I suggested we could get another piece to match the floor and make a coffee table. Alex enthusiastically agreed. So we were decided. We would no longer have tiles fitted in the living room. We would have pink marble floors and a matching pink marble coffee table.

Now we only had two problems. First, we needed to return to Glyfada quickly and tell Stavros before he started the tiling. We would have to fight him as his tiling company was due in a few days, but I was ready. Secondly: how to fund seventy square metres of pink marble? I'd only paid for this meal by rummaging around the glove compartment for a few stray coins.

Back in Glyfada, Stavros was standing outside the apartment block chatting with our dastardly neighbour Pandelis. I wondered what they were scheming. Whatever it was, it would not be to our advantage. As far as we were concerned, Pandelis was taking far too much interest in our building, which was worrying. Alex jumped out of the car and interrupted their conversation. Pandelis didn't leave but took a few steps backwards and pretended to look into the shop window so he could still hear our conversation with Stavros.

'We're having marble floors,' Alex announced.

'No, you are not,' Stavros replied. 'The tiling contractors are starting in five days' time,' he said, 'so it's too late to change your mind. And who's paying for it?'

We had now set our hearts on the pink marble flooring, so we would not back down, whatever it took. We undertook to pay for the fitting of the marble, as well as the marble itself, and we decided not to ask him to credit us for the price of the tiles.

This would be a good deal for him, but he still felt that he had to protest. It was in his nature. It would be most inconvenient, he said, as the levels would all be wrong, given that marble was thicker than tiles. But it would be simple to raise the level of the tiling in the bathroom, I replied, and of the hardwood floor in the bedroom. After argument and counter-argument, he agreed as long as we had the marble there within ten days. End of story. We went off to find some marble.

First things first, though I was not looking forward to this, I called my bank manager in the UK. He was a decent enough chap but was one of that new breed of bank managers who no longer made their own decisions but was governed by a computer database and had to tick all the boxes before the machine spat out a yes or no to my request. He asked me how much I needed. I had no idea but aimed high. '£2000 should do it,' I ventured hopefully. I held my breath while listening to the tapping of a keyboard. His voice came back online. That would be fine, he said. The bank would extend my overdraft temporarily.

We drove along the coast to a nearby marble yard and walked around it, surveying the large chunks of granite and onyx. At last we found some pink marble. It was all stacked up vertically in racks and far too heavy to move for a closer inspection. The yard owner came out of his wooden shack and shook our hands and introduced himself as Milos. Alex pointed at the huge block of pink marble and asked the price for seventy square metres.

He grinned. 'That's a lot of marble,' he said. 'We don't have that much in stock. You'll have to wait a few months for them to quarry more out of the mountain.'

This was not going well. We only had ten days before Stavros's deadline.

'How much is it anyway?' Alex asked.

Milos went back into his shack and returned with a grubby folder containing the price list. He scanned through it, found the pink marble and informed us of the price. Alex and I felt deflated. He was quoting 150 euros per metre. My bank manager was a nice chap, but he would never allow an overdraft of that size.

'Sorry, Milos, we can't afford that much. Is there anything cheaper?' Alex said.

Milos was a kind-looking man. He'd seen the disappointment on our faces and was keen to help. We told him of our plans. Apparently we'd chosen the most expensive marble, the type that was usually used only for small decorative areas and was not suitable for floors. It would be better to use marble tiles, he told us. These were still pure marble but a lot less expensive and easy to fit. Alex cautiously asked how much they were.

'You can get a lovely pink marble for between fifteen and twenty euros a metre.'

He had saved us. Our dream of a marble floor was back on track.

Milos beckoned us into his shed, rummaged behind his desk and produced a piece of beautiful shiny pink marble. Alex put it on the floor. We both stood back to admire it and imagine what a whole room would look like covered in this wonderful stone. We loved it and asked when he could deliver.

Milos's face fell as he told us that this was the only piece he had. 'But I can get some from my brother in Evia in two or three weeks' time.'

This being Greece, where nothing happened fast, we knew that two weeks would likely extend to two months.

'Is there any way we can get it in a week?' Alex pleaded.

Milos felt sorry for us. 'Wait a moment, I will call my brother.' He picked up the phone and after a brief conversation told us that his brother had an excellent selection and plenty in stock at his yard in north Evia. 'But you have to go there to choose the right shade,' he said.

We agreed to visit Milos's bother. Milos would fit it for us at a cost of five euros a metre, and he could do this for us next week.

The island of Evia, or Euboea, was a three-hour drive from Glyfada, via the suspension bridge over the Euripus Strait, the narrow sea channel that separates it from the mainland. Although it's the second-largest island in Greece, few British people have ever heard of it, probably because it's not a traditional holiday resort and has no airport. It's long and thin, measuring 180 kilometres from top to bottom and just six kilometres across at its narrowest point. The southernmost tip is close to the islands of Andros, Tinos and Mykonos, while its northern coast looks across the sea towards Skiathos and Skopelos.

Once across the bridge and on the island, we drove under the arches of the old Roman viaduct to the seafront at Chalkida, Evia's capital. This is the only place in Greece where there are tides, and they are unique in the world. The current in the strait separating Chalkida from the mainland moves in a northerly direction for six hours at a time. After this period there follow eight minutes of calm before the direction of the current reverses. This strange phenomenon has fascinated humans since ancient times. The Greek philosopher Aristotle travelled here to study it, and various other scientists and philosophers have also tried to solve the riddle of these tides. It's thought that the strait takes its name from a man called Euripus who drowned in his attempt to work it out.

The speed of the current peaks at about twelve kilometres per hour, northwards and southwards, which causes small boats a lot of trouble, and sometimes there is the added hazard of whirlpools. When the tide withdraws, it reveals a rich supply of molluscs in the sand, which makes the birds happy. We watched as Chalkida's large beach filled with thousands of wading birds pecking the sand, looking for their breakfast.

Leaving Chalkida behind us, we started the climb up the mountain and soon entered a pine forest. Most of its trees had containers strapped to their trunks; some were buckets, others were just bags, and they all held a milky liquid. They were harvesting pine resin. This is done by making a cut in the bark, which sets off a type of defence mechanism whereby the tree will try to heal the wound by directing its sap to that point. The resin then drips out, slowly but continuously. The harvesters sometimes leave the containers in place for years to gather the sap. There are now more modern methods for extracting this valuable commodity, but Greeks have been doing it this way for centuries, so why rush. The resin is sold and used for flavouring the national wine, retsina, or as the essence for the production of perfumes and essential oils.

The road continued to wind its way higher and higher up the mountain. We stopped at the summit to admire the view. Behind us and far below was the city of Chalkida, with the sun glistening off the calm waters beyond. Ahead of us was an ocean of green pine trees extending through the valleys as far as we could see. It was cold up there, and I imagined trying to navigate that road in the snow, aided by the metal poles at the sides of the road to mark out the highway in the event of snow-drifts. In the distance was a white-topped mountain, but it was springtime and that was not snow but white marble that we were looking at.

As we followed the serpentine road down the other side, flowers began to dot the grass verges between the trees. We started to notice multi-coloured beehives in every clearing until we were passing blocks of hundreds bunched together, creating miniature villages along the side of the valley. We didn't see another vehicle for the next hour, but we had to drive carefully as it wasn't unusual to round a bend and be met by a herd of goats standing nonchalantly in the middle of the road, chewing away. They all wore bells around their necks, on leather collars, and after giving us accusing looks for having disturbed their peace, they would trot off into the pine forest, accompanied by a symphony of tinkling as they went. We saw no sign of the island's eponymous oxen, however – its name, Evia, literally meaning the land of well-fed oxen.

An hour later we entered a small village called Prokopi and were surprised to see a line of coaches parked end to end and displaying the name of tour operators from all over Greece. This had to be a famous village to attract so much tourism, especially being so remote. We stopped to explore. A huge off-white church stood proudly at the end of the village square and all around the perimeter were a selection of tavernas and coffee bars, with tables and chairs spread across the pavement. Shops displayed a selection of religious icons as well as bags of multi-coloured pasta, sweet nougat and ornate walking sticks hanging from bright canopies.

The cool air of the village carried with it the wonderful smell of roasting lamb and my mouth began to water. We followed our noses to the taverna in question, and got chatting to the owner. It surprised him that we'd never heard of the village, which he said was perhaps the best-known pilgrimage destination for Orthodox Christians.

Within Prokopi's church lay the body of St John the Russian. Born in around 1690 in what is now Ukraine, John fought for Peter the Great in the Russo-Turkish war, was taken captive by the Turks and sold as a slave to a Muslim master in the village of Prokopion in what is now central Anatolia. Despite being abused by his captors, John resisted their orders to convert to Islam, remained devoutly Christian, and was credited with performing several miracles. After his death in 1730, he was given a Christian burial there; three years later, a priest in the village had a dream that John's body was still intact, which turned out to be true. He became venerated as a saint by Orthodox Christians living in central Anatolia, most of whom were ethnically Greek, and over the next hundred years many miracles were attributed to St John the Russian. When in 1924 the Greek population of Turkey was expelled during the dying days of the Ottoman Empire, they brought the relics of St John the Russian to Greece with them, to the island of Evia.

There are some amazing entries in the records of the recent miracles performed by St John the Russian. They include multiple healings of extremely sick people. It is said that St

John has a special love for children, and pilgrims from all over the world visit to ask for his blessing. Of all the miracles performed through the saint's prayers, the most striking is the number of people with cancer who have been healed.

It is not only the Orthodox Greeks that receive help from St John. In 1998 the baby daughter of a young family of Orthodox Muscovites was diagnosed with blood cancer. For the first few years of her life, both she and her mother rarely left the hospital. The whole family prayed for the girl, but despite trying every possible treatment, she was dying. As a last resort, the parents were advised to try a bone-marrow transplant, an operation that would cost tens of thousands of dollars. The search for sponsors began, but it proved impossible raise the full amount. The parents went to ask for advice from the father at the Holy Trinity, the spiritual centre of the Russian Orthodox Church, about seventy kilometres from Moscow. Father Kirill recommended that the couple use the money raised to take their sick daughter to Evia and pray there to St John the Russian.

The family stayed on Evia for several days, ordering prayer services for their daughter's health. At their request, the priest opened the reliquary so that they could position the sick girl on the relics of St John. At this point, the child began to feel much better. And then a genuine miracle happened. Upon returning home, the girl's tests showed that she had been healed of her illness.

After lunch, we crossed the road to visit the church ourselves. We lit a few candles and put some coins into the collection tray, then joined the queue to pay our respects to the saint. He was lying in a casket with a glass top. A golden mask covered half his face. One arm showed, the other was hidden in the folds of a blue satin gown. He looked peaceful. I glanced over at Alex. She had tears streaming down her face and was sobbing quietly.

We hadn't realised that Prokopi was one of the most beautiful areas not only of Evia but of the whole of Greece. We had stumbled across this incredible place by accident. We drove on through the valley alongside a fast-running river with willows dipping their branches into the crystal-clear water, a highly unusual sight in Greece. Small trout were dancing in the water, some jumping to catch flies. The river disappeared around a bend where a grey heron was sitting on a rock, looking for his lunch. As we stood in the cool green forest staring into the sparkling river, we felt at peace with the world. We could have stayed there for another hour, but we'd forgotten the reason for our trip and needed to get ourselves back on track because we had a deadline to get our marble.

Alex called Milos's brother from the car. As it was Saturday, the yard was closed, but he had agreed to open up especially for us. An hour later we arrived at the rusty metal gates leading to his yard. A smiling man beckoned us inside and introduced himself as Demitri. We followed him in, past large slabs of raw marble upended in racks, piles of dusty cutting equipment and aged forklift trucks scattered across the open space.

Demitri had already assembled a selection of pink tiles for us to choose from. These ranged from almost white to shades of dark red. Alex pointed at a deeper pink stone with veins of grey threading through it. 'Can I see that one?' she asked.

Demitri left the office and returned with two matching tiles and laid them on the desk. They looked beautiful. Alex took them one by one off the desk and laid them on the floor. We both stood back and admired the pattern and unusual colour. We both agreed that these were the ones for us. Now it was crunch time. They looked expensive, and we didn't want to get too excited until we were sure we could afford them. We cautiously asked the price.

Demitri thought about it. 'I will do a special deal for you,' he said. 'Fifteen euros a metre.'

Not wishing to push our luck, I asked how much it would cost to deliver.

'That's including delivery. I have a shipment going to Athens on Monday, so I will send it at the same time.'

I wanted to kiss him, but Alex beat me to it. So I just shook his hand. Our dream had come true. We had secured the marble at a fabulous price, and Milos would fit it for us, all within a timeframe that would avoid us holding up the building progress.

We had booked into a hotel near the marble yard in the village of Pefki and were so pleased with our deal that we asked if Demetri would join us for a meal later. He accepted and suggested a fish taverna in Elinika. I made a point of insisting that we would pay, and he waved his hand in agreement. We followed him there, through the never-ending pine forest until we reached a small village spread over a hilltop. It was idyllic. The white houses were built into the side of the hill in a series of steps, nestled among pine trees and fruit orchards, their red-tiled roofs glowing in the late-afternoon sunshine. Demitri turned down a narrow track towards the sea and just shy off the beach pulled into a small yard behind a house. I looked around but couldn't see a restaurant or any signs for one, but Demitri was already out of his truck and waving for us to follow.

We walked down three steps and through a blue door. Ahead of us was a spacious area with wooden tables and chairs with blue tablecloths and a vase of flowers on each. A smiling lady came out of the kitchen and kissed Demitri on the cheek. He introduced us. She kissed Alex and shook my hand and led us through the restaurant and onto the large balcony terrace.

The view took my breath away. I stood at the wall and my eyes lapped up the panorama. Below us through the trees was a narrow sandy beach, then the sea, with some small boats at anchor. The water was so clear, they looked to be floating in air. A little further out there was a small green island with a church perched on the top. It was only about two hundred metres away, so the details were clear. The church was Agios Nikolaos. It had pure white walls, a white bell tower, and a dark red roof. A path led from the water up a few steps to the entrance. The only way to visit would be to swim the short distance from the beach. A little further out to sea was a slightly larger island in the shape of a turtle covered in pine trees, where the only land showing was a white, rocky perimeter. In the distance, over the flat calm Aegean Sea, was the island of Skiathos. I had visited many beautiful places in my life, but this was by far the most incredible view I had ever seen.

The owner took a seat next to Alex and introduced herself as Helen. She told us about a nice selection of fish that her husband had caught that day and asked us to follow her to the kitchen to see them. Lying on a bed of ice in a refrigerated drawer was a selection of silver and red fish, all looking fresh and smelling of the sea. We chose a few of the silver ones, ordered a salad, fries and some vegetables and returned to our seats while she cooked our meal.

The food was delicious and was complemented by the ice-cold homemade white wine that just kept coming in small tin jugs. We sat and chatted to Demitri about our building in Glyfada, Helen finished in the kitchen and came to join the conversation. Her husband finished cleaning the kitchen and came over too. Helen had inherited the restaurant from her mother and now ran it with her husband and two daughters. As with most businesses in Greece, it was a family concern. She was the cook, her husband provided the fish, and their daughters were the waiters. Business was good. I asked Helen if many tourists visited.

'Only in August we get a few,' she replied. 'The rest of the year it's locals like Demitri.'

I couldn't help thinking that if more tourists knew about this delightful place, they would be famous, but perhaps they preferred it this way. They made a living, had time to get to know their clients, and didn't lead a stressful life.

Slowly the light faded, and I asked Helen for the bill. She apologised and told me that Demitri had asked her not to accept money from me, as we were his guests and he would deal with it later. I pushed a tip into her hand and we left our new friends, assuring them that we would return soon.

Two days later, our marble arrived in Glyfada. We watched as it was offloaded from the truck in large wooden crates. Alex telephoned Milos, who would send his technicians the next day to put it in place and polish it.

The following day, we stayed away from the site. We didn't want to get in their way and preferred to see the floor only once it had been completed. We spent our day aimlessly wandering around Athens, but our minds were still on the works at home. Late in the afternoon we could resist no longer. Alex called Milos to ask how it was going. She ended the conversation, looked at me with a big smile and told me they'd finished it. We could wait no longer. We had to see it.

We got almost to the top of the stairs to our apartment and looked ahead. There it was in all its glory. It looked like glass. As we stepped onto the marble, it shone. The tiles had been laid so snugly there were no gaps in between and the polishing had made it look like one continuous slab of marble, with no joins visible. The only clue that it wasn't one giant piece was the fact that the grain on each tile differed slightly, and this simply added to the beauty of this floor. It was perfect.

Stavros appeared. He'd watched the floor being laid and grudgingly agreed that it was nice. But he complained that he now had to cover it during the rest of the work, to prevent it from getting dirty or scratched. We didn't care. We had our floor.

We headed off to Milos's yard, to thank him and pay him. He was outside his office chatting to one of his workers. When he saw us, he waved and smiled. 'Follow me,' he said. 'I have a present for you.'

He had heard from his brother on Evia we were thinking of a marble coffee table to match our floor. We walked with him around the side of his office, and there stood a large slice of pink marble which matched our floor exactly. It was roughly triangular in shape and was sparkling in the afternoon sunshine. Next to it were three small Greek columns. We would place these at each corner to support the slab. It was such a thoughtful gift, and we didn't know how to thank him.

The kindness of Greek people never ceases to surprise me. We had set out to buy some marble, had accidentally stumbled on the most beautiful village in Greece on the most beautiful island, had made new lifelong friends and realised our dream. Life was good.

# 19

## BLOOD-RED EASTER EGGS AND SPIT-ROASTED LAMB

I t was Easter Week, the beginning of one of the most important periods in Greece. Traditionally, we always celebrated this seven-day festival with our extended family; it's a time full of different rituals that allow Greeks to mourn the loss of Jesus Christ and to contemplate his life and celebrate his rebirth. This year, however, we were living in a temporary flat above a shop, and Debbie and Zissis had remained in the UK, so Alex and I would have a scaled-down Easter. We would still do the visits to the church and get involved in the village traditions, but it wouldn't be the same without the family. We promised ourselves that we would hold an even bigger celebration next year, once our new home was finished and the family was back together.

The religious observances for Easter actually start forty-eight days prior to Easter Sunday, with Kathari Deftera – Clean Monday or Pure Monday. This marks the beginning of Lent and is sometimes also known as Ash Monday, just as Ash Wednesday is the first day of Lent in Western Christianity. The Orthodox Church in some countries, including Greece, calculates the date for Easter according to the Julian rather than the Gregorian calendar, which means that Greek Easter is usually a week or two later than the UK celebration. The Julian calendar was brought into effect by Julius Caesar in 45 BC and remained in common usage until Pope Gregory authorised revisions in 1582 in light of advances in astronomy whereby the length of the solar year was calculated even more precisely; the revised Gregorian calendar was adopted in Great Britain in 1752.

Clean Monday begins with a special service in which all present bow down before one another and ask for forgiveness. In this way, people can start Lent with a clean conscience. It's a public holiday, celebrated with outdoor excursions, family picnics, the traditional flying of kites and a meal of shellfish and other fasting food. Eating meat, eggs and dairy products is forbidden to Orthodox Christians throughout Lent, with fish being eaten only on major feast days, but shellfish are allowed; Debbie maintained that this was because shellfish don't have red blood and are therefore pure.

Not all Greeks observe the fasting. The Church grants dispensation for manual labourers, soldiers and sailors. Although Debbie observed most of the Orthodox protocols, she refrained from eating meat or dairy only on Good Friday and part of Easter Saturday. She laughingly told me that she enjoyed being fat and needed her strength so could not afford the weight loss.

Alex tends to be a little stricter. She refrains from eating meat but still eats dairy products and fish. One year, she and I decided to observe the fast together. We vowed to cut out all dairy produce and meat for the required forty days. I was commuting to England for work at the time, returning to Glyfada every weekend. After a few days in England, I was suffering. I replaced my morning cappuccino from Starbucks with a strong black coffee without sugar. Although I tried, I could not get to like it. I had no idea what to eat. Beans on toast was just not the same without butter on the bread, so I decided to explore the local takeaways. I knew that I was allowed to eat octopus and calamari, but McDonald's didn't sell that, so I settled for a nut burger. It was disgusting, so I threw it in the bin and ordered a Big Mac. I telephoned Alex to confess. She laughed as she owned up to having broken the fast too. She missed cheese and just could not drink coffee without milk. That weekend I arrived in Athens and took the family to Vari for barbecued pork and kokoretsi; we could always try fasting again the following year.

Before Lent begins, however, there is carnival: one last chance to enjoy ourselves before the fasting starts. The best place to do this is in Patras, the main port for ferries to Italy, around 230 kilometres northwest of Glyfada. The city hosts one of the largest carnivals in the world, attracting almost half a million visitors every year during the season, which runs from 17 January until the Sunday before Clean Monday. The festival originated in ancient Greece and has since been much influenced by Venetian customs, thanks to the city's proximity to Italy. The tradition of dressing up comes from the practice of women wearing masks to hide their identity. The Greeks took this a step further. Now everyone dresses up.

The first time Alex and I went to carnival, Alex decided that she would dress as an Amazon warrior – highly appropriate, we agreed, given that, like Alex, the Amazons were famed for their aggression and brutality, with their primary concern in life being war. She decreed that I would dress as Conan the Barbarian. As we had no chance of finding a hotel, we'd planned to sleep in the car. This had presented problems with getting into our costumes, but we managed. Alex looked magnificent: slim and very sexy in her short leather skirt. After touching up her own make-up, she turned her attention to mine. She wanted to paint black flashes across my face to make me appear macho and fit the part of Conan the Barbarian. I sat patiently as she got to work but had no idea how I looked as the car mirror had recently fallen off my old Citroen and I hadn't had time to replace it.

I pulled on my platinum-blonde wig borrowed from Alex's beauty salon and we set off to join the festivities. The atmosphere in the crowded streets was lively. Thousands of people were dancing to loud, thumping music outside bars and filling main squares, all wearing colourful costumes and having a great time. A procession of decorated flatbed lorries passed us, decked out with statues of ancient Greek gods, Disney characters and replicas of wooden ships and fishing boats. It was a beautiful and exotic mix of cultures. There were troops of marching bands, and children representing their schools, all dressed in matching outfits. Then came the float bearing the effigy of the king of the carnival, bidding farewell to his subjects on his way to the harbour, where he would be sent out to sea and set alight to mark the end of the celebration and the start of Lent. The king is always a representation of evil and a hated figure. Sometimes it's an effigy of Judas, but it can also be an unpopular politician or an enemy of the country. The figure is usually portrayed with sharp teeth, an enormous nose and a long tail and is surrounded by smaller monstrous creatures. It's meant to reflect all the 'crimes' of the country.

As I stood watching the procession, I received a lot of attention from passing revellers. Some blew kisses in my direction, others grabbed my bottom and squeezed it before walking away with a smile on their faces. I looked at Alex. She was giggling, her eyes wet with tears. She'd been watching and relishing the reactions I was getting. It took me a long time to cotton on, but finally I realised why she'd taken such a long time painting my face earlier. I rushed over to a nearby shop window to try and catch my reflection. It confirmed my suspicions. Staring back at me was not a warlike barbarian with black flashes, but a pantomime dame with dark blue eye shadow, bright red lipstick and deep pink blusher, further enhanced by the blond wig. I had spent the afternoon walking around proudly, assuming I resembled Arnold Schwarzenegger, whereas I actually resembled one of my more eccentric aunties.

Towards the end of Lent, during the daytime on Holy (or Great) Thursday, equivalent to Maundy Thursday, the traditional Easter bread, tsoureki, is baked. This is made from a sweet yeast dough of flour, sugar, butter, orange peel, tree resin (mastika) and milk, with several hardboiled eggs, dyed red in honour of Easter, pressed into the top. The red eggs represent the blood of Christ and remind us of the renewal of life. For the rest of that day, it's common to see people wandering around with red fingers, having dipped them into the coloured water to retrieve the eggs. On Easter Sunday, everyone in the household takes a red egg each, holds it in their hand and allows the person next to them to tap it with theirs while saying 'Christos anesti' (Christ has risen). The person with the strongest, uncracked egg wins. The eggs are then eaten as part of the meal.

Holy Thursday commemorates the day of the Last Supper. Church services include a symbolic representation of the Crucifixion, and the period of mourning begins. In most villages, people will stay in church throughout the night, in traditional mourning.

Most Greeks do not cook on Holy Friday. If they do, it will be simple food that can be boiled in water. Alex always cooks a cauldron of plain lentils, representing the tears of Christ, which are shared with the family. This is the day to remember the Crucifixion, and the overwhelming feeling in the home is of sadness. In the morning, flowers are taken to the church to decorate the epitaphios, the symbolic bier of Christ, which bears his image; the bier will be at the heart of the Service of Lamentation that evening, which mourns the death of Christ. The crucial events begin after the sun goes down, when everyone in the village makes their way to the church holding brown candles in small paper cups to protect the flame from the breeze. This ritual happens in every village in Greece and is observed by everyone, young or old.

Two years earlier, Debbie, Alex and I had celebrated Easter together for the last time in the old house, Zissis being away working on a cruise ship in the Caribbean. On Holy Friday, we arrived at the church, which was full to overflowing. Crowds of people stood outside in the courtyard waiting for the priests to appear while the church bell tolled intermittently to announce Christ's death. After a while, the priests and bishops exited the church, the priests dressed in black and the bishops in pure white robes with gold embroidery and golden crowns. They were followed by the epitaphios, a litter bearing the symbolic body of Christ. This was about the size of a single bed; its base and sides were covered in sweet-smelling lilies, stocks and carnations, and it had a flowered dome and a cross on top. Four volunteers had been given the honour of carrying it on their shoulders, one at each corner.

More priests followed as the procession lined up behind the village band, which comprised the local scout troop, all of them in uniform and holding an assortment of instruments. A drum beat rhythmically as the trumpets, trombones and baritone horns started to play sad music. As usual, the band was noticeably out of tune, which made me think of the opening scene of *The Godfather*. Alex poked me in the ribs when I reminded her about the film as she tried not to giggle. After all, this was a sad occasion and levity had no place. But I told her that some people really do laugh during funerals, as a way of expressing grief. If this band had played at the funerals I'd attended, mourners would have been rolling in the aisles.

We villagers followed behind the band, the priests and the epitaphios, holding our candles as we walked, listening to the mournful music as we reflected on our sadness and grief. Across the country, entire villages would have been doing exactly the same as we were, carrying their candles in silence.

Together we processed slowly around the village and then for a short distance along the main road before turning and heading back to the church. All traffic was held up for the duration, and drivers stepped out of their cars with their heads bowed as we passed. Back at the church, some of the faithful remained there with the epitaphios through the night, holding a vigil and praying.

The next day, preparations for the Easter feast began, ready for Sunday's celebration of the Resurrection. Most families in Greece cook a whole lamb for this, and we were no exception. This is traditionally a job for the head of the family, but as Zissis was away, it fell to me, as the man of the house, to take it on.

Like most men, I love playing with fire, but my barbecue experience had so far only encompassed grilling a few sausages on a warm day, and maybe a hamburger or two. The prospect of cooking a whole twenty-five-kilogram lamb was therefore a little worrying, but I was keen to give it a go.

The rickety old barbecue had been sitting beneath a tarpaulin under a plum tree in the garden since the previous Easter. It was just a large rusty tin box on four iron legs, with some notched steel bars protruding above the box and a black oily bicycle chain wrapped around them. Slotted into the chain was a selection of two-metre-long steel skewers with forks threaded onto them to secure the meat in place. To the side of the box was an old stained motor with a wire and plug dangling down. This was unlike any barbecue I had ever seen, but although it was ancient and wobbly, it looked functional.

We cleared away the cobwebs and gave it a good hose down, and once dried it looked quite respectable. Alex took one end and I took the other, and together we manoeuvred it up the back staircase to the patio. Once in position, I plugged in the motor to test the system. It whirred into life. The steel skewers turned at a slow rate, I put my hand on the rotating metal and felt the power of the motor. It was certainly strong enough to turn a lamb, so we were ready.

The next thing on the list was to get the lamb. We went off to the central meat market in Athens to choose one. I had done nothing like this in Greece before, and hoped that the lamb would not be one of the ones that was still wandering around. I would never be able to slaughter it myself, in which case we'd likely end up with sausages and a disappointed family.

The meat market was a collection of small independent traders all lined up separately around the perimeter. It smelled of raw meat and sawdust and was pleasantly cool. Porters were pushing carts up and down the central aisle and yelling at people that were too slow to move out of their way. Vendors screamed out their prices and assured us that their produce was the best. They all seemed to be selling the same thing, lamb, and all of these were thankfully prepared and skinned and ready to cook.

Even so, it felt like the lambs were watching me in an accusing manner with their wide-open eyes as I browsed the stalls in search of my victim. I tried to avoid their lifeless gaze and asked one of the butchers to take down and weigh a plump-looking animal hanging near the counter. This came in at just over twenty-five kilograms, a little more than we needed, but it looked good, so I handed over the payment and he packed it into a large bin bag with its head sticking out of the top. Alex suggested that while we were there, we should also buy some intestines and other lamb innards for kokoretsi, which we would cook on the charcoal at the same time as the lamb.

Our car was small, so the lamb didn't fit into the boot. I squeezed it onto the back seat and left its legs hanging out of the window. Back at the house, Debbie was in a flurry of activity, cutting vegetables for Russian salad and making filo pastry for a cheese pie. Bubbling in a saucepan there was a concoction of offal, lettuce, onions and dill for the making of the customary mayiritsa soup, to which would be added the organs and intestines of the lamb. We would eat this after the midnight service. The idea is that a bowl of mayiritsa soup protects your stomach and eases you gently back into eating proper food after your forty days of meatless fasting. The soup is a vegetarian's nightmare. The first time I tried it, my face went greener than the soup. But, always happy to embrace the traditions of my adopted family, I have since made sure to develop a taste for it.

I spent the afternoon creating the kokoretsi ready for the barbecue the following day. This task I was not enjoying. I had already threaded the chunks of heart, lung, spleen, kidney and other unidentified organs onto the skewer but was now struggling with a large bucket of water containing the tangled and slippery mess of intestines, which kept tying themselves in knots and refused to be pulled out of the bucket in suitable lengths without breaking. Finally, after an hour of mummifying the offal inside the greasy innards, I was done. These kokoretsi looked nothing like the perfect specimens I had seen in restaurants, but they would have to do. I took them into the house and wrapped them up in wet towels with the whole lamb ready for cooking tomorrow.

This was Holy (or Great) Saturday and we were looking forward to tonight's celebration. We'd already watched the television footage of the arrival of the eternal flame. As always, it was brought out of Christ's tomb in Jerusalem by an Orthodox bishop, then flown to Greece by the national airline, to be distributed to waiting priests who carried it to their local churches, including ours. Now, as midnight approached, it was time to join the rest of our village and return to the church for the midnight Service of the Resurrection.

Everyone who is able to do so attends this service, including children, and this was as true of Glyfada as everywhere else. We took with us our white Easter candles, called labatha, made especially for this celebration. Everyone brings a labatha with them; parents and godparents often give labatha to children as gifts, sometimes decorated with favourite storybook characters.

As always, the crowds were so big that the church filled up fast and many people had to gather outside. Anticipation mounted. Shortly before midnight, all lights were extinguished, and the church was illuminated only by the flicker of the eternal flame on the altar. It was beautifully atmospheric. Then the clock struck midnight and the priest called out 'Christos anesti' (Christ is risen) and passed the flame, the light of the Resurrection, to the person nearest him, to light their labatha. The flame was then passed from person to person. Before long, the church and courtyard were glowing with candlelight.

All the sadness had now been forgotten, and the celebrations began. The night air was alive with the singing of the Byzantine chant 'Christos anesti' as friends and neighbours exchanged the ritual kiss of peace, said 'Christos anesti' to each other as a way of wishing them well and replied 'Alithos anesti' (Truly, he is risen') or 'Alithinos o Kyrios' (True is the Lord). The church bells began ringing nonstop and great bursts of fireworks were released into the sky. We headed home for our long-awaited midnight feast, starting with the green soup.

Easter Sunday dawned. It was time for me to cook the lamb and kokoretsi.

Having worked briefly in a butcher's shop, I was not a complete novice in meat preparation. I had experience in cutting and knew which bits belonged where, but cooking it was a mystery. I loaded the tin barbecue with charcoal and a pack of firelighters and set it ablaze. Meanwhile, I threaded the lamb onto the long steel skewer and tightened up the forks. It looked good. I lifted it over the hot coals, secured the skewer to the black bicycle chain and switched on the motor. To my delight, it turned.

I pulled up a chair and watched as the roasting began. I was feeling pleased with myself, but then the noise started. On every rotation, the middle of the lamb rose when it reached the top of the arc and with a loud thump then dropped away from the spit. Something was wrong.

I took everything off the fire and studied the partially cooked body on the table in front of me. I worked it out. As the lamb cooked, it shrank and become floppy. Although I had secured each end of the lamb, I had omitted to tie the middle. I found some wire, wrapped it around the body and twisted it tight. Back on the spit, it looked okay and was turning without the thumps. But after a few more moments, there was a grinding sound as the beast split into two halves, which continued to wrap themselves around the spit before dropping off into the charcoal. The wire that I had wrapped around the lamb had cut through the whole thing and severed it.

Both halves were now on fire and burning in the inferno, with the flames being fed by the fat running out of the lamb. I was in big trouble. Debbie and Alex had trusted me with the job of cooking the most important meal of the year; I had assured them that I was up to the task and that they shouldn't worry about anything. But I was now looking at our half-cremated lunch and desperately trying to drag it out of the barbecue.

After suffering several mild third-degree burns, I recovered all the charred, smoking lamb remnants. These were now in front of me on the table. I admitted defeat and sheepishly went downstairs to break the news to the family. Alex and Debbie were waiting for me with grins on their faces. They had heard the commotion and the swearing and had been expecting me. I began to explain, but Debbie cut me off.

'Did the lamb fall into the fire?' she asked knowingly.

Embarrassed, I nodded.

They both laughed. 'Don't worry,' Alex said, 'that always happens.'

Relieved that my father-in-law was just as inept as me at

seasonal lamb cooking, I accompanied them back to the terrace to discuss the next step. We decided on the solution that they had used the previous year, which was to cut the animal into chunks and line these up on the spit individually. Once we'd finished, it looked nothing like a lamb, more like some sort of mutation found in black lagoons. We added the kokoretsi to the barbecue and all sat back to watch. A few hours later it was ready. It tasted wonderful, and together with the other dishes prepared by Debbie, turned out to be the best meal I'd ever eaten. Friends and family arrived to join us, and to a backdrop of Greek music we all continued chatting, eating, and drinking wine in the sunshine and then on into the evening, until the sun sank below the horizon.

Easter may be the primary celebration in Greece, but religion is central to many other aspects of Greek culture. As in the old Glyfada house, most homes will have a dedicated prayer corner with an icon or two, and likely a cross as well as an oil burner with a flame constantly flickering. Greeks will always cross themselves when passing a church and will always light a candle and kiss the icon when they enter one.

Priests seem to have more power than politicians and influence a large proportion of laws and regulations. And yet, if you see a priest in the street, it's considered to be bad luck. Alex and I were wandering through Athens one day when we noticed that a priest was walking towards us. 'Quick, grab your balls,' Alex said.

This seemed a strange command. But the convention is that you should turn and run away, holding your testicles. This harks back to when Christianity took hold of the ancient Greek world. There was widespread destruction of Hellenic nude statues, especially their genitals; the early Christians broke off the penis and testicles from every sculpture. After that, whenever ethnic Greeks saw a priest coming, they would tell each other to hold on to their balls. When Alex and I were on the island of Tinos, making our pilgrimage to the hilltop Panagia Evangelistria, there were so many priests around, my hand never left my crotch during the entire visit. Priests all over the world are greeted in so many different ways, so presumably Greek priests are used to this by now.

Every Greek knows all the saints' days, of which there are many. They are always observed in conjunction with other events and seem to crop up almost monthly, justifying a public holiday. Many of these are cleverly scheduled on a Wednesday. As this is in the middle of the week, there's not much point in going to work on the Monday or Tuesday, and Thursday and Friday will need to be taken as days off, to recover. So a day's national holiday will usually turn into a week's holiday. After all, the Greek word for work, douleiá, also means slavery.

In the UK, things have changed. We need to reflect on the demise of our own culture and think about what brings meaning to our lives. Some traditions bind us to each other and should be shared. I have adopted the Greek way of life and sometimes look back with sadness at my home country, where this has been lost. I'm not suggesting that we grab our private bits every time we encounter a religious leader, as this will likely get us all arrested. Or that we copy the Greek system of having a week off to celebrate every saint's day. But it would be good to know why it is we have that long weekend off in the spring. A hot-cross bun and a chocolate Easter egg do not make up for losing sight of our cultural heritage. In the UK, we pride ourselves on our multi-cultural society. Each religion adds to the fabulous spectrum of our evolving culture. It's okay to celebrate Ramadan, it's fine to be part of the Jewish celebration of Yom Kippur. Many Hindus in the country share Diwali, the festival of light, every year and we all join in. The Greeks do not care what religion you are. They are happy to include anyone that wants to come. Why not use the Greek example and bring some meaning back to Easter?

## 20

## BLOODSUCKERS ON KEA

We were deep into our plans to use classical Greek architecture as a theme for our interior decoration and keen to gather ideas. The Acropolis being a sore point, as most of it was sitting in the British Museum, I was trying to steer attention away from that embarrassment and look elsewhere for inspiration. Alex suggested that we visit the famous temple in Sounion, which was not far away.

It was a warm sunny morning as we drove south along the coast road from Glyfada. The beaches were already getting busy and the sea was filling with inflatable toys and early swimmers. We passed Agia Marina and then continued along the rocky shoreline of the bright blue Aegean. It was a lovely route as we were never out of sight of the sea.

An hour later, we arrived at the Temple of Poseidon and made straight for the cafeteria, where we sat sipping coffee near the cliff edge while Alex relayed the story of King Aegeus, who, according to Greek mythology, threw himself into the sea from those very rocks. Aegeus's son Theseus had left for Crete on a mission to kill the Minotaur. Aegeus had told him to hoist white sails on his ship when returning home if he'd been successful and had killed the Minotaur. If the Minotaur had killed him, then Theseus's army was to hoist black sails instead. Theseus, however, forgot these instructions, even though he had been victorious over the Minotaur. When Aegeus saw the black sails coming into view, he believed that his son had died; stricken with grief, he committed suicide by jumping off the rocks into the sea. This area of the Mediterranean, the stretch of sea located between Greece in the west, Turkey in the east and the island of Crete to the south, now carries the unfortunate king's name.

The temple looked like a smaller version of the Parthenon. Its marble base was studded with golden-hued columns that towered into the air against a perfect backdrop of clear blue sky and shimmering water. I would have loved to have walked among the columns and touched the stone, but the temple was fenced off. This may have been because of all the people who'd carved their names into the stone, leaving a trail of ancient graffiti. Lord Byron was one of them. He inscribed his name at the base of one of the stones when he visited during his grand tour. But the Greeks forgave him for that act of vandalism after he assisted them in their struggle for independence against the Ottoman Turks. He writes about his trip to the temple in his poem 'The Isles of Greece'.

We walked around the temple. I was as fascinated by the panoramic view as by the ruins themselves. We were standing in our lofty position, gazing down on the land and sea surrounding us. Out to sea there were a few tiny, uninhabited islands, but a little further out, to the east, was a larger one. If I squinted, I could make out the shape of buildings. 'I think that might be Kea,' Alex said uncertainly. Neither of us knew anything about it, and nor it turned out did the cafe owner, but we did discover that the nearby port ran ferries to the island every couple of hours. That was all the incentive we needed.

A short ferry ride later, we landed on Kea. The first thing I noticed were the strange shapes around the mountains. Every hillside had been terraced, creating a vast series of stepped fields, and this was true of the entire island. It was as if every mountain and hill was surrounded by hoops. The island had no naturally flat land on which to grow crops, so terracing provided islanders with level surfaces and prevented the valuable soil from washing away. The scale of this undertaking was immense and would have taken many generations to complete; doubtless it continued to take a lot of effort to maintain. The main crop was acorns, which had long been central to the island's economy. For centuries, acorns were used as a raw material in the tanneries; nowadays they're ground into flour for biscuits.

Kea is only about nineteen kilometres long and nine kilometres wide, with a population of around two thousand. Its main town, Ioulis, is built into the side of a hill and is out of bounds to cars, so we parked outside it and ambled up. Everywhere we walked involved either climbing steps or descending them. Most of the whitewashed houses had blue shutters and they all had red-tiled roofs. There was an overwhelming feeling of peace to the place, and the air smelled fresh, laced with the scent of sideritis (ironwort), used to make mountain tea, and oregano.

We found a small taverna along one of the narrow streets and sat at a table outside on the cobbled road. We asked the owner what was on the menu.

'Sausages,' he replied.

'Anything else?'

'No, just sausages. But we have lots of different ones. And we also have salads, cheese pie, fried cheese, chips and boiled vegetables.'

This was a sausage taverna. We had never heard of such a thing and were interested to try out the selection. The interior was lined with racks and racks of many-coloured sausages. We asked for a meze of different ones, just to try. They were all delicious, as was the local wine. It wasn't an enormous meal, but we felt full and needed to walk a little. So we set about exploring the village. It was delightful.

As we turned a corner, the road opened into a small square with a cafeteria and tables dotted around. There was an ancient Greek theme to its decor, notably at the entrance, with its pair of columns to either side and a triangular pediment spanning the top, and in the ornate plasterwork surrounding the window, which had been made to look like marble with carvings of Greek Olympians running, wrestling and jumping.

While Alex went inside to see further designs, I sat enjoying my ice cream and staring over the top of the terracotta roofs at the valley and the sea beyond. There was not a sound. No persistent rumble of traffic, no buzzing of air conditioners. Even the birds had ceased their chatter. I was wondering what it would be like to live in that magical village and wake up to the views and silence every day when Alex interrupted my dream and asked me to come inside as she wanted to show me something.

My eyes quickly adjusted to the dim interior. Alex pointed to the columns lining the walls. In between the columns, the walls had been covered with pink marble. This was the exact colour and pattern of the floor tiles recently laid in our new home. It looked great but would cost us a fortune to replicate. Alex smiled at me. The owner winked at her and nodded. 'It's not marble.' Alex laughed. 'It's paint.'

I held out my hand and touched the wall. It felt warm and not at all like marble.

'It's Venetian stock,' said the owner.

He explained that this was a painting technique designed to give the illusion of marble; it was commonly employed in Venetian palaces, he said. I was impressed. But if lining our walls with marble would be expensive, hand-painting the same walls would likely cost us more, and where would we find a craftsman with the ability to do it?

Alex was still smiling, as was the owner. They were obviously sharing a joke. Alex introduced me to her new friend, whose name was Adonis. He explained that his son had painted the walls and was a student at an art college in Athens; for a little pocket money, he would do our walls for us too.

The cafeteria was empty, so Adonis took away our ice-cream bowls and replaced them with a bottle of ouzo and a bucket of ice. He put three glasses on the table and half-filled each of them before sitting down to discuss his suggestions for our apartment. Alex was keen on entire walls being painted with the Venetian stock, but Adonis counselled against this as it would make the room feel dark and smaller. He recommended just using it to make a feature. After a few ouzos and an exchange of ideas, Alex finally settled on painting only our semi-circular chimney breast with the stock to match the floors. As the chimney would be the main focal point in the living area, this made sense. We would also paint the bathroom ceiling to mimic a blue sky with puffy clouds. It was all agreed. Adonis's son Nick would come to Glyfada tomorrow to make the deal.

It was getting late. I'd forgotten how many glasses of ouzo I'd consumed. Judging by the fuzziness of my vision, it was probably too many. It was unusual for Alex to drink, but she liked ouzo and had sipped two measures, so she didn't feel that she should drive either. We hadn't planned on staying away from Athens for the night, but here we were. Alex asked Adonis if there was a hotel or guest house within walking distance. Luckily, he had a room that he rented to visitors in the summer and it happened to be unoccupied that night, so problem solved.

He led us away from the square and along a narrow passage to a blue door with a small window at the top. The paint was flaking and a huge red bougainvillea had grown up the wall and around the frame. He opened the door and flung back the shutters. Light flooded in. It was like a brown cave. The walls were covered top to bottom in bamboo matting. We looked up. The ceiling was also covered in bamboo. Even the double bed was made of bamboo.

Before settling in, we needed to get a few basics from the local shop. Namely toothbrushes and mosquito repellent. I hate mosquitoes, but they love me. Apart from the brutal Greek bureaucracy, the only thing I dislike about Greece is its blood-sucking monsters who invariably know when I'm around and gang up to have a party. Any bit of exposed flesh gets attacked, bitten and sucked. If I am sitting with my family on a warm summer evening, it's only ever me that's targeted.

Before I go outside into the night air, I cover every inch of skin with super-strength Jungle Formula, which, according to the bottle, protects the wearer from many tropical biting insects as well as scorpions. But the mosquitoes in Greece seem to love it. They probably think it's some spicy sauce to go with their meal. Alex is immune and is sure that I overreact. She seems to ignore the large angry red lumps all over my body and the others on my scalp, hidden under my hair.

There is always someone willing to give me advice on how to avoid being eaten alive. My mother-in-law suggested eating large quantities of garlic. The mosquitoes apparently found this delicious, but no one else would come near me. A friend recommended that I rub basil onto my skin, but I discovered that the local insects preferred green skin, so I gave up on that idea. An old fisherman confided that imbibing large doses of ouzo before bed always did the trick for him. I drank half a bottle of the fiery spirit, passed out and woke up with two huge raw patches on the end of my nose and an intoxicated mosquito lying on the pillow beside me. After a great deal of painful trial and error, I had learned that the only way to get a decent night's sleep without these vampires devouring me was to set up a special burner in the room; this slowly heated a blue tablet that seemed to keep the mosquitoes away.

I was in a panic. I would be sleeping in a bamboo room that offered the bloodsuckers a million places to hide before launching their attack once I'd closed my eyes. Toothpaste was not my priority. I needed a burner and mosquito-repelling tablets. We found the local shop, and I purchased two burners and a jumbo pack of tablets. We got back to the room and I plugged both heaters into the wall and waited to see if I could detect any insects buzzing around. There was no sign of any, but I was convinced they were loitering between the bamboo sticks, biding their time. I decided not to take any chances.

I selected one of the blue pads, pinched it between my finger and thumb and lit it. It burned, releasing a stream of acrid smoke which I wafted around the room. Now it began to rain mosquitoes! I was right. The little buggers had been lurking in the cracks, proboscises watering at the thought of a good meal when the lights went out. Once I'd burned the fourth blue pad, the insects stopped falling. I was having trouble breathing, but that was a small price to pay. Alex couldn't stand the smell and had gone for a walk to allow me to hunt in peace. By the time she returned, there were hundreds of little bodies lying on the stone floor with their skinny legs in the air. I had won.

Adonis's son, Nick, was even more enthusiastic than his father. He wandered around our apartment pointing at walls which would look good painted in his style and suggesting designs for the external balcony. We were not too keen on most of his ideas, and we vetoed his proposal that we have Zeus sitting on a cloud on the bathroom ceiling, which seemed a little pretentious. But we didn't want to dampen his spirits so assured him we would bear his other suggestions in mind once he'd done the chimney breast. He sat on the pink marble floor, looked up at the wall and began planning the design in his head.

We had nearly finished the building. The ceilings had ornate plaster coving that matched the top of the cupboards beautifully and was complemented by similarly styled door architraves and skirting boards. We walked up the grey marble staircase and out onto the roof terrace, waiting a moment until our eyes had adjusted to the intense sunshine. The terrace floor was covered with pale cream cement tiles which would reflect the heat of the sun and help to keep the apartment below cool during the long summer. We stood on the pane of reinforced glass and gazed down at the pink marble floor beneath. It shone in the sunlight. Fancy iron balustrades surrounded the entire deck, allowing us to peer over the edge and appreciate the great height of our apartment block.

In silence we strolled across our rooftop, pivoting to admire the panorama. Most of Athens was, as usual on warm days, shrouded in a haze that served only to magnify the sun's rays and make the city even hotter. The mountains were studded with clumps of greenery, outcrops of white rock and a little church nestling between them, halfway up the slope. Islands dotted the distant blue Aegean, and below us, moored along the harbour wall, was a line of little fishing boats selling their catch.

In our minds, we had already designed our own mini-Acropolis for the terrace, and now we stood back to visualise the effect. This was to be purely a folly and would serve no purpose other than being a huge decorative feature. We would place it at the back of the terrace, with the door from the apartment below opening into it. No roof was planned, only the columns and the frieze, with a triangular pediment at the front, intended to mimic the real Parthenon. We imagined sitting there, transported back to ancient Greece, watching the stars on warm summer evenings and enjoying the views from atop what was now the tallest structure in Glyfada.

We descended the stairs to survey the rest of our domain, in particular our shop, on the ground floor. It was almost complete. They had fitted large plate-glass windows to the side and the front, with a glass door to match, which made the whole place look enormous. A spiral staircase in blue steel connected the shop area with the mezzanine and the basement.

Just as we were completing our tour there was a tap at the shop door. There was Stavros, standing with a man in his early forties wearing a pinstriped suit and red tie and holding a clip-board. This was Michalis, a real-estate agent, Stavros told us.

'Could I have a look around?' Michalis asked. 'I have someone who is interested in renting your shop.'

We readily agreed and removed ourselves across the road for a coffee, keeping our fingers crossed as we left. We watched the two men emerge a few moments later. They stood outside the two shops, had a brief discussion, and then entered Stavros's shop, which was larger.

Within minutes they had joined us at our table and ordered their coffees. Michalis began his pitch. His eyes looked sad as he told us that rental prices were not what they used to be. 'In order to get reliable tenants who will pay their rent regularly, you will have to go low on the rent,' he said sagely. Stavros nodded in agreement. Michalis waited for this to sink in before continuing. His eyes brightened as he suggested a solution. 'The tenant that is taking Stavros's shop is looking to expand and would be most interested in taking yours too.'

Alex looked at me for my reaction. It was not positive.

Stavros chipped in. 'I would collect the rent for you and pay you every month,' he said, before going on to explain how he could remove the central wall and create one big shop.

I could tell that Alex was thinking the same as me. Once all the building work had been completed, we didn't want to continue as business partners with Stavros, and we were both sure that we'd be given only the crumbs from his plate rather than receive our full market share. So we thanked them for the offer and told them we would test the waters ourselves and let them know.

Our shop had not been decorated because any potential tenant would bring their own fitters; it was ready to rent. We didn't really want to use a local agent as we suspected that most of them swam in the same pool as Stavros. So we went to the stationery shop and purchased some big red banners with 'Shop to Rent' written in large bold letters together with a space for our phone number. We fixed them to the inside of the windows with Blu Tack and went to Meat Street for lunch.

As the wine arrived, Alex's phone rang. 'That was someone interested in the shop.' She smiled. 'They are outside now and want to look at it.'

We called over the waiter and asked him to put our lunch on hold, assuring him that we'd be back soon. We turned the corner towards home and there outside our building was a well-dressed couple waiting for us. The woman wore a fashionable designer suit and had perfectly coiffed hair, and her partner was equally stylish in a tailored suit and black bow tie, which seemed a little overdressed for the middle of the day. We introduced ourselves and exchanged handshakes. Realising that I wasn't Greek, they both immediately switched to perfect English. They were on their way to a wedding reception, they said, and had just happened across our sign.

All of Greece knew of Mr and Mrs Papas, fabric designers for the well-heeled of Athens, because of their own cable TV channel. They already had several shops and a factory but were looking for a property in Glyfada, which had become the fashion centre of Greece. Being just off the main high street, our shop was in the perfect position, giving their famous clients a little more privacy.

Alex and I followed them around as they inspected every corner of all three floors. Then Mr Papas politely asked us to step outside for a moment so that they could discuss it with each other before making an offer. Alex pulled at my T-shirt and whispered, 'Leave them alone,' so we crossed the road and feigned an interest in a coffee menu in a glass case screwed to the wall.

After a while, Mr and Mrs Papas emerged and waved us over. 'So how much rent are you looking for?' Mrs Papas asked.

Alex and I looked at each other. We had no idea of the market rate and hadn't even considered the price.

Mr Papas assisted us. 'Yesterday, we saw a shop similar to yours, but we weren't keen on the area. That was being rented at three thousand euros a month.'

I tried to remain impassive. Alex squeezed my hand while maintaining a neutral expression.

'So,' he continued, 'as this shop's in a better location, we'll offer you 3,500 euros a month. We'd like to sign a five-year agreement, with a five per cent increase per year. We'll give you one month's holding deposit and four months' rent in advance, which you'll hold onto until the end of the term.'

Still reeling after hearing that the market rate was more than three thousand euros a month, my mind blanked out the rest of the offer. We were both in shock. Alex recovered before me and shook their hands to seal the agreement. They told us that their lawyer could prepare the contracts by the morning, and we could meet them again tomorrow to complete the deal. With that, they climbed into their limousine and left.

Still trying to process this momentous event, we held hands and walked silently back to Meat Street. We resumed our seats, and the waiter put our wine on the table along with two upturned glasses.

'What just happened?' Alex asked, her eyes glassy.

'I think we just rented our shop,' I replied.

I suggested we tell Stavros, but Alex had a twinkle in her eye as she explained the game she wanted to play.

# 21

# MEMBERS ONLY

The next day we were still walking on air. Now that we had rented out our shop, we had money in our pockets. This meant that we could enjoy a little financial freedom to complete our home. We drove to the building company that had agreed to fit our columns – two in the salon, and the rest on the roof terrace – completed the deal and agreed on a payment plan.

Next on the list was to wind up Stavros. He didn't yet know that we'd found a tenant for our shop, so we thought we'd catch him before the news broke on the local grapevine. In Glyfada, nothing stays secret for long, so we had to act fast.

Alex called him to ask about the renter he was proposing for our shop. Within minutes he was at the site, keen to give us the info on his deal.

'I thought you would change your mind.' He grinned.

We grinned back and asked how much rent he was offering.

Stavros scratched his chin and considered this question. 'Well, he's offering eight hundred euros a month, but I may push him up to a thousand.' He looked at us for a reaction.

We both smiled. Stavros took our expression as agreement and assured us he would do the deal on our behalf, so not to worry. He would collect the rent and pay it into our bank account, so there would be no need for us to even speak to the potential tenant.

Alex was no longer smiling now that the attempted con had become clearer. She stealthily launched her attack. It started with a question. 'So you don't want us to meet the tenant then?' she said sweetly.

Stavros's eyebrows twitched. 'It's not that,' he replied. 'I just want to make things easier for you by doing all the paperwork.' A bead of sweat appeared on his forehead and trickled down into his eye, making him blink.

'How much rent are you getting from your shop?' Alex asked.

'That's not the point,' he replied.

'I think it is,' she said. 'If we're going into partnership with you on our shop, we'll need to know the full rental value of both shops so a proper agreement can be considered based on the overall value.'

Then he lit the dynamite. 'But my shop is twice the size of yours,' he shot back, before immediately realising what he'd said.

But it was too late. Alex was already reaching for his throat and I was trying to hold her back. The frustration that had built up through the two years of the building project flooded out.

Neighbours came out to watch. People leaned over their balconies, keen to observe the developing show as the verbal assault continued.

As usual, Stella was in position on her terrace, watering can in hand as if she were tending to her geraniums though making no attempt to pretend she wasn't listening. Every so often she would yell encouragement. 'You tell him, Alex,' she screeched. 'He thinks he's better than us because he has a big car. And he doesn't like cats.'

Everything went temporarily quiet while Alex paused to absorb this information. She realised it was a meaningless Stella rant and continued her attack.

Pandelis was standing on the forecourt of his apartment block with a clipboard in hand, seemingly writing down every word of the exchange and storing it up for future use. If Alex finally killed Stavros, he could be a witness at the trial, and how he would relish such a perfect chance to take Alex down at last.

Alex tried to free herself from my grip. Screaming insults at this *malaka* was not enough. She needed to see blood. The *malaka* knew he was in danger and backed away, raising his arms in a gesture of surrender. Alex was in no mood to take prisoners and continued to try and wriggle out my grasp so she could conclude the matter with his slaughter. I yelled at Stavros to get lost quickly. He turned and ran.

We decided to focus on the positives, of which there were a great many. Skilled tradespeople were putting the finishing touches to our home: the kitchen and the bathroom had been installed and everything was working; the decorating was done; Nick had finished applying the special paint to the chimney breast, which now matched the marble floor; and the bathroom ceiling was a lovely shade of blue with lightly painted clouds. The interior looked even better than we'd imagined. All that was left to complete the building was the lift, which still needed to be fitted into the empty shaft.

Meanwhile, Alex started to feel sorry for Stavros. Although she would happily have killed him yesterday, today her anger had subsided. She took a walk to the local pudding shop, found a large sticky cake and went to his office to make amends. I held the door open for her as she needed both hands to steady the cake as we entered.

Stavros was sitting behind his desk with his eyes focused on the box Alex was carrying towards him. He looked both fearful and curious as she approached. Given her anger towards him the previous day, it wouldn't have surprised him if it were a bomb, even if it was gift-wrapped.

Alex apologised to him for yesterday's outburst, but suggested that he shouldn't be trying to con us. She wanted this to mark an end to our disagreements, she said, and for there to be no more bad feeling between us.

Stavros lifted the lid of the box and peered inside. It was an ornately decorated chocolate cake topped with dried fruit and piped cream. He asked his secretary to bring some plates and cut each of us a slice. Then he dug his fork into his portion, took a large dollop, put it in his mouth and chewed happily.

Alex ignored her slice and asked Stavros if things were okay now.

He smiled, put down his fork and assured us that all was fine and that there would be no more hard feelings once we'd paid him for the meters.

'What meters?' Alex asked.

'The electricity meters,' he replied.

Alex asked him to explain.

He slid his cake plate to the side and opened a blue folder on his desk. 'You're going to have to pay for one electricity meter for each of your properties,' he told her. 'Plus another one for the communal areas.'

The temperature in the room escalated. Even without looking at Alex, I could sense her fury rising.

'Why didn't you tell us about this at the beginning?' she asked.

'It's in the contract,' he retorted.

Alex's voice got louder as she asked what the cost was.

Stavros looked smug. 'It's five hundred euros per property. You have four, so that will be two thousand euros. Plus the communal meter, which is another five hundred.'

Suddenly, the slice of cake that had previously been sitting on the desk in front of Alex was flying, still on its plate, like a sticky brown Frisbee, towards Stavros's head. He must have been expecting this as with a quick movement he ducked to the side. The cake hit the wall behind him with a squelch.

Alex stood up, kicked the chair across the room behind her and slammed his office door on her way out, leaving me watching Stavros, and the newly decorated office wall.

'Is there anything else that we should know?' I asked before leaving to join Alex.

'Yes. You also have to pay for the water meters.'

I returned to the site and found Alex looking at a small pile of rubble outside our building. She had picked up a hefty chunk of wood about the size of a baseball bat and was tapping it against the wall thoughtfully. I put my arm around her and gave her a hug. I suggested it was probably a bad idea to hit Stavros with it today, as she would only feel sorry tomorrow. She agreed and threw her weapon back onto the pile. I thought it best that I didn't mention the water meters yet, as she seemed to be calming down and the large lump of wood was still within reach.

The next day, the lift arrived. Teams of technicians swarmed up and down the elevator shaft, suspended on ropes and harnesses. Others banged and clanked in the basement, the noise of their work amplified by the empty shaft and radiating around the building. Finally, by the end of the afternoon, they'd completed their tests and adjusted the new doors, leaving us to play with our new toy. It was wonderful.

We stood near the building entrance on the ground floor. Alex pressed the call button. A soft purring sound announced the lift's arrival. We heard a loud click as the door unlocked, so I grabbed the handle and it swung open. It was beautiful. Not only would we avoid the arduous climb up five floors to our apartment, we would also travel in style.

We stepped onto its green marble floor. The walls were clad in matching marble to waist height, and above were silver architraves around antique-effect mirrors. At the top of the bank of buttons was a large one announcing 'Penthouse Suite' with a keyhole beside it. We inserted our key. With a satisfying clunk, the door locked and we ascended towards our home. A few seconds later, we stepped out directly into our living room.

Immediately to our left was our main front door. This opened onto the staircase to the lower floors. Ahead of us was the white marble staircase leading up to the terrace, now fitted with elaborate gold-plated rails for banisters. To the right, rising out of the pink marble floor of the main living room, were two majestic Corinthian columns that reached up to the ceiling. Past these was a wall of glass and then the balcony. We had created our dream home. All the stress, money troubles and fighting of the last two years had been worth it. We now owned a millionaire's apartment.

It was such a refreshing change to arrive in our home without aching legs and heaving chests. We were so happy, like a couple of kids with a new plaything, visiting every floor simply for the pleasures of going up and down, stepping in and out, and pressing buttons.

We took one more ride in our new elevator to the ground floor and then strolled down to the harbour for lunch. As usual, it was sunny. We took a seat at one of the plastic tables in front of the simple fish taverna nestled among the fishing boats tied up along the harbour wall. Each of the small boats had set up a trestle table alongside, with a selection of their catch on beds of ice, under multi-coloured umbrellas to protect the fish from the sun. We ordered a simple Greek salad and some calamari with a bottle of rough retsina and watched the fishers haggle with their customers while we enjoyed our meal.

This was a lovely restaurant, but you had to be willing to share your meal with the local wildlife. Today was no different. I felt something touching my leg and a purring sound coming from under the table.

Cats rule in Greece. They are charming little roamers that offer their love to anyone willing to feed them. Most hang around tavernas, rubbing their bodies against your leg and meowing at you while you're eating, trying to charm you into offering them a piece of meat or fish.

Greek sparrows are equally persistent. They will sit on your table staring at you until you look away. They then steal chips from your plate and fly away fully loaded. If they drop something, they'll chase away any cats lurking under the table, quickly collect their ill-gotten gains and leave the cat cowering.

Seagulls in Greece have a stealth mode. Unlike the noisy creatures of seaside resorts in England, here they are silent. They flock together around the harbours, picking up scraps from the fishing boats, then circle in the air without a sound until they spot an unguarded piece of calamari on your plate. One noiseless swoop and they've snaffled it.

We were quite happy to share our meal, as today self-congratulations were in order. For the last two years we'd struggled to turn our dreams into a reality, but now we'd done it. We had a pristine new building, a luxury apartment for ourselves, another for the parents, an apartment to rent as income for Alex's parents, and a shop providing a decent revenue for Alex and me. All that remained was to bring in the furniture and move in.

We had put quite a lot of items from the old house into storage, but most of that belonged to Debbie and Zissis. Alex and I had very few belongings in Greece; most of our stuff was at our home in England. We were still going to keep our house in the UK as, although Alex would live in Glyfada permanently, I would commute for my work and split my time between both countries until I could get a decent job in Greece. We decided we'd pack up some furniture from our home in England, buy some more on eBay and arrange for an international removals company to bring it all over for us.

We also needed to relocate our dogs. Alex's parents had been living in the UK for the last couple of years, so they'd been taking care of our animals during our regular trips to Glyfada, but Debbie and Zissis would soon be returning to live permanently in Greece. So our dogs would need to become Greek nationals too.

We finished our lunch and headed back home to play with

the lift some more. As we turned the corner into our road, there was a giant yellow crane blocking the road, with a large grey Corinthian column dangling from its chain. This was being hoisted towards the two men who were leaning over the railings of our roof terrace waiting to receive it. Our own private Parthenon had arrived.

Over the next few days, it all came together. There were ten columns arranged in a square, and these were drilled into the roof terrace and sealed in place. A plain stone frieze ran around the top of the structure, with ornate plaster coving along its interior. At the front was a triangular pediment. It was magnificent, exactly like a simplified, miniature version of the Parthenon on top of the Acropolis.

We set up two floodlights and directed them at the structure, then waited for night to fall. Once it was dark, we went upstairs to enjoy our folly. It was majestic. We spent some time fiddling with the lights at different angles until it looked just right. Illuminated against the black sky, it really did appear uncannily like a genuine building from antiquity.

Pleased with this addition to our terrace, Alex suggested we take a walk around the neighbourhood to admire it from a distance. As our building was now the tallest in the village, we would be able to see our creation from anywhere. We headed off, deliberately not looking back until we were two streets away. Then we turned, lifted our gaze and took it all in, displayed to its very best advantage. Our own mini-Parthenon lit up the night sky like a golden crown.

We both stood there with our mouths open, not believing this was ours. A chap came out of a nearby restaurant, stopped beside us and followed our gaze. Alex asked him what he thought of it. He took a puff on his cigarette, waved his hand towards the illuminations and said, 'It's a private nightclub. Members only.' Then, 'I've been there. It's very nice.'

The following day we arrived for a last inspection before returning to England. As we were finishing up, the intercom buzzed. I looked at the monitor, and there on the screen were two police officers. I pressed the button to open the door and told them to come to the fourth floor. A few moments later, they stepped out of the elevator into our living room.

Greek police do not make social calls, so we knew we were in trouble. I was trying to remember where I'd parked the car. Had I blocked a driveway? I couldn't call to mind any other offence. Perhaps Stavros had made a complaint about Alex trying to kill him (again), though surely he was used to that by now.

The reason for their visit became clear when they asked to see the terrace.

In Greece, police have the power to enforce planning regulations and punish any related transgressions. We had not bothered to seek permission to erect our roof structure. We didn't even know if permission was required, though ignorance of the law was no excuse.

We nervously followed the officers up the stairs and watched as they surveyed the roof and columns. They took tape measures out of their pockets and measured the heights of the columns, the length and width of the structure and the amount of space between the columns.

Finally, one of them turned to me and said, 'You are under arrest.'

Well, this was inconvenient. We were due back in England the following day, but with me likely to be wearing handcuffs and incarcerated at the local police station, that didn't look too hopeful.

Alex stepped in. 'So what exactly is the problem?' she asked.

A conversation ensued in rapid Greek and was far too fast for me to follow. I just observed the body language and expressions for clues as to who was winning. Finally, the two police officers nodded in agreement and left.

I was still a free man. Once she had seen them into the elevator, Alex returned to explain.

There had been a complaint from a neighbour. The police had received word that we'd built something on our roof terrace without permission. I leaned over the balustrade and gazed out over the neighbourhood. Pandelis was sitting on his balcony, smiling up at me. He had obviously enjoyed the show.

After measuring and taking notes, the police officers had decided that although the columns and top links were okay and didn't break planning rules, the pediment at the front was in contravention. It was one metre too high. Alex had immediately assured them that this had been a mistake and promised to remove it immediately, thus saving me from my day in court.

We called the column company, who sent a team to take the pediment down. It was a shame because it looked majestic, but the last thing we needed was to fall foul of the authorities and end up in a Greek prison. I would have considered that a most ungrateful response, as the last Englishman to have concerned himself with a Parthenon had purloined most of it and given it to the British Museum. I, on the other hand, had done the public a favour by constructing another one. There was no pleasing some people. But I still had my freedom, so we had got away lightly.

I looked at the stonework that was now lying on the tiles and wondered what to do with it. Alex, meanwhile, was staring out over the railings at the houses opposite, trying to work out which of our neighbours had complained. We both suspected

Pandelis, but if it wasn't him, it had certainly been someone local. Everyone knew of Alex and her temper, so no one would ever admit to having reported us. Their identity has remained a mystery, but we have our strong suspicions.

We were just recovering from the unwelcome official visit when the intercom buzzed again. My heart stopped. Had they changed their mind and come back to arrest me after all? I looked at the screen and was only slightly relieved to see that, instead of the police officers, Stella's face was staring at the camera. Reluctantly, Alex pressed the button to let her in. A few moments later we heard her voice in the lift shaft; she was already speaking, although there was no one to hear. But this had never mattered to Stella, who simply loved to talk at people and never expected a reply.

She told us that she'd been worried about us when she'd seen the police arrive. More likely, she wanted the gossip. Alex explained that they'd been there because of the building on the roof.

'Yes, I've seen it from my balcony,' Stella replied. 'What is it?'

'It's the Parthenon,' Alex said.

'So what do you do with it?'

Alex told her that on warm summer evenings we would sit between the columns under a starry sky and watch the waters of the Aegean Sea shimmer in the moonlight while sipping a glass of ouzo and toasting the ancient gods.

'What else does it do?' Stella asked.

'Nothing. It's just for decoration.'

This made no sense to Stella. She turned and got into the lift. As she made her way down to the ground floor, her voice carried up the lift shaft. She was on a roll, talking to herself about how stupid this Englishman was. 'Why can't they put chickens in it?' she shrieked. 'At least it would be useful then.'

# 22

## GREEK CATS CHASE DOGS

T he day of our departure from England arrived. This time we would not be travelling alone. We would take our two dogs, Jack and Bella. Jack was an eight-month-old golden Labrador who considered everything to be edible. He was very fond of chair legs and had developed a taste for door frames. Being the doggie equivalent of a toddler, he needed constant supervision. Bella was a grumpy six-year-old golden retriever who spent most of her time being annoyed by Jack. She showed her disapproval by emitting a continual low growl whenever he was in the room, usually while having her ear chewed.

In Greece, dogs are mostly mixed breed and lazy. All government departments have a sleeping dog lying on the front step, and all supermarkets possess a dozing mutt curled up under the trolleys. These animals are not owned but are adopted and fed by whoever works in the buildings; this is normal practice. Dogs that are actually owned by people seem to spend their time yapping at passers-by from the safety of high balconies.

Now we were bringing Jack and Bella to join the canine family of Glyfada. They were already bilingual, so we expected them to adapt well. There were just two problems that I could foresee. The first was the heat. We would need to give the dogs a haircut; being used to cool and rainy England, they'd likely find the relentless summer temperatures of Athens difficult to deal with. The other problem was cultural. In Greece, cats chase dogs.

On their daily walk and sniff around our local park in England, Jack and Bella would meet their doggie friends and race after a few sticks and sometimes a ball. They knew exactly where the neighbourhood cats lived and would sit in wait, hoping to find one unwise enough to have ventured out during walkies time. If spotted, the games ensued. The cat would run, the dogs would chase. The cat invariably scarpered up a tree, and the dogs barked at the base of it until they got bored and left to investigate other corners of the park. The cat would go home, and the games would resume the following day.

In Greece, though, dogs avoid cats. If they see one, they'll cross the road. If confronted by one inadvertently, the dog will always run away, pursued by a screaming blur of fur and sharp claws intent on inflicting as much damage as possible. Unfortunately, dogs cannot climb trees to avoid these predators, so most of them have battle-scarred faces from encounters with these feline relatives of leopards. Our dogs would be in for a culture shock.

Jack and Bella's boisterous temperaments would be a challenge during our drive through Europe. We'd had to plan carefully. First, the dogs needed a passport. Then we had to find pet-friendly hotels at each of our stopping points.

The first of these was near Reims in northeastern France. We had chosen a castle hotel in the Champagne region, complete with moat, stained-glass windows and tiny arrow slits in its imposing grey stone walls. It looked magnificent. We drove across the drawbridge and opened the back door to release the dogs. Bella just wandered around the gravel courtyard, discovering new and exotic smells. Jack, however, sped off, found a slope and jumped into the moat. By the time I got to the water's edge, all I could see was his wagging tail protruding above the water like a periscope as he disappeared around the side of the castle.

The website of this five-star hotel had proudly announced that it was dog-friendly. We were about to find out just how far that friendliness would extend when applied to a wet and muddy Labrador that had just completed two laps of their green and foul-smelling moat.

Our room was enormous, with ceilings as high as a barn's, a beautiful four-poster bed, an antique wardrobe and matching roll-top desk, and a chaise longue and leather armchair. The staff had laid out two dog beds at the foot of the four-poster. Directly below our window was the moat. I suggested to Alex that we keep the window closed in case Jack fancied another swim.

Dogs weren't allowed in the dining room, so we left Jack and Bella upstairs while we went for dinner. The menu was in French. I don't speak a word. Although Alex speaks Greek, English, Italian and Spanish, she never studied French so was no help. Luckily, the waiter begrudgingly admitted to having a little English, so we asked him to translate.

Alex pointed at the first item.

'It's very nice,' he assured us. 'It's pigeon in its own blood. We take a young pigeon and wring its neck.' He clasped his hands together and twisted them in opposite directions. 'We save the blood and add this to the sauce and serve the dish slightly cooked and pink.'

Alex turned a little green. We ordered the fish.

Back upstairs, Jack had made the most of his time alone in our room. It was chaos in there. He'd dragged all the bedclothes onto the floor, been into the bathroom, found the freshly laundered towels and added them to the pile. The bedsheet was perforated with giant holes where Jack had eaten it, and there were teeth marks on the antique wardrobe's legs and around the base of the door. Going by the expression on the hotel manager's face, I doubted that establishment would remain dog-friendly for much longer.

Our next stop was near Lucerne in Switzerland. Jack had dived into the Reims hotel moat as a pre-departure treat, but by the time we reached the Alps, the smell of wet dog had subsided and the mud had mostly dropped off his fur and onto the car seat, with just a few flecks lingering around his ears. We arrived at our Lucerne hotel just as the sun was sinking behind the mountains on the other side of the vast and glittering lake. The village looked like a series of cuckoo clocks set into the side of the green hill that swept down to the lakeshore. It was beautiful.

Our hotel was right on the lake, and our room had large double doors leading to a patio that dipped into the water. Jack was already pulling on his lead, keen to leap straight in, but the bedroom was immaculate, with white walls, a white carpet and a pure white quilt on the bed. There were two white dog beds to one side of the room, and white bowls for food and water set beside each. We were at risk of going snowblind. Even the pictures on the walls were of snowy white Alps.

Predictably, another disastrous night of canine misadventures ensued, this time involving runaway dogs, cheese fondue, takeaway pizza and bedsheets that had no chance of staying white for long. We made a swift getaway the following morning.

The scenery was spectacular. Snow-capped mountains surrounded us as we drove through green valleys full of sheep peacefully grazing the slopes and past ornate timber-framed houses that stood on the edge of pine forests enjoying fine Alpine views. At times we went not over the mountains but through them. In places, the motorway had been cut straight through the middle of the mountains in a series of long tunnels, one of which was more than thirty kilometres long.

Eventually, we started our descent, crossing the border into Italy and skirting Lake Como as we continued on to Venice, where we could catch the ferry to Greece. Loath to indulge Jack's passion for water any further at this point in our trip, we'd decided not to linger in Venice itself, despite the tantalisingly magical glimpses of narrow canals and terracotta towers rising above sunshine-coloured houses. Instead, we made straight for the ferry port.

As we climbed the stairs to the reception deck of the Venice–Patras ferry, a young woman in naval uniform bent down to stroke Jack and Bella. Pets being banned from the cabin, she was there to take them to the kennels on the top deck. Meanwhile, a porter picked up our bag and led us human passengers to our accommodation. The dogs whined as they watched the lift door close behind us.

The cabin was lovely. It had thick, plush carpet, a fully stocked fridge, a double bed and, best of all, two enormous expanses of plate-glass window offering a panoramic view of the ship's bow and the open sea beyond. This was a not a traditional ferry, it was more like an upmarket cruise ship.

The restaurant was equally luxurious, staffed by a row of chefs busily dishing out Greek specialities from silver trays behind curved glass counters. Further back was a series of bars, all with finely dressed waiters bustling around with trays of drinks. We found a vacant table by a huge window offering an unparalleled view of Venice, and placed our order.

As Alex went to check on the dogs, I sipped my beer and gazed out over the city. She returned just as the ship began its slow departure from the harbour. Within moments, we were sailing along the Grand Canal, looking down onto the splendour of St Mark's Square, which was full of tourists wandering around with their mobile phones on sticks, taking selfies against the grand facades. Clouds of pigeons swarmed above them, some swooping down to perch on willing shoulders for the reward of a few grains of corn purchased from the vendors spread around the square.

All too soon, St Mark's was behind us as the ship turned and headed for the open sea. As the last great buildings of

Venice vanished from view and the coastline of Trieste took shape in the distance, we tucked into a delicious lunch. I asked Alex how the dogs were. 'Fine,' she replied.

It had been a long drive from Switzerland, and now that we were safely aboard the ship, we could relax a little. We returned to our cabin for a siesta. I tapped the key-card reader outside our door, depressed the handle, and entered a warzone.

When Alex had gone to check on the dogs, she'd found them in a kennel block next to the ship's funnels. The place stank of the urine that was sitting in pools across the metal deck. There was a long row of cages, all of them empty apart from the one at the end containing Jack and Bella. They looked miserable. We'd seen lots of dogs being led upstairs from the car decks, and there'd been at least four in reception when we checked in. So where were they? Certainly not in that smelly prison.

Alex felt she had no choice but to liberate Bella and Jack. Given that all the cages were empty, she assumed that every other dog owner on the ship had broken the rules and smuggled their beloved pets into their cabins. So she felt justified in doing the same.

She found their leads hanging on a hook and sneaked them down the stairs, along the corridor and into our cabin. With her finger at her lips, she'd hushed them to silence and promised that we would be back soon.

While we'd been enjoying our lunch-with-a-view, our two tearaways had dragged the bedclothes onto the carpet, balled up the sheets in the corner, ripped feathers from a now half-eaten pillow, chewed chunks out of my bedside book, and shredded a fifty-euro note left on the table.

Unbeknown to us, the ship did offer pet-friendly cabins, in which it was completely legal to keep your dogs. Our cabin, however, being advertised as VIP, was not on that list. But the damage was done, so I agreed to keep them with us.

My last visit to Patras had been at carnival time, when I'd spent the day inadvertently dressed as a pantomime dame. As we drove off the ferry and onto the streets of Patras, I was pleased that the car had darkened glass in its windows. The sun was shining and the air felt warm as we headed towards the motorway. It would be a good three-hour drive to Glyfada, so we found an area of grassland bordering a small sandy beach and stopped to give the dogs some much needed exercise before the trip.

Both dogs sniffed the air, enjoying the new smells. Suddenly, Jack lifted his head, saw the sea and set off at high speed towards the beach. He had never seen salt water before; his swims in the UK were normally either in local rivers or involved chasing ducks around the village pond. This smelled strange. He stopped short of the water and gazed into the distance, deciding whether to take the plunge. Soon, though, he was in, happily swimming and splashing, racing in and out of the water. He was having a great time. Then he took a drink.

I hurtled across the grass, rushed into the sea up to my waist, gripped his collar and pulled him towards the beach while he continued to lap at the salty water. By the time we got to shore, he'd already quenched his thirst and was now vomiting. I got a bowl from the car, filled it to the brim with fresh water and held it out for him until he'd emptied it. Jack never learned his lesson, and most of our future walks ended with a vomiting dog on a beach and me forcing bottled water into his mouth.

Arriving in Glyfada, we turned into our road. There it was: our giant white tower, dominating the street, its upper floors illuminated by bright sunshine, the lower floors in the shadow of neighbouring buildings. Our shop was open for business, its windows displaying lengths of fabric artfully draped over marble statues. There was a large stone table on the forecourt, at which customers were studying home-decor designs from colourful catalogues.

Next door, Stavros's shop had opened as a cafeteria. Its forecourt was humming with people drinking coffee and enjoying sandwiches under cream-coloured parasols. I recalled standing in that very spot just two years before and waving to Alex and Debbie as they sat at the little table at the top of the stairs outside our beloved old home. All that was now lost forever and would exist only as a happy memory. But this was something else. We now owned three luxury apartments and a busy shop in the most affluent part of Greece. We had our own Parthenon on the roof terrace, with views of the mountains, the sea and distant islands. And much more. The ghost of the old house was still there, and we would build on all those years of happiness and forge many more joyous memories in our new home.

As we pulled up onto our freshly paved driveway, Stavros appeared. Alex and I had decided to forgive him for his dodgy dealings and wily manoeuvring. Little Red Riding Hood couldn't blame the big bad wolf for eating her grandmother; it was in his nature. Being sharp-elbowed was in Stavros's nature. We had what we wanted. It was just that he had more. But that was yesterday. We were thrilled with our brand-new building. Alex kissed him on the cheek and I shook him by the hand. We parted as friends.

We took our keys, opened the door to our shiny apartment block and entered. As we stepped into the hallway and pressed the button to call the lift, an overpowering smell of sewers filled our nostrils. It was so bad that my eyes were stinging. We ignored the click of the lift door and followed the stench down the stairs to the basement. In the plant room, the odour was even more pungent. I bent down and lifted a piece of tin sheeting to reveal a concrete pit with a small yellow sump pump in the bottom, sitting in a pool of human excrement.

Realising that the local sewers were not deep enough to discharge the waste from his cafe's customer toilets, which were located in the basement under the cafe, Stavros had directed all the waste from those washrooms into a concrete pit. He'd put this pit on our side of the building, so as not to upset his tenant and their customers.

Alex stood up. Her face was dark with rage. 'Where's Stavros?' she screamed. 'I'm *definitely* going to kill him this time.'

# EPILOGUE
## TIME IS A DOCTOR WHO HEALS ALL GRIEFS

Home of philosophy, birthplace of democracy, Greece has a proud culture that's been forged over thousands of years of adversity. Across the millennia, Greeks have repeatedly fought the occupation of their territory by nations that sought to control their resilient race, from the Persian invaders of the fifth century BC to the Nazi armies of the Second World War.

My own Greek family played their role in protecting their homeland. Alex's grandfather, Jannis, was a hero of the Second World War, forced into temporary exile in Canada for actively supporting the resistance efforts against the Nazi occupiers. His wife, Alex's beloved grandmother Bia, fed many people in Castella during the wartime famine, hunting tirelessly for black-market food, which she paid for with the gold sovereigns smuggled into Greece via Jannis's resistance network. Decades later, their son, Alex's uncle Vasilis, gave up a lucrative career as a ship's captain rather than go against his conscience and carry a cargo of weapons.

I feel honoured to have become a part of this complex, diverse, ancient culture. Yes, Greece is beautiful and lauded by tourists across the world for its sunny weather, warm seas and fresh food. But below the surface there is so much more wonder to appreciate; you just need to look a little deeper.

Being married to a Greek woman, I have adopted the best of her culture. I now think more deeply, and I experience, and show, emotions that I'd closed off for many years. If I'm happy,

I say so; if I'm sad, I express that too. I feel more complete than ever before. Alex, meanwhile, has realised that we Brits are not a cold race. She has seen the genuine goodness in people she previously considered to be stiff and unfeeling. She's learned that when our protective shell is stripped away, we are just like her: loving, kind and caring. As a couple relishing the multiple pleasures of discovery in our cross-cultural marriage, we're representatives of the wider world. Our own lived experience tells us that there's nothing to be gained in prejudging others on colour, nationality or religion, for we are all the same underneath.

Stavros, our architect, drove us to distraction throughout the construction period, but the culture permitted the raging arguments and countless fights. It was his business to gain as much as possible from all of his projects and our business to protect ourselves. We didn't take it personally, and neither did he. We are now the best of friends. He continues to help us whenever he can. Greeks are survivors. History tells us that.

As I write this book, Greece is just emerging from the most serious economic collapse it's ever experienced. Unemployment has hit record levels. People have little money; some have trouble feeding their families. Covid arrived to add to the troubles, decimating the tourist industry, leaving hotels and resorts empty.

In 2010 Greece asked the European Union and the International Monetary Fund for a financial rescue. Bailouts and emergency loans were proffered. But they came at a price. Greece was forced to agree to a series of crippling austerity measures, including spending restrictions, higher taxes and multiple cuts to pensions. The unemployment rate peaked at 27.5 per cent but for those under twenty-five it was fifty-eight per cent.

The Greek economy is now twenty-five per cent smaller

than when the crisis began and it will take decades to pay off its huge debt. But Greeks are a pragmatic race and used to hardship. Ask the average Greek their opinion on all this and they'll likely quote a famous line from Diphilus, one of their ancient poets: 'Time is a doctor who heals all griefs.'

Some things will never change. They still grow the grapes for the wine that fills the little tin jugs that bead with droplets of condensation on a hot day; they still catch fish in their old wooden boats, in the same nets deployed by their grandfathers before them; they still cultivate and press olives to make the golden oil that glistens atop every Greek salad.

I have found a better way to live. The love of my life still surprises me every day with her energy, sparky nature and unpredictability. We no longer suffer the pain of being away from each other. We wake up together every morning, be that in Greece or England, a true multi-cultural marriage that spans both countries. At this very moment I can feel her breath on the back of my neck. She is watching me type, casting her eyes over the script to ensure I don't wander off into a fantasy. She agreed to my writing this book on the condition it would be an accurate account of our lives to date.

Which it is.

# WHAT HAPPENED NEXT?

Clearly, Stavros was more afraid of upsetting his new tenant than he was of Alex. This showed either remarkable bravery or ultimate stupidity.

We arrived home to find our new apartment block smelling like a swamp and traced the overpowering odour to the basement. Stavros had installed a small yellow pump in an open pit to take away all the kitchen and toilet waste from his cafeteria next door. Large globules of congealed fat were floating around in a brown sludge with sheets of toilet paper. Foul liquid overflowed from the pit and ran under the door towards the lift shaft.

Alex bounded up the stairs from the cellar two at a time and slammed the front door as she stormed out in search of Stavros. I rushed after her as she entered his office. She was back out when I arrived.

"He's not there," Alex yelled as I reached her.

She took out her phone and called his number. It rang once and ended. He obviously saw her number, got scared and cancelled the call. This just infuriated Alex more. With her anger mounting and no-one to express it to, she stormed back across the road and entered the cafeteria. She pushed her way past tables outside and entered the kitchen. A small man was standing at a table making sandwiches as a wild, red-faced, furious Alex approached. He held up the butter knife to defend himself from this angry invader.

"What do you want?" he asked in a shaky voice.

"I'm your neighbour, and I have something of yours. Follow me." Alex was silent as the confused man followed her next door into our apartment block with me trailing behind trying to catch up.

"Does that belong to you?" Alex asked, pointing at the ever-deepening river of sludge with floating pieces of toilet paper running through our basement.

Alex explained that this was his drain discharging his waste into our property.

"I did not know," he said. "I think we should call Stamos."

This time, Stamos answered. He felt safe to answer the call because it wasn't Alex.

Alex snatched the phone off him and screamed, "Get here NOW. You are in big trouble!" She handed the phone back.

"Get here now!" echoed his tenant, then turned to Alex.

"Look, my name is Nico. Stamos never told me about this when I rented the shop. We can't wait here. My eyes are watering with this stink. Let's go back, I will make you a nice coffee while we wait for him."

Alex took his offered hand and shook it. Her normal colour was returning, but the blackness around her eyes was darkening.

"I'm not blaming you," she assured Nico, "but I am going to kill Stamos."

"Yes. I have a nice sharp knife next door," he smiled. "You are well within your rights."

Alex sat looking at her untouched coffee. Her leg trembled nervously as her foot vibrated on the floor. Then Stamos crossed the road towards us.

I reached for Alex's sleeve and missed as she jumped up, knocking over a chair in her haste to get to him. I chased, grabbed one arm as she flayed out towards Stamos with the other and gripped his throat. He stepped back from the assault as I tightened my grip on Alex to restrain her.

"You *Malaka!*" she screamed, struggling to get to him.

People sitting outside the cafeteria had seen the furniture flying as this furious woman launched the attack and were happily watching the show. Balconies along the road filled with residents keen to find out what the fuss was all about. Then Nico came out and added his voice to Alex's.

"Expect no more rent from me," Nikos told him. "You didn't tell me I didn't have any drains when you rented me the shop. This poor woman's home smells like a sewage factory and it is all your fault."

Stamos held up his hands in surrender.

"It's only temporary. I have already ordered the proper pumping station and it will be fitted soon," he assured us.

"Sorry, but that isn't good enough. You will not receive rent from me this month. And by the look of Alex, she is after more than money. Perhaps your life?"

In the end, we received a settlement from Stamos for the nuisance, and for sneakily putting the sewerage pump on our side. He lost two months' rent from Nico, who also realised Stamos could not be trusted. He left a few months later to find another more agreeable landlord in another part of Glyfada.

We had our magnificent structure on our roof terrace, looking like a crown above our town. It looked fantastic, floodlit at night and reflecting the sun by day. It was beautiful. But soon we realised the downside. A little like the real Parthenon on top of the nearby Acropolis, it looks majestic perched on the hill dominating the Athens skyline, but when you get up close, it's nice but you don't want to spend too much time there in the full Greek sunshine.

So, we put some parasols inside to protect the seating area from the sun. But Glyfada, being a seaside village, is windy. The first parasol flew through the open roof and disappeared over the side of the terrace. We bought another one and secured it in a bucket of concrete. The wind blew and dragged the umbrella across the terrace, taking the chairs with it, and got itself wedged between the columns. The pole broke, and the parasol launched into the sky and flew off towards the distant mountains.

We needed a Plan B.

We saved up some money, and employed a builder to put a roof over the Parthenon on our roof, fit some windows and glass doors between the columns. It looked great. The Parthenon became a bedroom. We installed plug sockets and lights, and a marble floor. We dragged our bed upstairs. Alex put up curtains and arranged flowers.

Then it rained. We stood in the middle of the bedroom, checked the windows, all dry. It was watertight. Alex left me to make coffee.

"It's raining," she yelled from downstairs.

"I know it's raining," I yelled back. "I can see it from the window."

"No, it's raining down here," she called back.

I ran downstairs. It was indeed raining, but in our living room. Fat drops of water were squeezing through the ceiling, dropping out of the spotlights and running in little rivers across our pink marble floor.

When the column company had built our Parthenon, they had drilled into the roof to secure it, but had drilled straight through the roof waterproofing layer.

We looked on the bright side. Not only did we have a Parthenon on our roof, we had an indoor swimming pool, too.

That was nice.

To find out more, join Peter and Alex in the sequel,
A Parthenon in Pefki

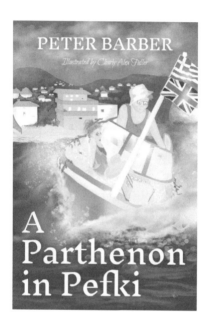

After perfecting their new apartment (complete with mini Parthenon) in a cosmopolitan suburb of Athens, Englishman Peter and his Greek wife Alexandra check out life in an authentic fishing village on a Greek island. They instantly fall in love with Pefki and plan to build a house there.

But all is not as it seems. As Peter and his feisty wife delve below the surface, they discover the sleepy village is hiding a wealth of secrets. Unperturbed, they embrace the fascinating village culture with unexpected and hilarious results.

What could possibly go wrong in paradise?

# A PARTHENON IN PEFKI
## AN EXCERPT

The first thing you see when entering Pefki is the majestic Pefka trees, the gateway to the village. Under the green arch, the road leads a few meters around a bend. Ahead is the sparkling blue Aegean Sea, with the village harbour closed to the sea on one side by a stone wall. Multi-coloured fishing boats of all sizes are tied up, awaiting their crew for the night's fishing trip. A few small pleasure crafts, secured to buoys, are scattered around the centre of the bay.

Beyond the harbour wall across the expanse of water are the high mountains of the mainland, with green trees at the base touching the sea and rising to grey barren peaks too high to support vegetation. This land wraps its way around the northern coast of Evia.

Looking to the right, in the distance, is the island of Skiathos with its blurred green landscape shimmering under the perfect blue sky, and just visible a little further into the distance is the island of Skopelos.

The road led past the harbour is lined with characteristic fish tavernas with sky-blue tables and chairs, some under wicker roofs, others sat below large canvas umbrellas. Waiters cross the road, busily holding trays of food and glass carafes of wine to fulfil the lunch orders of hungry diners relaxing on the paved terraces above the small sandy beach and crystal-clear water.

Further into the village, palm trees line the road. There are no buildings to obscure the view of the sea, and tables, chairs, sunbeds, and parasols spread in tidy blocks along the beach and serviced by the many cafeterias across the quiet road where you can sit and watch the world slowly pass.

Leaving the village behind, we drove along the road parallel with the shingle beach. Although it was midsummer, and the height of the tourist season, the beach was almost deserted. Being one of the longest beaches in Greece, you can pick a spot and swim in complete privacy in the clear blue water overlooking distant islands.

A right turn away from the sea, we found our hotel, our home for the next week.

The next few days passed enjoying the beach and village. We found a section of beach well away from other sunbathers and swimmers and let the dogs run and swim freely. Lunch would be at a taverna near the harbour, or one of the small establishments dotted along the coast, all with their typical blue tin tables sitting outside under trees or canopies.

Quickly, we realised how much we loved this village. Although tourist season was well underway, it still felt peaceful. The people we met were charming and genuine, the views over the straights of Artemision were spectacular. We were falling in love with this place.

So, on the fourth day, we accidentally bought land. Well, I say we bought land but more truthfully, we agreed to buy it, but with no money in our pockets. My bank manager was still angry with me for splashing out on pink marble floors for our new home in Glyfada.

One day, we were relaxing in a picturesque taverna overlooking the harbour. I sipped an ice-cold glass of wine, a nice

Greek salad covered with glistening olive oil with a sprinkle of oregano sat on the table with incredible views of mountains in the distance across the shimmering blue sea. The dogs snoozed happily under the blue tin table.

Alex left me at the table and crossed the road to pick up some dog food from the small supermarket opposite. A few moments later, she came running back towards me.

"Leave the meal, bring the dogs and follow that car," she yelled.

Amazon Link to A Parthenon in Pefki
https://bit.ly/Parthenon-2

# A NOTE FROM THE AUTHOR

I write about Greece. It doesn't take too much imagination. I just look out of the window and see the beauty of my subject spread around me. The bright Greek sunshine in an unreal blue sky. Orange and lemon trees swaying gently in the cool breeze. The sound of crickets. The perfume of mountain herbs invading my senses, the distant tinkle of bells tied to the collars of goats grazing happily on the hills.

Writers are a strange bunch. We isolate ourselves in closed rooms with only a keyboard for company. We rip out our souls and spend months and years obsessively perfecting our art.

Few of us will ever become rich, but this is not why we do it. We write for love.

The most incredible compliment any writer can get is to hear from you. It's such a wonderful experience to look online to see someone who I have never met has enjoyed my book and taken some of their valuable time to tell me.

If you have enjoyed my book, please let me know by spending a few moments to leave a review for *A Parthenon on our Roof*.

*Peter Barber, 2023*

# ABOUT THE AUTHOR

Peter Barber was born in Watford, in the UK, and flits between Bedfordshire and Athens with his Greek wife. He spends as much time as possible in Greece messing about in boats, enjoying both the weather and the company, but mostly the food and wine.

Having nothing to do on a Greek island is time-consuming. When not trying to sink his boat and amusing the locals, Peter writes books.

The Parthenon series is a trilogy based on Greek life.

Book 1: A Parthenon on our Roof
Book 2: A Parthenon in Pefki
Book 3: to follow

# CONTACTS AND LINKS

Email: peterbarberbooks@gmail.com
Website: https://peterbarberwriter.com/
Facebook: www.facebook.com/peter.barber.771/
Twitter: www.twitter.com/greekwriting

## Writing About Greece

Join the Facebook community, Writing about Greece, a group founded by Peter Barber and his wife, Alex, dedicated to Greece and people who love Greece.

www.facebook.com/groups/3690103324939088
or type
Writing About Greece in the Facebook search box.

# ACKNOWLEDGEMENTS

I would like to thank my editor, Lucy Ridout, who guided me through the several rewrites with patience and professionalism. I would also like to thank my Greek reader and friend Athena who gave me valuable insight on Greek culture.

I would like to thank the people of Greece who have opened my mind and allowed me to become part of their valuable culture.

## We Love Memoirs

Join Peter Barber and other memoir authors and readers in the **We Love Memoirs Facebook group**, the friendliest group on Facebook.

www.facebook.com/groups/welovememoirs/

# ANT PRESS BOOKS
## AWESOME AUTHORS ~ AWESOME BOOKS

**Ant Press**

If you enjoyed this book, you may also enjoy these Ant Press memoirs. All titles are available in ebook, paperback, hardback and large print editions from **Amazon** (recommended). Paperbacks can also be ordered from **Blackwell's** (World-wide free delivery), **Waterstones** (Europe delivery), **Booktopia** (Australia), **Barnes & Noble** (USA), and all good bookstores.

PETER BARBER - Award winning bestselling author

A Parthenon on our Roof
A Parthenon in Pefki

VICTORIA TWEAD - New York Times bestselling Author

Chickens, Mules and Two Old Fools
Two Old Fools ~ Olé!
Two Old Fools on a Camel
Two Old Fools in Spain Again
Two Old Fools in Turmoil
Two Old Fools Down Under

Two Old Fools Fair Dinkum
One Young Fool in Dorset (Prequel)
One Young Fool in South Africa (Prequel)
Dear Fran, Love Dulcie: Life and Death in the Hills
and Hollows of Bygone Australia

DIANE ELLIOTT

Butting Heads in Spain: Lady Goatherder 1
El Maestro: Lady Goatherder 2 (to follow)

BETH HASLAM

*Fat Dogs and French Estates ~ Part I*
*Fat Dogs and French Estates ~ Part II*
*Fat Dogs and French Estates ~ Part III*
*Fat Dogs and French Estates ~ Part IV*
*Fat Dogs and French Estates ~ Part V*
*Fat Dogs and Welsh Estates ~ The Prequel*

EJ Bauer

*From Moulin Rouge to Gaudi's City*
*From Gaudi's City to Granada's Red Palace*

MIKE CAVANAGH

*One of its Legs are Both the Same*
*A Pocket Full of Days, Part 1*
*A Pocket Full of Days, Part 2*

NICK ALBERT

*Fresh Eggs and Dog Beds: Living the Dream in Rural Ireland Fresh Eggs and Dog Beds 2: Still Living the Dream in Rural Ireland*
*Fresh Eggs and Dog Beds 3: More Living the Dream in Rural Ireland*
*Fresh Eggs and Dog Beds 4: More Living the Dream in Rural Ireland*

For more information about stockists, Ant Press titles or how to publish with Ant Press, please visit our website or contact us by email.

WEBSITE: www.antpress.org

EMAIL: admin@antpress.org

FACEBOOK: https://www.facebook.com/AntPress/

INSTAGRAM: https://instagram.com/publishwithantpress